YO-AAK-572

SUPER HOROSCOPE

CAPRICORN 19 99

December 21 - January 19

B
BERKLEY BOOKS, NEW YORK

The publishers regret that they cannot answer
individual letters requesting personal horoscope information.

1999 SUPER HOROSCOPE CAPRICORN

PRINTING HISTORY
Berkley Trade Edition / August 1998

The Penguin Putnam Inc. World Wide Web site address is
http://www.penguinputnam.com

ISBN: 0-425-16333-4

BERKLEY®
Berkley Books are published by The Berkley Publishing Group,
a member of Penguin Putnam Inc.,
200 Madison Avenue, New York, New York 10016.
"BERKLEY" and the "B" logo
are trademarks belonging to Berkley Publishing Corporation.

PRINTED IN THE UNITED STATES OF AMERICA

10 9 8 7 6 5 4 3 2 1

CONTENTS

THE CUSP-BORN CAPRICORN

Are you *really* a Capricorn? If your birthday falls around Christmas, at the very beginning of Capricorn, will you still retain the traits of Sagittarius, the sign of the Zodiac before Capricorn? And what if you were born during the third week of January—are you more Aquarius than Capricorn? Many people born at the edge, or cusp, of a sign have great difficulty determining exactly what sign they are. If you are one of these people, here's how you can figure it out, once and for all.

Consult the cusp table on the facing page, then locate the year of your birth. The table will tell you the precise days on which the Sun entered and left your sign for the year of your birth. In that way you can determine if you are a true Capricorn—or whether you are a Sagittarius or Aquarius—according to the variations in cusp dates from year to year (see also page 17).

Whether you were born at the beginning or end of Capricorn, yours is a lifetime reflecting a process of subtle transformation. Your life on Earth will symbolize a significant change in consciousness, for you are either about to enter a whole new way of living, or are leaving one behind.

If you were born at the beginning of Capricorn, you may want to read the horoscope book for Sagittarius as well as Capricorn, for Sagittarius is a deep—often hidden—part of your spirit. You were born with the special gift of being able to bring your dreams into reality and put your talents and ambitions to practical use. You need to conquer worry and depression and learn to take life seriously, but without losing your sense of humor and hope. You need to find a balance between believing nothing and believing too much. You need to find the middle ground between cynicism and idealism.

If you were born at the end of Capricorn, you may want to read the horoscope book on Aquarius, for you are a dynamic mixture of both the Capricorn and Aquarius natures. You are in a transitional state of consciousness, about to enter a whole new way of living, but still duty-bound to perform responsibilities before you are set free. You are bound by two lifestyles, one conservative, the other freedom-oriented. You combine the talents of regularity and discipline with rebellious spontaneity and flashing genius. You can be troubled by reversals and setbacks, despite your serious

4

planning, and find great conflict between strong, personal ambitions and deep desires for freedom.

You have a great pull toward the future, but you are powerfully drawn back to society and cultural conditioning. Try to concentrate on your newly found enthusiasms and build a solid foundation on which to achieve the success you long for.

THE CUSPS OF CAPRICORN

DATES SUN ENTERS CAPRICORN (LEAVES SAGITTARIUS)

December 22 every year from 1900 to 2000, except for the following:

December 21

1912	1944	1964	1977	1989
16	48	65	80	92
20	52	68	81	93
23	53	69	84	94
28	56	72	85	96
32	57	73	86	97
36	60	76	88	98
40	61			

DATES SUN LEAVES CAPRICORN (ENTERS AQUARIUS)

January 20 every year from 1900 to 2000, except for the following:

January 19		January 21		
1977	1989	1903	1920	1932
81	93	04	24	36
85	97	08	28	44
		12		

THE ASCENDANT: CAPRICORN RISING

Could you be a "double" Capricorn? That is, could you have Capricorn as your Rising sign as well as your Sun sign? The tables on pages 8–9 will tell you Capricorns what your Rising sign happens to be. Just find the hour of your birth, then find the day of your birth, and you will see which sign of the Zodiac is your Ascendant, as the Rising sign is called. The Ascendant is called that because it is the sign rising on the eastern horizon at the time of your birth. For a more detailed discussion of the Rising sign and the twelve houses of the Zodiac, see pages 17–20.

The Ascendant, or Rising sign, is placed on the 1st house in a horoscope, of which there are twelve houses. The 1st house represents your response to the environment—your unique response. Call it identity, personality, ego, self-image, facade, come-on, body-mind-spirit—whatever term best conveys to you the meaning of the you that acts and reacts in the world. It is a you that is always changing, discovering a new you. Your identity started with birth and early environment, over which you had little conscious control, and continues to experience, to adjust, to express itself. The 1st house also represents how others see you. Has anyone ever guessed your sign to be your Rising sign? People may respond to that personality, that facade, that body type governed by your Rising sign.

Your Ascendant, or Rising sign, modifies your basic Sun sign personality, and it affects the way you act out the daily predictions for your Sun sign. If your rising sign is indeed Capricorn, what follows is a description of its effects on your horoscope. If your Rising sign is not Capricorn, but some other sign of the Zodiac, you may wish to read the horoscope book for that sign.

For those of you with Capricorn Rising, that is, in the 1st house, the planet that is rising in the 1st house is Saturn, ruler of Capricorn. Saturn here gives you an extraordinary philosophical capacity and at the same a penchant for lone pursuits. You can see reality from many perspectives, and you feel impelled to test the viability of each framework you discover. But you would rather do it your own way, not other people's, and be accountable only to yourself, not to anyone else. Saturn in this position also gives you a melancholy turn of mind.

You have an immense respect for the best order of things, for the way people should relate to each other in order to support each other. And you want to weave this order and support not only into the fabric of your own life but also into the larger tapestry of society as a whole. Thus you are very social, but your underlying drive is to integrate concepts of how people should behave with your self-concept. You start with a principle and you try to expand it. You are not concerned with peer pressure or popularity. Indeed, your aloofness, combined with your solitary habits, taciturn moods, and great powers of concentration, make some people think that you do not care at all or that you have an undeveloped conscience. Quite the opposite is true.

Because of these traits you have a remarkable ability to create far-reaching plans and to see them through. You can put kaleidoscopic images into focus, you can galvanize scattered energies into a powerful momentum. You are an excellent manipulator of ideas and a good manager of people. You are happiest when such tasks face you and when you have unlimited responsibility to carry them out. A family or a company is grist for your mill. Power to you means the ability to achieve your aims. Power is not fame, fortune, fondness, or any other measure of how people judge you. You are your own judge.

On the other hand, Capricorn Rising individuals are quite sensitive to the ways in which people treat your principles. In your mind your identity and your principles are merged, so when your ideas are insulted, you are insulted. You dislike rule breakers, and for that you may earn a reputation for sternness. You detest traitors, philanderers, cheats of all kinds, and for that you may be called rigid or old-fashioned. You consider a breach of support or trust dishonorable because it is harmful, and you can be pitiless in your scorn of the perpetrator.

Your persona may be so identified with your principles that you check impulses, shun spontaneity. You could refuse to let mirth show in your face even though you are probably the first peson to see humor in a situation. You could insulate your feelings because they don't seem to fit your preconceptions; contradiction is a theme you seldom tolerate. And only until you have generalized the meaning of an event, an interaction, an emotion, will you then relax into it.

The key words for those of you with Capricorn Rising are form and focus. Your own uphill struggle is a model of success for those who would despair and give in. Don't conserve your talents in seclusion.

RISING SIGNS FOR CAPRICORN

Hour of Birth	Day of Birth		
	December 21–26	December 27–31	January 1–5
Midnight	Virgo;	Libra	Libra
1 AM	Libra 12/22	Libra	Libra
2 AM	Libra	Libra; Scorpio 12/29	Scorpio
3 AM	Scorpio	Scorpio	Scorpio
4 AM	Scorpio	Scorpio	Scorpio; Sagittarius 1/5
5 AM	Sagittarius	Sagittarius	Sagittarius
6 AM	Sagittarius	Sagittarius	Sagittarius
7 AM	Sagittarius	Capricorn	Capricorn
8 AM	Capricorn	Capricorn	Capricorn
9 AM	Capricorn; Aquarius 12/26	Aquarius	Aquarius
10 AM	Aquarius	Aquarius	Aquarius; Pisces 1/2
11 AM	Pisces	Pisces	Pisces
Noon	Pisces; Aries 12/22	Aries	Aries
1 PM	Aries; Taurus 12/26	Taurus	Taurus
2 PM	Taurus	Taurus	Gemini
3 PM	Gemini	Gemini	Gemini
4 PM	Gemini	Gemini	Cancer
5 PM	Cancer	Cancer	Cancer
6 PM	Cancer	Cancer	Cancer
7 PM	Cancer; Leo 12/22	Leo	Leo
8 PM	Leo	Leo	Leo
9 PM	Leo	Leo; Virgo 12/30	Virgo
10 PM	Virgo	Virgo	Virgo
11 PM	Virgo	Virgo	Virgo

Hour of Birth	Day of Birth		
	January 6–10	January 11–15	January 16–21
Midnight	Libra	Libra	Libra
1 AM	Libra	Libra; Scorpio 1/13	Libra
2 AM	Scorpio	Scorpio	Scorpio
3 AM	Scorpio	Scorpio	Scorpio; Sagittarius 1/21
4 AM	Sagittarius	Sagittarius	Sagittarius
5 AM	Sagittarius	Sagittarius	Sagittarius
6 AM	Sagittarius; Capricorn 1/7	Capricorn	Capricorn
7 AM	Capricorn	Capricorn	Capricorn
8 AM	Capricorn; Aquarius 1/7	Aquarius	Aquarius
9 AM	Aquarius	Aquarius	Aquarius; Pisces 1/17
10 AM	Pisces	Pisces	Pisces; Aries 1/21
11 AM	Aries	Aries	Aries
Noon	Aries; Taurus 1/10	Taurus	Taurus
1 PM	Taurus	Taurus; Gemini 1/15	Gemini
2 PM	Gemini	Gemini	Gemini
3 PM	Gemini	Gemini; Cancer 1/15	Cancer
4 PM	Cancer	Cancer	Cancer
5 PM	Cancer	Cancer	Cancer; Leo 1/21
6 PM	Leo	Leo	Leo
7 PM	Leo	Leo	Leo
8 PM	Leo	Leo; Virgo 1/14	Virgo
9 PM	Virgo	Virgo	Virgo
10 PM	Virgo	Virgo	Virgo; Libra 1/21
11 PM	Libra	Libra	Libra

THE PLACE OF ASTROLOGY IN TODAY'S WORLD

Does astrology have a place in the fast-moving, ultra-scientific world we live in today? Can it be justified in a sophisticated society whose outriders are already preparing to step off the moon into the deep space of the planets themselves? Or is it just a hangover of ancient superstition, a psychological dummy for neurotics and dreamers of every historical age?

These are the kind of questions that any inquiring person can be expected to ask when they approach a subject like astrology which goes beyond, but never excludes, the materialistic side of life.

The simple, single answer is that astrology works. It works for many millions of people in the western world alone. In the United States there are 10 million followers and in Europe, an estimated 25 million. America has more than 4000 practicing astrologers, Europe nearly three times as many. Even down-under Australia has its hundreds of thousands of adherents. In the eastern countries, astrology has enormous followings, again, because it has been proved to work. In India, for example, brides and grooms for centuries have been chosen on the basis of their astrological compatibility.

Astrology today is more vital than ever before, more practicable because all over the world the media devotes much space and time to it, more valid because science itself is confirming the precepts of astrological knowledge with every new exciting step. The ordinary person who daily applies astrology intelligently does not have to wonder whether it is true nor believe in it blindly. He can see it working for himself. And, if he can use it—and this book is designed to help the reader to do just that—he can make living a far richer experience, and become a more developed personality and a better person.

Astrology and Relationships

Astrology is the science of relationships. It is not just a study of planetary influences on man and his environment. It is the study of man himself.

We are at the center of our personal universe, of all our relationships. And our happiness or sadness depends on how we act, how we relate to the people and things that surround us. The emotions that we generate have a distinct effect—for better or worse—on the world around us. Our friends and our enemies will confirm this. Just look in the mirror the next time you are angry. In other words, each of us is a kind of sun or planet or star radiating our feelings on the environment around us. Our influence on our personal universe, whether loving, helpful, or destructive, varies with our changing moods, expressed through our individual character.

Our personal "radiations" are potent in the way they affect our moods and our ability to control them. But we usually are able to throw off our emotion in some sort of action—we have a good cry, walk it off, or tell someone our troubles—before it can build up too far and make us physically ill. Astrology helps us to understand the universal forces working on us, and through this understanding, we can become more properly adjusted to our surroundings so that we find ourselves coping where others may flounder.

The Challenge of Love

The challenge of love lies in recognizing the difference between infatuation, emotion, sex, and, sometimes, the intentional deceit of the other person. Mankind, with its record of broken marriages, despair, and disillusionment, is obviously not very good at making these distinctions.

Can astrology help?

Yes. In the same way that advance knowledge can usually help in any human situation. And there is probably no situation as human, as poignant, as pathetic and universal, as the failure of man's love.

Love, of course, is not just between man and woman. It involves love of children, parents, home, and friends. But the big problems usually involve the choice of partner.

Astrology has established degrees of compatibility that exist between people born under the various signs of the Zodiac. Because people are individuals, there are numerous variations and modifications. So the astrologer, when approached on mate and marriage matters, makes allowances for them. But the fact remains that some groups of people are suited for each other and some are not, and astrology has expressed this in terms of characteristics we all can study and use as a personal guide.

No matter how much enjoyment and pleasure we find in the different aspects of each other's character, if it is not an overall compatibility, the chances of our finding fulfillment or enduring happiness in each other are pretty hopeless. And astrology can help us to find someone compatible.

Astrology and Science

Closely related to our emotions is the "other side" of our personal universe, our physical welfare. Our body, of course, is largely influenced by things around us over which we have very little control. The phone rings, we hear it. The train runs late. We snag our stocking or cut our face shaving. Our body is under a constant bombardment of events that influence our daily lives to varying degrees.

The question that arises from all this is, what makes each of us act so that we have to involve other people and keep the ball of activity and evolution rolling? This is the question that both science and astrology are involved with. The scientists have attacked it from different angles: anthropology, the study of human evolution as body, mind and response to environment; anatomy, the study of bodily structure; psychology, the science of the human mind; and so on. These studies have produced very impressive classifications and valuable information, but because the approach to the problem is fragmented, so is the result. They remain "branches" of science. Science generally studies effects. It keeps turning up wonderful answers but no lasting solutions. Astrology, on the other hand, approaches the question from the broader viewpoint. Astrology began its inquiry with the totality of human experience and saw it as an effect. It then looked to find the cause, or at least the prime movers, and during thousands of years of observation of man and his *universal* environment came up with the extraordinary principle of planetary influence—or astrology, which, from the Greek, means the science of the stars.

Modern science, as we shall see, has confirmed much of astrology's foundations—most of it unintentionally, some of it reluctantly, but still, indisputably.

It is not difficult to imagine that there must be a connection between outer space and Earth. Even today, scientists are not too sure how our Earth was created, but it is generally agreed that it is only a tiny part of the universe. And as a part of the universe, people on Earth see and feel the influence of heavenly bodies in almost every aspect of our existence. There is no doubt that the Sun has the greatest influence on life on this planet. Without it there would be no life, for without it there would be no warmth, no division into day and night, no cycles of time or season at all. This is clear and easy to see. The influence of the Moon, on the other hand, is more subtle, though no less definite.

There are many ways in which the influence of the Moon manifests itself here on Earth, both on human and animal life. It is a well-known fact, for instance, that the large movements of water on our planet—that is the ebb and flow of the tides—are caused by the Moon's gravitational pull. Since this is so, it follows that these water movements do not occur only in the oceans, but that all bodies of water are affected, even down to the tiniest puddle.

The human body, too, which consists of about 70 percent water, falls within the scope of this lunar influence. For example the menstrual cycle of most women corresponds to the 28-day lunar month; the period of pregnancy in humans is 273 days, or equal to nine lunar months. Similarly, many illnesses reach a crisis at the change of the Moon, and statistics in many countries have shown that the crime rate is highest at the time of the Full Moon. Even human sexual desire has been associated with the phases of the Moon. But it is in the movement of the tides that we get the clearest demonstration of planetary influence, which leads to the irresistible correspondence between the so-called metaphysical and the physical.

Tide tables are prepared years in advance by calculating the future positions of the Moon. Science has known for a long time that the Moon is the main cause of tidal action. But only in the last few years has it begun to realize the possible extent of this influence on mankind. To begin with, the ocean tides do not rise and fall as we might imagine from our personal observations of them. The Moon as it orbits around Earth sets up a circular wave of attraction which pulls the oceans of the world after it, broadly in an east to west direction. This influence is like a phantom wave crest, a loop of power stretching from pole to pole which passes over and around the Earth like an invisible shadow. It travels with equal effect across the land masses and, as scientists were recently amazed to observe, caused oysters placed in the dark in the middle of the United States where there is no sea to open their shells to receive the nonexistent tide. If the land-locked oysters react to this invisible signal, what effect does it have on us who not so long ago in evolutionary time came out of the sea and still have its salt in our blood and sweat?

Less well known is the fact that the Moon is also the primary force behind the circulation of blood in human beings and animals, and the movement of sap in trees and plants. Agriculturists have established that the Moon has a distinct influence on crops, which explains why for centuries people have planted according to Moon cycles. The habits of many animals, too, are directed by the movement of the Moon. Migratory birds, for instance, depart only at or near the time of the Full Moon. And certain sea creatures, eels in particular, move only in accordance with certain phases of the Moon.

Know Thyself—Why?

In today's fast-changing world, everyone still longs to know what the future holds. It is the one thing that everyone has in common: rich and poor, famous and infamous, all are deeply concerned about tomorrow.

But the key to the future, as every historian knows, lies in the past. This is as true of individual people as it is of nations. You cannot understand your future without first understanding your past, which is simply another way of saying that you must first of all know yourself.

The motto "know thyself" seems obvious enough nowadays, but it was originally put forward as the foundation of wisdom by the ancient Greek philosophers. It was then adopted by the "mystery religions" of the ancient Middle East, Greece, Rome, and is still used in all genuine schools of mind training or mystical discipline, both in those of the East, based on yoga, and those of the West. So it is universally accepted now, and has been through the ages.

But how do you go about discovering what sort of person you are? The first step is usually classification into some sort of system of types. Astrology did this long before the birth of Christ. Psychology has also done it. So has modern medicine, in its way.

One system classifies people according to the source of the impulses they respond to most readily: the muscles, leading to direct bodily action; the digestive organs, resulting in emotion; or the brain and nerves, giving rise to thinking. Another such system says that character is determined by the endocrine glands, and gives us such labels as "pituitary," "thyroid," and "hyperthyroid" types. These different systems are neither contradictory nor mutually exclusive. In fact, they are very often different ways of saying the same thing.

Very popular, useful classifications were devised by Carl Jung, the eminent disciple of Freud. Jung observed among the different faculties of the mind, four which have a predominant influence on character. These four faculties exist in all of us without exception, but not in perfect balance. So when we say, for instance, that someone is a "thinking type," it means that in any situation he or she tries to be rational. Emotion, which may be the opposite of thinking, will be his or her weakest function. This thinking type can be sensible and reasonable, or calculating and unsympathetic. The emotional type, on the other hand, can often be recognized by exaggerated language—everything is either marvelous or terrible—and in extreme cases they even invent dramas and quarrels out of nothing just to make life more interesting.

The other two faculties are intuition and physical sensation. The sensation type does not only care for food and drink, nice clothes and furniture; he or she is also interested in all forms of physical experience. Many scientists are sensation types as are athletes and nature-lovers. Like sensation, intuition is a form of perception and we all possess it. But it works through that part of the mind which is not under conscious control—consequently it sees meanings and connections which are not obvious to thought or emotion. Inventors and original thinkers are always intuitive, but so, too, are superstitious people who see meanings where none exist.

Thus, sensation tells us what is going on in the world, feeling (that is, emotion) tells us how important it is to ourselves, thinking enables us to interpret it and work out what we should do about it, and intuition tells us what it means to ourselves and others. All four faculties are essential, and all are present in every one of us. But some people are guided chiefly by one, others by another. In addition, Jung also observed a division of the human personality into the extrovert and the introvert, which cuts across these four types.

A disadvantage of all these systems of classification is that one cannot tell very easily where to place oneself. Some people are reluctant to admit that they act to please their emotions. So they deceive themselves for years by trying to belong to whichever type they think is the "best." Of course, there is no best; each has its faults and each has its good points.

The advantage of the signs of the Zodiac is that they simplify classification. Not only that, but your date of birth is personal—it is unarguably yours. What better way to know yourself than by going back as far as possible to the very moment of your birth? And this is precisely what your horoscope is all about, as we shall see in the next section.

WHAT IS A HOROSCOPE?

If you had been able to take a picture of the skies at the moment of your birth, that photograph would be your horoscope. Lacking such a snapshot, it is still possible to recreate the picture—and this is at the basis of the astrologer's art. In other words, your horoscope is a representation of the skies with the planets in the exact positions they occupied at the time you were born.

The year of birth tells an astrologer the positions of the distant, slow-moving planets Jupiter, Saturn, Uranus, Neptune, and Pluto. The month of birth indicates the Sun sign, or birth sign as it is commonly called, as well as indicating the positions of the rapidly moving planets Venus, Mercury, and Mars. The day and time of birth will locate the position of our Moon. And the moment—the exact hour and minute—of birth determines the houses through what is called the Ascendant, or Rising sign.

With this information the astrologer consults various tables to calculate the specific positions of the Sun, Moon, and other planets relative to your birthplace at the moment you were born. Then he or she locates them by means of the Zodiac.

The Zodiac

The Zodiac is a band of stars (constellations) in the skies, centered on the Sun's apparent path around the Earth, and is divided into twelve equal segments, or signs. What we are actually dividing up is the Earth's path around the Sun. But from our point of view here on Earth, it seems as if the Sun is making a great circle around our planet in the sky, so we say it is the Sun's apparent path. This twelvefold division, the Zodiac, is a reference system for the astrologer. At any given moment the planets—and in astrology both the Sun and Moon are considered to be planets—can all be located at a specific point along this path.

Now where in all this are you, the subject of the horoscope? Your character is largely determined by the sign the Sun is in. So that is where the astrologer looks first in your horoscope, at your Sun sign.

The Sun Sign and the Cusp

There are twelve signs in the Zodiac, and the Sun spends approximately one month in each sign. But because of the motion of the Earth around the Sun—the Sun's apparent motion—the dates when the Sun enters and leaves each sign may change from year to year. Some people born near the cusp, or edge, of a sign have difficulty determining which is their Sun sign. But in this book a Table of Cusps is provided for the years 1900 to 2000 (page 5) so you can find out what your true Sun sign is.

Here are the twelve signs of the Zodiac, their ancient zodiacal symbol, and the dates when the Sun enters and leaves each sign for the year 1999. Remember, these dates may change from year to year.

ARIES	Ram	March 20–April 20
TAURUS	Bull	April 20–May 21
GEMINI	Twins	May 21–June 21
CANCER	Crab	June 21–July 23
LEO	Lion	July 23–August 23
VIRGO	Virgin	August 23–September 23
LIBRA	Scales	September 23–October 23
SCORPIO	Scorpion	October 23–November 22
SAGITTARIUS	Archer	November 22–December 22
CAPRICORN	Sea Goat	December 22–January 20
AQUARIUS	Water Bearer	January 20–February 18
PISCES	Fish	February 18–March 20

It is possible to draw significant conclusions and make meaningful predictions based simply on the Sun sign of a person. There are many people who have been amazed at the accuracy of the description of their own character based only on the Sun sign. But an astrologer needs more information than just your Sun sign to interpret the photograph that is your horoscope.

The Rising Sign and the Zodiacal Houses

An astrologer needs the exact time and place of your birth in order to construct and interpret your horoscope. The illustration on the next page shows the flat chart, or natural wheel, an astrologer uses. Note the inner circle of the wheel labeled 1 through 12. These 12 divisions are known as the houses of the Zodiac.

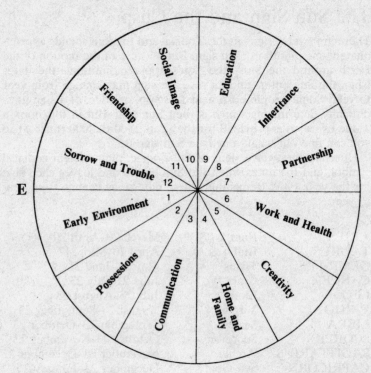

The 1st house always starts from the position marked E, which corresponds to the eastern horizon. The rest of the houses 2 through 12 follow around in a "counterclockwise" direction. The point where each house starts is known as a cusp, or edge.

The cusp, or edge, of the 1st house (point E) is where an astrologer would place your Rising sign, the Ascendant. And, as already noted, the exact time of your birth determines your Rising sign. Let's see how this works.

As the Earth rotates on its axis once every 24 hours, each one of the twelve signs of the Zodiac appears to be "rising" on the horizon, with a new one appearing about every 2 hours. Actually it is the turning of the Earth that exposes each sign to view, but in our astrological work we are discussing apparent motion. This Rising sign marks the Ascendant, and it colors the whole orientation of a horoscope. It indicates the sign governing the 1st house of the chart, and will thus determine which signs will govern all the other houses.

To visualize this idea, imagine two color wheels with twelve divisions superimposed upon each other. For just as the Zodiac is divided into twelve constellations that we identify as the signs, another twelvefold division is used to denote the houses. Now imagine one wheel (the signs) moving slowly while the other wheel (the houses) remains still. This analogy may help you see how the signs keep shifting the "color" of the houses as the Rising sign continues to change every two hours. To simplify things, a Table of Rising Signs has been provided (pages 8–9) for your specific Sun sign.

Once your Rising sign has been placed on the cusp of the 1st house, the signs that govern the rest of the 11 houses can be placed on the chart. In any individual's horoscope the signs do not necessarily correspond with the houses. For example, it could be that a sign covers part of two adjacent houses. It is the interpretation of such variations in an individual's horoscope that marks the professional astrologer.

But to gain a workable understanding of astrology, it is not necessary to go into great detail. In fact, we just need a description of the houses and their meanings, as is shown in the illustration above and in the table below.

THE 12 HOUSES OF THE ZODIAC

1st	Individuality, body appearance, general outlook on life	Personality house
2nd	Finance, possessions, ethical principles, gain or loss	Money house
3rd	Relatives, communication, short journeys, writing, education	Relatives house
4th	Family and home, parental ties, land and property, security	Home house
5th	Pleasure, children, creativity, entertainment, risk	Pleasure house
6th	Health, harvest, hygiene, work and service, employees	Health house
7th	Marriage and divorce, the law, partnerships and alliances	Marriage house
8th	Inheritance, secret deals, sex, death, regeneration	Inheritance house
9th	Travel, sports, study, philosophy and religion	Travel house
10th	Career, social standing, success and honor	Business house
11th	Friendship, social life, hopes and wishes	Friends house
12th	Troubles, illness, secret enemies, hidden agendas	Trouble house

The Planets in the Houses

An astrologer, knowing the exact time and place of your birth, will use tables of planetary motion in order to locate the planets in your horoscope chart. He or she will determine which planet or planets are in which sign and in which house. It is not uncommon, in an individual's horoscope, for there to be two or more planets in the same sign and in the same house.

The characteristics of the planets modify the influence of the Sun according to their natures and strengths.

Sun: Source of life. Basic temperament according to the Sun sign. The conscious will. Human potential.

Moon: Emotions. Moods. Customs. Habits. Changeable. Adaptive. Nurturing.

Mercury: Communication. Intellect. Reasoning power. Curiosity. Short travels.

Venus: Love. Delight. Charm. Harmony. Balance. Art. Beautiful possessions.

Mars: Energy. Initiative. War. Anger. Adventure. Courage. Daring. Impulse.

Jupiter: Luck. Optimism. Generous. Expansive. Opportunities. Protection.

Saturn: Pessimism. Privation. Obstacles. Delay. Hard work. Research. Lasting rewards after long struggle.

Uranus: Fashion. Electricity. Revolution. Independence. Freedom. Sudden changes. Modern science.

Neptune: Sensationalism. Theater. Dreams. Inspiration. Illusion. Deception.

Pluto: Creation and destruction. Total transformation. Lust for power. Strong obsessions.

Superimpose the characteristics of the planets on the functions of the house in which they appear. Express the result through the character of the Sun sign, and you will get the basic idea.

Of course, many other considerations have been taken into account in producing the carefully worked out predictions in this book: the aspects of the planets to each other; their strength according to position and sign; whether they are in a house of exaltation or decline; whether they are natural enemies or not; whether a planet occupies its own sign; the position of a planet in relation to its own house or sign; whether the sign is male or female; whether the sign is a fire, earth, water, or air sign. These are only a few of the colors on the astrologer's pallet which he or she must mix with the inspiration of the artist and the accuracy of the mathematician.

How To Use These Predictions

A person reading the predictions in this book should understand that they are produced from the daily position of the planets for a group of people and are not, of course, individually specialized. To get the full benefit of them our readers should relate the predictions to their own character and circumstances, coordinate them, and draw their own conclusions from them.

If you are a serious observer of your own life, you should find a definite pattern emerging that will be a helpful and reliable guide.

The point is that we always retain our free will. The stars indicate certain directional tendencies but we are not compelled to follow. We can do or not do, and wisdom must make the choice.

We all have our good and bad days. Sometimes they extend into cycles of weeks. It is therefore advisable to study daily predictions in a span ranging from the day before to several days ahead.

Daily predictions should be taken very generally. The word "difficult" does not necessarily indicate a whole day of obstruction or inconvenience. It is a warning to you to be cautious. Your caution will often see you around the difficulty before you are involved. This is the correct use of astrology.

In another section (pages 78–84), detailed information is given about the influence of the Moon as it passes through each of the twelve signs of the Zodiac. There are instructions on how to use the Moon Tables (pages 85–92), which provide Moon Sign Dates throughout the year as well as the Moon's role in health and daily affairs. This information should be used in conjunction with the daily forecasts to give a fuller picture of the astrological trends.

HISTORY OF ASTROLOGY

The origins of astrology have been lost far back in history, but we do know that reference is made to it as far back as the first written records of the human race. It is not hard to see why. Even in primitive times, people must have looked for an explanation for the various happenings in their lives. They must have wanted to know why people were different from one another. And in their search they turned to the regular movements of the Sun, Moon, and stars to see if they could provide an answer.

It is interesting to note that as soon as man learned to use his tools in any type of design, or his mind in any kind of calculation, he turned his attention to the heavens. Ancient cave dwellings reveal dim crescents and circles representative of the Sun and Moon, rulers of day and night. Mesopotamia and the civilization of Chaldea, in itself the foundation of those of Babylonia and Assyria, show a complete picture of astronomical observation and well-developed astrological interpretation.

Humanity has a natural instinct for order. The study of anthropology reveals that primitive people—even as far back as prehistoric times—were striving to achieve a certain order in their lives. They tried to organize the apparent chaos of the universe. They had the desire to attach meaning to things. This demand for order has persisted throughout the history of man. So that observing the regularity of the heavenly bodies made it logical that primitive peoples should turn heavenward in their search for an understanding of the world in which they found themselves so random and alone.

And they did find a significance in the movements of the stars. Shepherds tending their flocks, for instance, observed that when the cluster of stars now known as the constellation Aries was in sight, it was the time of fertility and they associated it with the Ram. And they noticed that the growth of plants and plant life corresponded with different phases of the Moon, so that certain times were favorable for the planting of crops, and other times were not. In this way, there grew up a tradition of seasons and causes connected with the passage of the Sun through the twelve signs of the Zodiac.

Astrology was valued so highly that the king was kept informed of the daily and monthly changes in the heavenly bodies, and the results of astrological studies regarding events of the future. Head astrologers were clearly men of great rank and position, and the office was said to be a hereditary one.

Omens were taken, not only from eclipses and conjunctions of the Moon or Sun with one of the planets, but also from storms and earthquakes. In the eastern civilizations, particularly, the reverence inspired by astrology appears to have remained unbroken since the very earliest days. In ancient China, astrology, astronomy, and religion went hand in hand. The astrologer, who was also an astronomer, was part of the official government service and had his own corner in the Imperial Palace. The duties of the Imperial astrologer, whose office was one of the most important in the land, were clearly defined, as this extract from early records shows:

> This exalted gentleman must concern himself with the stars in the heavens, keeping a record of the changes and movements of the Planets, the Sun and the Moon, in order to examine the movements of the terrestrial world with the object of prognosticating good and bad fortune. He divides the territories of the nine regions of the empire in accordance with their dependence on particular celestial bodies. All the fiefs and principalities are connected with the stars and from this their prosperity or misfortune should be ascertained. He makes prognostications according to the twelve years of the Jupiter cycle of good and evil of the terrestrial world. From the colors of the five kinds of clouds, he determines the coming of floods or droughts, abundance or famine. From the twelve winds, he draws conclusions about the state of harmony of heaven and earth, and takes note of good and bad signs that result from their accord or disaccord. In general, he concerns himself with five kinds of phenomena so as to warn the Emperor to come to the aid of the government and to allow for variations in the ceremonies according to their circumstances.

The Chinese were also keen observers of the fixed stars, giving them such unusual names as Ghost Vehicle, Sun of Imperial Concubine, Imperial Prince, Pivot of Heaven, Twinkling Brilliance, Weaving Girl. But, great astrologers though they may have been, the Chinese lacked one aspect of mathematics that the Greeks applied to astrology—deductive geometry. Deductive geometry was the basis of much classical astrology in and after the time of the Greeks, and this explains the different methods of prognostication used in the East and West.

Down through the ages the astrologer's art has depended, not so much on the uncovering of new facts, though this is important, as on the interpretation of the facts already known. This is the essence of the astrologer's skill.

But why should the signs of the Zodiac have any effect at all on the formation of human character? It is easy to see why people thought they did, and even now we constantly use astrological expressions in our everyday speech. The thoughts of "lucky star," "ill-fated," "star-crossed," "mooning around," are interwoven into the very structure of our language.

Wherever the concept of the Zodiac is understood and used, it could well appear to have an influence on the human character. Does this mean, then, that the human race, in whose civilization the idea of the twelve signs of the Zodiac has long been embedded, is divided into only twelve types? Can we honestly believe that it is really as simple as that? If so, there must be pretty wide ranges of variation within each type. And if, to explain the variation, we call in heredity and environment, experiences in early childhood, the thyroid and other glands, and also the four functions of the mind together with extroversion and introversion, then one begins to wonder if the original classification was worth making at all. No sensible person believes that his favorite system explains everything. But even so, he will not find the system much use at all if it does not even save him the trouble of bothering with the others.

In the same way, if we were to put every person under only one sign of the Zodiac, the system becomes too rigid and unlike life. Besides, it was never intended to be used like that. It may be convenient to have only twelve types, but we know that in practice there is every possible gradation between aggressiveness and timidity, or between conscientiousness and laziness. How, then, do we account for this?

A person born under any given Sun sign can be mainly influenced by one or two of the other signs that appear in their individual horoscope. For instance, famous persons born under the sign of Gemini include Henry VIII, whom nothing and no one could have induced to abdicate, and Edward VIII, who did just that. Obviously, then, the sign Gemini does not fully explain the complete character of either of them.

Again, under the opposite sign, Sagittarius, were both Stalin, who was totally consumed with the notion of power, and Charles V, who freely gave up an empire because he preferred to go into a monastery. And we find under Scorpio many uncompromising characters such as Luther, de Gaulle, Indira Gandhi, and Montgomery, but also Petain, a successful commander whose name later became synonymous with collaboration.

A single sign is therefore obviously inadequate to explain the differences between people; it can only explain resemblances, such as the combativeness of the Scorpio group, or the far-reaching devotion of Charles V and Stalin to their respective ideals—the Christian heaven and the Communist utopia.

But very few people have only one sign in their horoscope chart. In addition to the month of birth, the day and, even more, the hour to the nearest minute if possible, ought to be considered. Without this, it is impossible to have an actual horoscope, for the word horoscope literally means "a consideration of the hour."

The month of birth tells you only which sign of the Zodiac was occupied by the Sun. The day and hour tell you what sign was occupied by the Moon. And the minute tells you which sign was rising on the eastern horizon. This is called the Ascendant, and, as some astrologers believe, it is supposed to be the most important thing in the whole horoscope.

The Sun is said to signify one's heart, that is to say, one's deepest desires and inmost nature. This is quite different from the Moon, which signifies one's superficial way of behaving. When the ancient Romans referred to the Emperor Augustus as a Capricorn, they meant that he had the Moon in Capricorn. Or, to take another example, a modern astrologer would call Disraeli a Scorpion because he had Scorpio Rising, but most people would call him Sagittarius because he had the Sun there. The Romans would have called him Leo because his Moon was in Leo.

So if one does not seem to fit one's birth month, it is always worthwhile reading the other signs, for one may have been born at a time when any of them were rising or occupied by the Moon. It also seems to be the case that the influence of the Sun develops as life goes on, so that the month of birth is easier to guess in people over the age of forty. The young are supposed to be influenced mainly by their Ascendant, the Rising sign, which characterizes the body and physical personality as a whole.

It is nonsense to assume that all people born at a certain time will exhibit the same characteristics, or that they will even behave in the same manner. It is quite obvious that, from the very moment of its birth, a child is subject to the effects of its environment, and that this in turn will influence its character and heritage to a decisive extent. Also to be taken into account are education and economic conditions, which play a very important part in the formation of one's character as well.

People have, in general, certain character traits and qualities which, according to their environment, develop in either a positive or a negative manner. Therefore, selfishness (inherent selfishness, that is) might emerge as unselfishness; kindness and consideration as cruelty and lack of consideration toward others. In the same way, a naturally constructive person may, through frustration, become destructive, and so on. The latent characteristics with which people are born can, therefore, through environment and good or bad training, become something that would appear to be its opposite, and so give the lie to the astrologer's description of their character. But this is not the case. The true character is still there, but it is buried deep beneath these external superficialities.

Careful study of the character traits of various signs of the Zodiac are of immeasurable help, and can render beneficial service to the intelligent person. Undoubtedly, the reader will already have discovered that, while he is able to get on very well with some people, he just "cannot stand" others. The causes sometimes seem inexplicable. At times there is intense dislike, at other times immediate sympathy. And there is, too, the phenomenon of love at first sight, which is also apparently inexplicable. People appear to be either sympathetic or unsympathetic toward each other for no apparent reason.

Now if we look at this in the light of the Zodiac, we find that people born under different signs are either compatible or incompatible with each other. In other words, there are good and bad interrelating factors among the various signs. This does not, of course, mean that humanity can be divided into groups of hostile camps. It would be quite wrong to be hostile or indifferent toward people who happen to be born under an incompatible sign. There is no reason why everybody should not, or cannot, learn to control and adjust their feelings and actions, especially after they are aware of the positive qualities of other people by studying their character analyses, among other things.

Every person born under a certain sign has both positive and negative qualities, which are developed more or less according to our free will. Nobody is entirely good or entirely bad, and it is up to each of us to learn to control ourselves on the one hand and at the same time to endeavor to learn about ourselves and others.

It cannot be emphasized often enough that it is free will that determines whether we will make really good use of our talents and abilities. Using our free will, we can either overcome our failings or allow them to rule us. Our free will enables us to exert sufficient willpower to control our failings so that they do not harm ourselves or others.

Astrology can reveal our inclinations and tendencies. Astrology can tell us about ourselves so that we are able to use our free will to overcome our shortcomings. In this way astrology helps us do our best to become needed and valuable members of society as well as helpmates to our family and our friends. Astrology also can save us a great deal of unhappiness and remorse.

Yet it may seem absurd that an ancient philosophy could be a prop to modern men and women. But below the materialistic surface of modern life, there are hidden streams of feeling and thought. Symbology is reappearing as a study worthy of the scholar; the psychosomatic factor in illness has passed from the writings of the crank to those of the specialist; spiritual healing in all its forms is no longer a pious hope but an accepted phenomenon. And it is into this context that we consider astrology, in the sense that it is an analysis of human types.

Astrology and medicine had a long journey together, and only parted company a couple of centuries ago. There still remain in medical language such astrological terms as "saturnine," "choleric," and "mercurial," used in the diagnosis of physical tendencies. The herbalist, for long the handyman of the medical profession, has been dominated by astrology since the days of the Greeks. Certain herbs traditionally respond to certain planetary influences, and diseases must therefore be treated to ensure harmony between the medicine and the disease.

But the stars are expected to foretell and not only to diagnose.

Astrological forecasting has been remarkably accurate, but often it is wide of the mark. The brave person who cares to predict world events takes dangerous chances. Individual forecasting is less clear cut; it can be a help or a disillusionment. Then we come to the nagging question: if it is possible to foreknow, is it right to foretell? This is a point of ethics on which it is hard to pronounce judgment. The doctor faces the same dilemma if he finds that symptoms of a mortal disease are present in his patient and that he can only prognosticate a steady decline. How much to tell an individual in a crisis is a problem that has perplexed many distinguished scholars. Honest and conscientious astrologers in this modern world, where so many people are seeking guidance, face the same problem.

Five hundred years ago it was customary to call in a learned man who was an astrologer who was probably also a doctor and a philosopher. By his knowledge of astrology, his study of planetary influences, he felt himself qualified to guide those in distress. The world has moved forward at a fantastic rate since then, and yet people are still uncertain of themselves. At first sight it seems fantastic in the light of modern thinking that they turn to the most ancient of all studies, and get someone to calculate a horoscope for them. But is it *really* so fantastic if you take a second look? For astrology is concerned with tomorrow, with survival. And in a world such as ours, tomorrow and survival are the keywords for the twenty-first century.

ASTROLOGICAL BRIDGE TO THE 21st CENTURY

As the last decade of the twentieth century comes to a close, planetary aspects for its final years connect you with the future. Major changes completed in 1995 and 1996 give rise to new planetary cycles that form the bridge to the twenty-first century and new horizons. The years 1996 through 1999 and into the year 2000 reveal hidden paths and personal hints for achieving your potential, for making the most of your message from the planets.

All the major planets begin new cycles in the late 1990s. Jupiter, planet of good fortune, transits four zodiacal signs from 1996 through 1999 and goes through a complete cycle in each of the elements earth, air, fire, and water. Jupiter is in Capricorn, then in Aquarius, next in Pisces, and finally in Aries as the century turns. With the dawning of the twenty-first century, each new yearly Jupiter cycle follows the natural progression of the Zodiac, from Aries in 2000, then Taurus in 2001, next Gemini in 2002, and so on through Pisces in 2011. The beneficent planet Jupiter promotes your professional and educational goals while urging informed choice and deliberation. Jupiter sharpens your focus and hones your skills. And while safeguarding good luck, Jupiter can turn unusual risks into achievable aims.

Saturn, planet of reason and responsibility, has begun a new cycle in the spring of 1996 when it entered fiery Aries. Saturn in Aries through March 1999 heightens a longing for independence. Your movements are freed from everyday restrictions, allowing you to travel, to explore, to act on a variety of choices. With Saturn in Aries you get set to blaze a new trail. Saturn enters earthy Taurus in March 1999 for a three-year stay over the turn of the century into the year 2002. Saturn in Taurus inspires industry and affection. Practicality, perseverance, and planning can reverse setbacks and minimize risk. Saturn in Taurus lends beauty, order, and structure to your life. In order to take advantage of opportunity through responsibility, to persevere against adversity, look to beautiful planet Saturn.

Uranus, planet of innovation and surprise, started an important new cycle in January of 1996. At that time Uranus entered its natural home in airy Aquarius. Uranus in Aquarius into the year 2003 has a profound effect on your personality and the lens through which you see the world. A basic change in the way you project yourself is just one impact of Uranus in Aquarius. More significantly, a whole new consciousness is evolving. Winds of change blowing your way emphasize movement and freedom. Uranus in Aquarius poses involvement in the larger community beyond self, family, friends, lovers, associates. Radical ideas and progressive thought signal a journey of liberation. As the century turns, follow Uranus on the path of humanitarianism. While you carve a prestigious niche in public life, while you preach social reform and justice, you will be striving to make the world a better place for all people.

Neptune, planet of vision and mystery, is in earthy Capricorn until late 1998. Neptune in Capricorn excites creativity while restraining fanciful thinking. Wise use of resources helps you build persona and prestige. Then Neptune enters airy Aquarius during November 1998 and is there into the year 2011. Neptune in Aquarius, the sign of the Water Bearer, represents two sides of the coin of wisdom: inspiration and reason. Here Neptune stirs powerful currents bearing a rich and varied harvest, the fertile breeding ground for idealistic aims and practical considerations. Neptune's fine intuition tunes in to your dreams, your imagination, your spirituality. You can never turn your back on the mysteries of life. Uranus and Neptune, the planets of enlightenment and renewed idealism both in the sign of Aquarius, give you glimpses into the future, letting you peek through secret doorways into the twenty-first century.

Pluto, planet of beginnings and endings, has completed one cycle of growth November 1995 in the sign of Scorpio. Pluto in Scorpio marked a long period of experimentation and rejuvenation. Then Pluto entered the fiery sign of Sagittarius on November 10, 1995 and is there into the year 2007. Pluto in Sagittarius during its long stay of twelve years can create significant change. The great power of Pluto in Sagittarius may already be starting its transformation of your character and lifestyle. Pluto in Sagittarius takes you on a new journey of exploration and learning. The awakening you experience on intellectual and artistic levels heralds a new cycle of growth. Uncompromising Pluto, seeker of truth, challenges your identity, persona, and self-expression. Uncovering the real you, Pluto holds the key to understanding and meaningful communication. Pluto in Sagittarius can be the guiding light illuminating the first decade of the twenty-first century. Good luck is riding on the waves of change.

THE SIGNS OF THE ZODIAC

Dominant Characteristics

Aries: March 21–April 20

The Positive Side of Aries

The Aries has many positive points to his character. People born under this first sign of the Zodiac are often quite strong and enthusiastic. On the whole, they are forward-looking people who are not easily discouraged by temporary setbacks. They know what they want out of life and they go out after it. Their personalities are strong. Others are usually quite impressed by the Ram's way of doing things. Quite often they are sources of inspiration for others traveling the same route. Aries men and women have a special zest for life that can be contagious; for others, they are a fine example of how life should be lived.

The Aries person usually has a quick and active mind. He is imaginative and inventive. He enjoys keeping busy and active. He generally gets along well with all kinds of people. He is interested in mankind, as a whole. He likes to be challenged. Some would say he thrives on opposition, for it is when he is set against that he often does his best. Getting over or around obstacles is a challenge he generally enjoys. All in all, Aries is quite positive and young-thinking. He likes to keep abreast of new things that are happening in the world. Aries are often fond of speed. They like things to be done quickly, and this sometimes aggravates their slower colleagues and associates.

The Aries man or woman always seems to remain young. Their whole approach to life is youthful and optimistic. They never say die, no matter what the odds. They may have an occasional setback, but it is not long before they are back on their feet again.

The Negative Side of Aries

Everybody has his less positive qualities—and Aries is no exception. Sometimes the Aries man or woman is not very tactful in communicating with others; in his hurry to get things done he is apt to be a little callous or inconsiderate. Sensitive people are likely to find him somewhat sharp-tongued in some situations. Often in his eagerness to get the show on the road, he misses the mark altogether and cannot achieve his aims.

At times Aries can be too impulsive. He can occasionally be stubborn and refuse to listen to reason. If things do not move quickly enough to suit the Aries man or woman, he or she is apt to become rather nervous or irritable. The uncultivated Aries is not unfamiliar with moments of doubt and fear. He is capable of being destructive if he does not get his way. He can overcome some of his emotional problems by steadily trying to express himself as he really is, but this requires effort.

Taurus: April 21–May 20

The Positive Side of Taurus

The Taurus person is known for his ability to concentrate and for his tenacity. These are perhaps his strongest qualities. The Taurus man or woman generally has very little trouble in getting along with others; it's his nature to be helpful toward people in need. He can always be depended on by his friends, especially those in trouble.

Taurus generally achieves what he wants through his ability to persevere. He never leaves anything unfinished but works on something until it has been completed. People can usually take him at his word; he is honest and forthright in most of his dealings. The Taurus person has a good chance to make a success of his life because of his many positive qualities. The Taurus who aims high seldom falls short of his mark. He learns well by experience. He is thorough and does not believe in shortcuts of any kind. The Bull's thoroughness pays off in the end, for through his deliberateness he learns how to rely on himself and what he has learned. The Taurus person tries to get along with others, as a rule. He is not overly critical and likes people to be themselves. He is a tolerant person and enjoys peace and harmony—especially in his home life.

Taurus is usually cautious in all that he does. He is not a person who believes in taking unnecessary risks. Before adopting any one line of action, he will weigh all of the pros and cons. The Taurus person is steadfast. Once his mind is made up it seldom changes. The person born under this sign usually is a good family person—reliable and loving.

The Negative Side of Taurus

Sometimes the Taurus man or woman is a bit too stubborn. He won't listen to other points of view if his mind is set on something. To others, this can be quite annoying. Taurus also does not like to be told what to do. He becomes rather angry if others think him not too bright. He does not like to be told he is wrong, even when he is. He dislikes being contradicted.

Some people who are born under this sign are very suspicious of others—even of those persons close to them. They find it difficult to trust people fully. They are often afraid of being deceived or taken advantage of. The Bull often finds it difficult to forget or forgive. His love of material things sometimes makes him rather avaricious and petty.

Gemini: May 21–June 20

The Positive Side of Gemini

The person born under this sign of the Heavenly Twins is usually quite bright and quick-witted. Some of them are capable of doing many different things. The Gemini person very often has many different interests. He keeps an open mind and is always anxious to learn new things.

Gemini is often an analytical person. He is a person who enjoys making use of his intellect. He is governed more by his mind than by his emotions. He is a person who is not confined to one view; he can often understand both sides to a problem or question. He knows how to reason, how to make rapid decisions if need be.

He is an adaptable person and can make himself at home almost anywhere. There are all kinds of situations he can adapt to. He is a person who seldom doubts himself; he is sure of his talents and his ability to think and reason. Gemini is generally most satisfied

when he is in a situation where he can make use of his intellect. Never short of imagination, he often has strong talents for invention. He is rather a modern person when it comes to life; Gemini almost always moves along with the times—perhaps that is why he remains so youthful throughout most of his life.

Literature and art appeal to the person born under this sign. Creativity in almost any form will interest and intrigue the Gemini man or woman.

The Gemini is often quite charming. A good talker, he often is the center of attraction at any gathering. People find it easy to like a person born under this sign because he can appear easygoing and usually has a good sense of humor.

The Negative Side of Gemini

Sometimes the Gemini person tries to do too many things at one time—and as a result, winds up finishing nothing. Some Twins are easily distracted and find it rather difficult to concentrate on one thing for too long a time. Sometimes they give in to trifling fancies and find it rather boring to become too serious about any one thing. Some of them are never dependable, no matter what they promise.

Although the Gemini man or woman often appears to be well-versed on many subjects, this is sometimes just a veneer. His knowledge may be only superficial, but because he speaks so well he gives people the impression of erudition. Some Geminis are sharp-tongued and inconsiderate; they think only of themselves and their own pleasure.

Cancer: June 21–July 20

The Positive Side of Cancer

The Moon Child's most positive point is his understanding nature. On the whole, he is a loving and sympathetic person. He would never go out of his way to hurt anyone. The Cancer man or woman is often very kind and tender; they give what they can to others. They hate to see others suffering and will do what they can to help someone in less fortunate circumstances than themselves. They are often very concerned about the world. Their interest in people generally goes beyond that of just their own families and close friends; they have a deep sense of community and respect humanitarian values. The Moon Child means what he says, as a rule; he is honest about his feelings.

The Cancer man or woman is a person who knows the art of patience. When something seems difficult, he is willing to wait until the situation becomes manageable again. He is a person who knows how to bide his time. Cancer knows how to concentrate on one thing at a time. When he has made his mind up he generally sticks with what he does, seeing it through to the end.

Cancer is a person who loves his home. He enjoys being surrounded by familiar things and the people he loves. Of all the signs, Cancer is the most maternal. Even the men born under this sign often have a motherly or protective quality about them. They like to take care of people in their family—to see that they are well loved and well provided for. They are usually loyal and faithful. Family ties mean a lot to the Cancer man or woman. Parents and in-laws are respected and loved. Young Cancer responds very well to adults who show faith in him. The Moon Child has a strong sense of tradition. He is very sensitive to the moods of others.

The Negative Side of Cancer

Sometimes Cancer finds it rather hard to face life. It becomes too much for him. He can be a little timid and retiring, when things don't go too well. When unfortunate things happen, he is apt to just shrug and say, "Whatever will be will be." He can be fatalistic to a fault. The uncultivated Cancer is a bit lazy. He doesn't have very much ambition. Anything that seems a bit difficult he'll gladly leave to others. He may be lacking in initiative. Too sensitive, when he feels he's been injured, he'll crawl back into his shell and nurse his imaginary wounds. The immature Moon Child often is given to crying when the smallest thing goes wrong.

Some Cancers find it difficult to enjoy themselves in environments outside their homes. They make heavy demands on others, and need to be constantly reassured that they are loved. Lacking such reassurance, they may resort to sulking in silence.

Leo: July 21–August 21

The Positive Side of Leo

Often Leos make good leaders. They seem to be good organizers and administrators. Usually they are quite popular with others. Whatever group it is that they belong to, the Leo man or woman is almost sure to be or become the leader. Loyalty, one of the Lion's noblest traits, enables him or her to maintain this leadership position.

Leo is generous most of the time. It is his best characteristic. He or she likes to give gifts and presents. In making others happy, the Leo person becomes happy himself. He likes to splurge when spending money on others. In some instances it may seem that the Lion's generosity knows no boundaries. A hospitable person, the Leo man or woman is very fond of welcoming people to his house and entertaining them. He is never short of company.

Leo has plenty of energy and drive. He enjoys working toward some specific goal. When he applies himself correctly, he gets what he wants most often. The Leo person is almost never unsure of himself. He has plenty of confidence and aplomb. He is a person who is direct in almost everything he does. He has a quick mind and can make a decision in a very short time.

He usually sets a good example for others because of his ambitious manner and positive ways. He knows how to stick to something once he's started. Although Leo may be good at making a joke, he is not superficial or glib. He is a loving person, kind and thoughtful.

There is generally nothing small or petty about the Leo man or woman. He does what he can for those who are deserving. He is a person others can rely upon at all times. He means what he says. An honest person, generally speaking, he is a friend who is valued and sought out.

The Negative Side of Leo

Leo, however, does have his faults. At times, he can be just a bit too arrogant. He thinks that no one deserves a leadership position except him. Only he is capable of doing things well. His opinion of himself is often much too high. Because of his conceit, he is

sometimes rather unpopular with a good many people. Some Leos are too materialistic; they can only think in terms of money and profit.

Some Leos enjoy lording it over others—at home or at their place of business. What is more, they feel they have the right to. Egocentric to an impossible degree, this sort of Leo cares little about how others think or feel. He can be rude and cutting.

Virgo: August 22–September 22

The Positive Side of Virgo

The person born under the sign of Virgo is generally a busy person. He knows how to arrange and organize things. He is a good planner. Above all, he is practical and is not afraid of hard work.

Often called the sign of the Harvester, Virgo knows how to attain what he desires. He sticks with something until it is finished. He never shirks his duties, and can always be depended upon. The Virgo person can be thoroughly trusted at all times.

The man or woman born under this sign tries to do everything to perfection. He doesn't believe in doing anything halfway. He always aims for the top. He is the sort of a person who is always learning and constantly striving to better himself—not because he wants more money or glory, but because it gives him a feeling of accomplishment.

The Virgo man or woman is a very observant person. He is sensitive to how others feel, and can see things below the surface of a situation. He usually puts this talent to constructive use.

It is not difficult for the Virgo to be open and earnest. He believes in putting his cards on the table. He is never secretive or underhanded. He's as good as his word. The Virgo person is generally plainspoken and down to earth. He has no trouble in expressing himself.

The Virgo person likes to keep up to date on new developments in his particular field. Well-informed, generally, he sometimes has a keen interest in the arts or literature. What he knows, he knows well. His ability to use his critical faculties is well-developed and sometimes startles others because of its accuracy.

Virgos adhere to a moderate way of life; they avoid excesses. Virgo is a responsible person and enjoys being of service.

The Negative Side of Virgo

Sometimes a Virgo person is too critical. He thinks that only he can do something the way it should be done. Whatever anyone else does is inferior. He can be rather annoying in the way he quibbles over insignificant details. In telling others how things should be done, he can be rather tactless and mean.

Some Virgos seem rather emotionless and cool. They feel emotional involvement is beneath them. They are sometimes too tidy, too neat. With money they can be rather miserly. Some Virgos try to force their opinions and ideas on others.

Libra: September 23–October 22

The Positive Side of Libra

Libras love harmony. It is one of their most outstanding character traits. They are interested in achieving balance; they admire beauty and grace in things as well as in people. Generally speaking, they are kind and considerate people. Libras are usually very sympathetic. They go out of their way not to hurt another person's feelings. They are outgoing and do what they can to help those in need.

People born under the sign of Libra almost always make good friends. They are loyal and amiable. They enjoy the company of others. Many of them are rather moderate in their views; they believe in keeping an open mind, however, and weighing both sides of an issue fairly before making a decision.

Alert and intelligent, Libra, often known as the Lawgiver, is always fair-minded and tries to put himself in the position of the other person. They are against injustice; quite often they take up for the underdog. In most of their social dealings, they try to be tactful and kind. They dislike discord and bickering, and most Libras strive for peace and harmony in all their relationships.

The Libra man or woman has a keen sense of beauty. They appreciate handsome furnishings and clothes. Many of them are artistically inclined. Their taste is usually impeccable. They know how to use color. Their homes are almost always attractively arranged and inviting. They enjoy entertaining people and see to it that their guests always feel at home and welcome.

Libra gets along with almost everyone. He is well-liked and socially much in demand.

The Negative Side of Libra

Some people born under this sign tend to be rather insincere. So eager are they to achieve harmony in all relationships that they will even go so far as to lie. Many of them are escapists. They find facing the truth an ordeal and prefer living in a world of make-believe.

In a serious argument, some Libras give in rather easily even when they know they are right. Arguing, even about something they believe in, is too unsettling for some of them.

Libras sometimes care too much for material things. They enjoy possessions and luxuries. Some are vain and tend to be jealous.

Scorpio: October 23–November 22

The Positive Side of Scorpio

The Scorpio man or woman generally knows what he or she wants out of life. He is a determined person. He sees something through to the end. Scorpio is quite sincere, and seldom says anything he doesn't mean. When he sets a goal for himself he tries to go about achieving it in a very direct way.

The Scorpion is brave and courageous. They are not afraid of hard work. Obstacles do not frighten them. They forge ahead until they achieve what they set out for. The Scorpio man or woman has a strong will.

Although Scorpio may seem rather fixed and determined, inside he is often quite tender and loving. He can care very much for others. He believes in sincerity in all relationships. His feelings about someone tend to last; they are profound and not superficial.

The Scorpio person is someone who adheres to his principles no matter what happens. He will not be deterred from a path he believes to be right.

Because of his many positive strengths, the Scorpion can often achieve happiness for himself and for those that he loves.

He is a constructive person by nature. He often has a deep understanding of people and of life, in general. He is perceptive and unafraid. Obstacles often seem to spur him on. He is a positive person who enjoys winning. He has many strengths and resources; challenge of any sort often brings out the best in him.

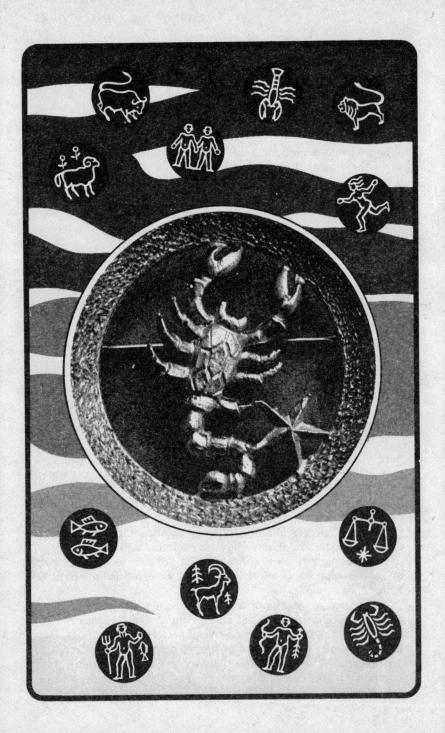

The Negative Side of Scorpio

The Scorpio person is sometimes hypersensitive. Often he imagines injury when there is none. He feels that others do not bother to recognize him for his true worth. Sometimes he is given to excessive boasting in order to compensate for what he feels is neglect.

Scorpio can be proud, arrogant, and competitive. They can be sly when they put their minds to it and they enjoy outwitting persons or institutions noted for their cleverness.

Their tactics for getting what they want are sometimes devious and ruthless. They don't care too much about what others may think. If they feel others have done them an injustice, they will do their best to seek revenge. The Scorpion often has a sudden, violent temper; and this person's interest in sex is sometimes quite unbalanced or excessive.

Sagittarius: November 23–December 20

The Positive Side of Sagittarius

People born under this sign are honest and forthright. Their approach to life is earnest and open. Sagittarius is often quite adult in his way of seeing things. They are broad-minded and tolerant people. When dealing with others the person born under the sign of the Archer is almost always open and forthright. He doesn't believe in deceit or pretension. His standards are high. People who associate with Sagittarius generally admire and respect his tolerant viewpoint.

The Archer trusts others easily and expects them to trust him. He is never suspicious or envious and almost always thinks well of others. People always enjoy his company because he is so friendly and easygoing. The Sagittarius man or woman is often good-humored. He can always be depended upon by his friends, family, and co-workers.

The person born under this sign of the Zodiac likes a good joke every now and then. Sagittarius is eager for fun and laughs, which makes him very popular with others.

A lively person, he enjoys sports and outdoor life. The Archer is fond of animals. Intelligent and interesting, he can begin an

animated conversation with ease. He likes exchanging ideas and discussing various views.

He is not selfish or proud. If someone proposes an idea or plan that is better than his, he will immediately adopt it. Imaginative yet practical, he knows how to put ideas into practice.

The Archer enjoys sport and games, and it doesn't matter if he wins or loses. He is a forgiving person, and never sulks over something that has not worked out in his favor.

He is seldom critical, and is almost always generous.

The Negative Side of Sagittarius

Some Sagittarius are restless. They take foolish risks and seldom learn from the mistakes they make. They don't have heads for money and are often mismanaging their finances. Some of them devote much of their time to gambling.

Some are too outspoken and tactless, always putting their feet in their mouths. They hurt others carelessly by being honest at the wrong time. Sometimes they make promises which they don't keep. They don't stick close enough to their plans and go from one failure to another. They are undisciplined and waste a lot of energy.

Capricorn: December 21–January 19

The Positive Side of Capricorn

The person born under the sign of Capricorn, known variously as the Mountain Goat or Sea Goat, is usually very stable and patient. He sticks to whatever tasks he has and sees them through. He can always be relied upon and he is not averse to work.

An honest person, Capricorn is generally serious about whatever he does. He does not take his duties lightly. He is a practical person and believes in keeping his feet on the ground.

Quite often the person born under this sign is ambitious and knows how to get what he wants out of life. The Goat forges ahead and never gives up his goal. When he is determined about something, he almost always wins. He is a good worker—a hard worker. Although things may not come easy to him, he will not complain, but continue working until his chores are finished.

He is usually good at business matters and knows the value of money. He is not a spendthrift and knows how to put something away for a rainy day; he dislikes waste and unnecessary loss.

Capricorn knows how to make use of his self-control. He can apply himself to almost anything once he puts his mind to it. His ability to concentrate sometimes astounds others. He is diligent and does well when involved in detail work.

The Capricorn man or woman is charitable, generally speaking, and will do what is possible to help others less fortunate. As a friend, he is loyal and trustworthy. He never shirks his duties or responsibilities. He is self-reliant and never expects too much of the other fellow. He does what he can on his own. If someone does him a good turn, then he will do his best to return the favor.

The Negative Side of Capricorn

Like everyone, Capricorn, too, has faults. At times, the Goat can be overcritical of others. He expects others to live up to his own high standards. He thinks highly of himself and tends to look down on others.

His interest in material things may be exaggerated. The Capricorn man or woman thinks too much about getting on in the world and having something to show for it. He may even be a little greedy.

He sometimes thinks he knows what's best for everyone. He is too bossy. He is always trying to organize and correct others. He may be a little narrow in his thinking.

Aquarius: January 20–February 18

The Positive Side of Aquarius

The Aquarius man or woman is usually very honest and forthright. These are his two greatest qualities. His standards for himself are generally very high. He can always be relied upon by others. His word is his bond.

Aquarius is perhaps the most tolerant of all the Zodiac personalities. He respects other people's beliefs and feels that everyone is entitled to his own approach to life.

He would never do anything to injure another's feelings. He is never unkind or cruel. Always considerate of others, the Water

Bearer is always willing to help a person in need. He feels a very strong tie between himself and all the other members of mankind.

The person born under this sign, called the Water Bearer, is almost always an individualist. He does not believe in teaming up with the masses, but prefers going his own way. His ideas about life and mankind are often quite advanced. There is a saying to the effect that the average Aquarius is fifty years ahead of his time.

Aquarius is community-minded. The problems of the world concern him greatly. He is interested in helping others no matter what part of the globe they live in. He is truly a humanitarian sort. He likes to be of service to others.

Giving, considerate, and without prejudice, Aquarius have no trouble getting along with others.

The Negative Side of Aquarius

Aquarius may be too much of a dreamer. He makes plans but seldom carries them out. He is rather unrealistic. His imagination has a tendency to run away with him. Because many of his plans are impractical, he is always in some sort of a dither.

Others may not approve of him at all times because of his unconventional behavior. He may be a bit eccentric. Sometimes he is so busy with his own thoughts that he loses touch with the realities of existence.

Some Aquarius feel they are more clever and intelligent than others. They seldom admit to their own faults, even when they are quite apparent. Some become rather fanatic in their views. Their criticism of others is sometimes destructive and negative.

Pisces: February 19–March 20

The Positive Side of Pisces

Known as the sign of the Fishes, Pisces has a sympathetic nature. Kindly, he is often dedicated in the way he goes about helping others. The sick and the troubled often turn to him for advice and assistance. Possessing keen intuition, Pisces can easily understand people's deepest problems.

He is very broad-minded and does not criticize others for their faults. He knows how to accept people for what they are. On the whole, he is a trustworthy and earnest person. He is loyal to his friends and will do what he can to help them in time of need. Generous and good-natured, he is a lover of peace; he is often willing to help others solve their differences. People who have taken a wrong turn in life often interest him and he will do what he can to persuade them to rehabilitate themselves.

He has a strong intuitive sense and most of the time he knows how to make it work for him. Pisces is unusually perceptive and often knows what is bothering someone before that person, himself, is aware of it. The Pisces man or woman is an idealistic person, basically, and is interested in making the world a better place in which to live. Pisces believes that everyone should help each other. He is willing to do more than his share in order to achieve cooperation with others.

The person born under this sign often is talented in music or art. He is a receptive person; he is able to take the ups and downs of life with philosophic calm.

The Negative Side of Pisces

Some Pisces are often depressed; their outlook on life is rather glum. They may feel that they have been given a bad deal in life and that others are always taking unfair advantage of them. Pisces sometimes feel that the world is a cold and cruel place. The Fishes can be easily discouraged. The Pisces man or woman may even withdraw from the harshness of reality into a secret shell of his own where he dreams and idles away a good deal of his time.

Pisces can be lazy. He lets things happen without giving the least bit of resistance. He drifts along, whether on the high road or on the low. He can be lacking in willpower.

Some Pisces people seek escape through drugs or alcohol. When temptation comes along they find it hard to resist. In matters of sex, they can be rather permissive.

Sun Sign Personalities

ARIES: Hans Christian Andersen, Pearl Bailey, Marlon Brando, Wernher Von Braun, Charlie Chaplin, Joan Crawford, Da Vinci, Bette Davis, Doris Day, W. C. Fields, Alec Guinness, Adolf Hitler, William Holden, Thomas Jefferson, Nikita Khrushchev, Elton John, Arturo Toscanini, J. P. Morgan, Paul Robeson, Gloria Steinem, Sarah Vaughn, Vincent van Gogh, Tennessee Williams

TAURUS: Fred Astaire, Charlotte Brontë, Carol Burnett, Irving Berlin, Bing Crosby, Salvador Dali, Tchaikovsky, Queen Elizabeth II, Duke Ellington, Ella Fitzgerald, Henry Fonda, Sigmund Freud, Orson Welles, Joe Louis, Lenin, Karl Marx, Golda Meir, Eva Peron, Bertrand Russell, Shakespeare, Kate Smith, Benjamin Spock, Barbra Streisand, Shirley Temple, Harry Truman

GEMINI: Ruth Benedict, Josephine Baker, Rachel Carson, Carlos Chavez, Walt Whitman, Bob Dylan, Ralph Waldo Emerson, Judy Garland, Paul Gauguin, Allen Ginsberg, Benny Goodman, Bob Hope, Burl Ives, John F. Kennedy, Peggy Lee, Marilyn Monroe, Joe Namath, Cole Porter, Laurence Olivier, Harriet Beecher Stowe, Queen Victoria, John Wayne, Frank Lloyd Wright

CANCER: "Dear Abby," Lizzie Borden, David Brinkley, Yul Brynner, Pearl Buck, Marc Chagall, Princess Diana, Babe Didrikson, Mary Baker Eddy, Henry VIII, John Glenn, Ernest Hemingway, Lena Horne, Oscar Hammerstein, Helen Keller, Ann Landers, George Orwell, Nancy Reagan, Rembrandt, Richard Rodgers, Ginger Rogers, Rubens, Jean-Paul Sartre, O. J. Simpson

LEO: Neil Armstrong, James Baldwin, Lucille Ball, Emily Brontë, Wilt Chamberlain, Julia Child, William J. Clinton, Cecil B. De Mille, Ogden Nash, Amelia Earhart, Edna Ferber, Arthur Goldberg, Alfred Hitchcock, Mick Jagger, George Meany, Annie Oakley, George Bernard Shaw, Napoleon, Jacqueline Onassis, Henry Ford, Francis Scott Key, Andy Warhol, Mae West, Orville Wright

VIRGO: Ingrid Bergman, Warren Burger, Maurice Chevalier, Agatha Christie, Sean Connery, Lafayette, Peter Falk, Greta Garbo, Althea Gibson, Arthur Godfrey, Goethe, Buddy Hackett, Michael Jackson, Lyndon Johnson, D. H. Lawrence, Sophia Loren, Grandma Moses, Arnold Palmer, Queen Elizabeth I, Walter Reuther, Peter Sellers, Lily Tomlin, George Wallace

LIBRA: Brigitte Bardot, Art Buchwald, Truman Capote, Dwight D. Eisenhower, William Faulkner, F. Scott Fitzgerald, Gandhi, George Gershwin, Micky Mantle, Helen Hayes, Vladimir Horowitz, Doris Lessing, Martina Navratalova, Eugene O'Neill, Luciano Pavarotti, Emily Post, Eleanor Roosevelt, Bruce Springsteen, Margaret Thatcher, Gore Vidal, Barbara Walters, Oscar Wilde

SCORPIO: Vivien Leigh, Richard Burton, Art Carney, Johnny Carson, Billy Graham, Grace Kelly, Walter Cronkite, Marie Curie, Charles de Gaulle, Linda Evans, Indira Gandhi, Theodore Roosevelt, Rock Hudson, Katherine Hepburn, Robert F. Kennedy, Billie Jean King, Martin Luther, Georgia O'Keeffe, Pablo Picasso, Jonas Salk, Alan Shepard, Robert Louis Stevenson

SAGITTARIUS: Jane Austen, Louisa May Alcott, Woody Allen, Beethoven, Willy Brandt, Mary Martin, William F. Buckley, Maria Callas, Winston Churchill, Noel Coward, Emily Dickinson, Walt Disney, Benjamin Disraeli, James Doolittle, Kirk Douglas, Chet Huntley, Jane Fonda, Chris Evert Lloyd, Margaret Mead, Charles Schulz, John Milton, Frank Sinatra, Steven Spielberg

CAPRICORN: Muhammad Ali, Isaac Asimov, Pablo Casals, Dizzy Dean, Marlene Dietrich, James Farmer, Ava Gardner, Barry Goldwater, Cary Grant, J. Edgar Hoover, Howard Hughes, Joan of Arc, Gypsy Rose Lee, Martin Luther King, Jr., Rudyard Kipling, Mao Tse-tung, Richard Nixon, Gamal Nasser, Louis Pasteur, Albert Schweitzer, Stalin, Benjamin Franklin, Elvis Presley

AQUARIUS: Marian Anderson, Susan B. Anthony, Jack Benny, John Barrymore, Mikhail Baryshnikov, Charles Darwin, Charles Dickens, Thomas Edison, Clark Gable, Jascha Heifetz, Abraham Lincoln, Yehudi Menuhin, Mozart, Jack Nicklaus, Ronald Reagan, Jackie Robinson, Norman Rockwell, Franklin D. Roosevelt, Gertrude Stein, Charles Lindbergh, Margaret Truman

PISCES: Edward Albee, Harry Belafonte, Alexander Graham Bell, Chopin, Adelle Davis, Albert Einstein, Golda Meir, Jackie Gleason, Winslow Homer, Edward M. Kennedy, Victor Hugo, Mike Mansfield, Michelangelo, Edna St. Vincent Millay, Liza Minelli, John Steinbeck, Linus Pauling, Ravel, Renoir, Diana Ross, William Shirer, Elizabeth Taylor, George Washington

The Signs and Their Key Words

		POSITIVE	NEGATIVE
ARIES	self	courage, initiative, pioneer instinct	brash rudeness, selfish impetuosity
TAURUS	money	endurance, loyalty, wealth	obstinacy, gluttony
GEMINI	mind	versatility	capriciousness, unreliability
CANCER	family	sympathy, homing instinct	clannishness, childishness
LEO	children	love, authority, integrity	egotism, force
VIRGO	work	purity, industry, analysis	faultfinding, cynicism
LIBRA	marriage	harmony, justice	vacillation, superficiality
SCORPIO	sex	survival, regeneration	vengeance, discord
SAGITTARIUS	travel	optimism, higher learning	lawlessness
CAPRICORN	career	depth	narrowness, gloom
AQUARIUS	friends	human fellowship, genius	perverse unpredictability
PISCES	confine-ment	spiritual love, universality	diffusion, escapism

The Elements and Qualities of The Signs

Every sign has both an *element* and a *quality* associated with it. The element indicates the basic makeup of the sign, and the quality describes the kind of activity associated with each.

Element	Sign	Quality	Sign
FIRE	ARIES LEO SAGITTARIUS	CARDINAL	ARIES LIBRA CANCER CAPRICORN
EARTH	TAURUS VIRGO CAPRICORN	FIXED	TAURUS LEO SCORPIO AQUARIUS
AIR	GEMINI LIBRA AQUARIUS		
WATER	CANCER SCORPIO PISCES	MUTABLE	GEMINI VIRGO SAGITTARIUS PISCES

Signs can be grouped together according to their element and quality. Signs of the same element share many basic traits in common. They tend to form stable configurations and ultimately harmonious relationships. Signs of the same quality are often less harmonious, but they share many dynamic potentials for growth as well as profound fulfillment.

Further discussion of each of these sign groupings is provided on the following pages.

The Fire Signs

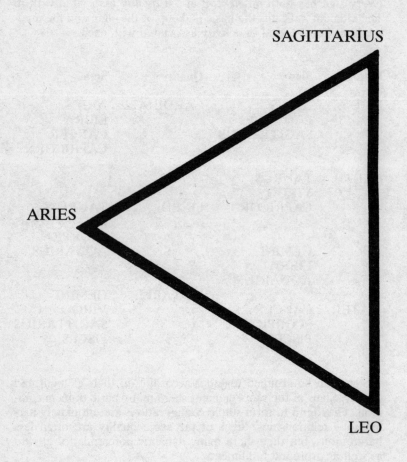

SAGITTARIUS

ARIES

LEO

This is the fire group. On the whole these are emotional, volatile types, quick to anger, quick to forgive. They are adventurous, powerful people and act as a source of inspiration for everyone. They spark into action with immediate exuberant impulses. They are intelligent, self-involved, creative, and idealistic. They all share a certain vibrancy and glow that outwardly reflects an inner flame and passion for living.

The Earth Signs

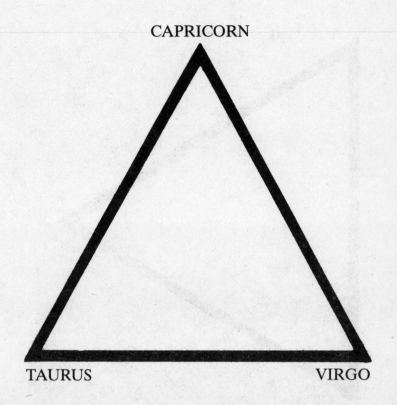

CAPRICORN

TAURUS   VIRGO

This is the earth group. They are in constant touch with the material world and tend to be conservative. Although they are all capable of spartan self-discipline, they are earthy, sensual people who are stimulated by the tangible, elegant, and luxurious. The thread of their lives is always practical, but they do fantasize and are often attracted to dark, mysterious, emotional people. They are like great cliffs overhanging the sea, forever married to the ocean but always resisting erosion from the dark, emotional forces that thunder at their feet.

The Air Signs

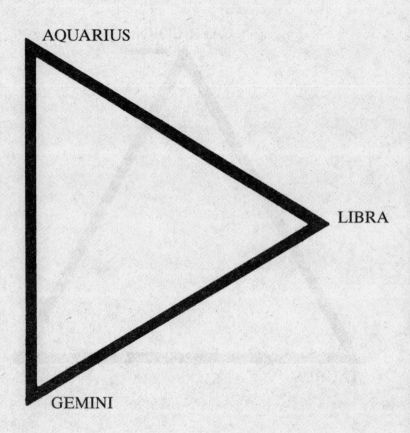

AQUARIUS

LIBRA

GEMINI

This is the air group. They are light, mental creatures desirous of contact, communication, and relationship. They are involved with people and the forming of ties on many levels. Original thinkers, they are the bearers of human news. Their language is their sense of word, color, style, and beauty. They provide an atmosphere suitable and pleasant for living. They add change and versatility to the scene, and it is through them that we can explore new territory of human intelligence and experience.

The Water Signs

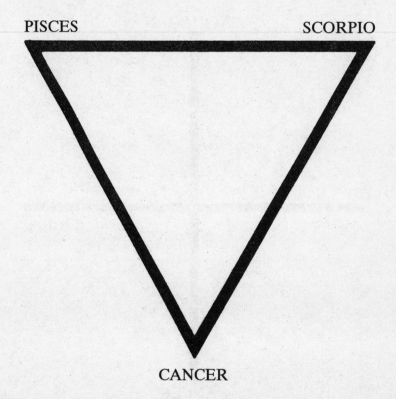

PISCES   SCORPIO

CANCER

This is the water group. Through the water people, we are all joined together on emotional, nonverbal levels. They are silent, mysterious types whose magic hypnotizes even the most determined realist. They have uncanny perceptions about people and are as rich as the oceans when it comes to feeling, emotion, or imagination. They are sensitive, mystical creatures with memories that go back beyond time. Through water, life is sustained. These people have the potential for the depths of darkness or the heights of mysticism and art.

The Cardinal Signs

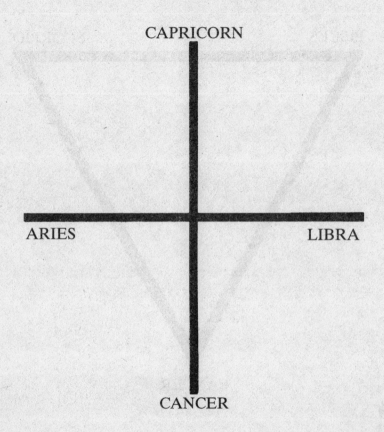

Put together, this is a clear-cut picture of dynamism, activity, tremendous stress, and remarkable achievement. These people know the meaning of great change since their lives are often characterized by significant crises and major successes. This combination is like a simultaneous storm of summer, fall, winter, and spring. The danger is chaotic diffusion of energy; the potential is irrepressible growth and victory.

The Fixed Signs

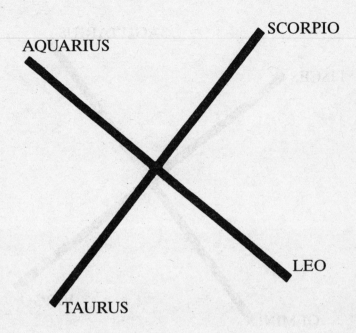

SCORPIO

AQUARIUS

LEO

TAURUS

Fixed signs are always establishing themselves in a given place or area of experience. Like explorers who arrive and plant a flag, these people claim a position from which they do not enjoy being deposed. They are staunch, stalwart, upright, trusty, honorable people, although their obstinacy is well-known. Their contribution is fixity, and they are the angels who support our visible world.

The Mutable Signs

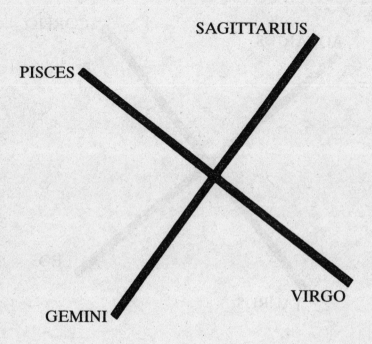

Mutable people are versatile, sensitive, intelligent, nervous, and deeply curious about life. They are the translators of all energy. They often carry out or complete tasks initiated by others. Combinations of these signs have highly developed minds; they are imaginative and jumpy and think and talk a lot. At worst their lives are a Tower of Babel. At best they are adaptable and ready creatures who can assimilate one kind of experience and enjoy it while anticipating coming changes.

THE PLANETS
OF THE SOLAR SYSTEM

This section describes the planets of the solar system. In astrology, both the Sun and the Moon are considered to be planets. Because of the Moon's influence in our day-to-day lives, the Moon is described in a separate section following this one.

The Planets and the Signs They Rule

The signs of the Zodiac are linked to the planets in the following way. Each sign is governed or ruled by one or more planets. No matter where the planets are located in the sky at any given moment, they still rule their respective signs, and when they travel through the signs they rule, they have special dignity and their effects are stronger.

Following is a list of the planets and the signs they rule. After looking at the list, read the definitions of the planets and see if you can determine how the planet ruling *your* Sun sign has affected your life.

SIGNS	RULING PLANETS
Aries	Mars, Pluto
Taurus	Venus
Gemini	Mercury
Cancer	Moon
Leo	Sun
Virgo	Mercury
Libra	Venus
Scorpio	Mars, Pluto
Sagittarius	Jupiter
Capricorn	Saturn
Aquarius	Saturn, Uranus
Pisces	Jupiter, Neptune

Characteristics of the Planets

The following pages give the meaning and characteristics of the planets of the solar system. They all travel around the Sun at different speeds and different distances. Taken with the Sun, they all distribute individual intelligence and ability throughout the entire chart.

The planets modify the influence of the Sun in a chart according to their own particular natures, strengths, and positions. Their positions must be calculated for each year and day, and their function and expression in a horoscope will change as they move from one area of the Zodiac to another.

We start with a description of the sun.

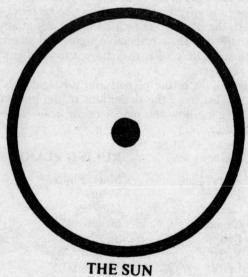

THE SUN

SUN

This is the center of existence. Around this flaming sphere all the planets revolve in endless orbits. Our star is constantly sending out its beams of light and energy without which no life on Earth would be possible. In astrology it symbolizes everything we are trying to become, the center around which all of our activity in life will always revolve. It is the symbol of our basic nature and describes the natural and constant thread that runs through everything that we do from birth to death on this planet.

To early astrologers, the Sun seemed to be another planet because it crossed the heavens every day, just like the rest of the bodies in the sky.

It is the only star near enough to be seen well—it is, in fact, a dwarf star. Approximately 860,000 miles in diameter, it is about ten times as wide as the giant planet Jupiter. The next nearest star is nearly 300,000 times as far away, and if the Sun were located as far away as most of the bright stars, it would be too faint to be seen without a telescope.

Everything in the horoscope ultimately revolves around this singular body. Although other forces may be prominent in the charts of some individuals, still the Sun is the total nucleus of being and symbolizes the complete potential of every human being alive. It is vitality and the life force. Your whole essence comes from the position of the Sun.

You are always trying to express the Sun according to its position by house and sign. Possibility for all development is found in the Sun, and it marks the fundamental character of your personal radiations all around you.

It is the symbol of strength, vigor, wisdom, dignity, ardor, and generosity, and the ability for a person to function as a mature individual. It is also a creative force in society. It is consciousness of the gift of life.

The underdeveloped solar nature is arrogant, pushy, undependable, and proud, and is constantly using force.

MERCURY

Mercury is the planet closest to the Sun. It races around our star, gathering information and translating it to the rest of the system. Mercury represents your capacity to understand the desires of your own will and to translate those desires into action.

In other words it is the planet of mind and the power of communication. Through Mercury we develop an ability to think, write, speak, and observe—to become aware of the world around us. It colors our attitudes and vision of the world, as well as our capacity to communicate our inner responses to the outside world. Some people who have serious disabilities in their power of verbal communication have often wrongly been described as people lacking intelligence.

Although this planet (and its position in the horoscope) indicates your power to communicate your thoughts and perceptions to the world, intelligence is something deeper. Intelligence is distributed throughout all the planets. It is the relationship of the planets to each other that truly describes what we call intelligence. Mercury rules speaking, language, mathematics, draft and design, students, messengers, young people, offices, teachers, and any pursuits where the mind of man has wings.

VENUS

Venus is beauty. It symbolizes the harmony and radiance of a rare and elusive quality: beauty itself. It is refinement and delicacy, softness and charm. In astrology it indicates grace, balance, and the aesthetic sense. Where Venus is we see beauty, a gentle drawing in of energy and the need for satisfaction and completion. It is a special touch that finishes off rough edges. It is sensitivity, and affection, and it is always the place for that other elusive phenomenon: love. Venus describes our sense of what is beautiful and loving. Poorly developed, it is vulgar, tasteless, and self-indulgent. But its ideal is the flame of spiritual love—Aphrodite, goddess of love, and the sweetness and power of personal beauty.

MARS

Mars is raw, crude energy. The planet next to Earth but outward from the Sun is a fiery red sphere that charges through the horoscope with force and fury. It represents the way you reach out for new adventure and new experience. It is energy and drive, initiative, courage, and daring. It is the power to start something and see it through. It can be thoughtless, cruel and wild, angry and hostile, causing cuts, burns, scalds, and wounds. It can stab its way through a chart, or it can be the symbol of healthy spirited adventure, well-channeled constructive power to begin and keep up the drive. If you have trouble starting things, if you lack the get-up-and-go to start the ball rolling, if you lack aggressiveness and self-confidence, chances are there's another planet influencing your Mars. Mars rules soldiers, butchers, surgeons, salesmen—any field that requires daring, bold skill, operational technique, or self-promotion.

JUPITER

This is the largest planet of the solar system. Scientists have recently learned that Jupiter reflects more light than it receives from the Sun. In a sense it is like a star itself. In astrology it rules good luck and good cheer, health, wealth, optimism, happiness, success, and joy. It is the symbol of opportunity and always opens the way for new possibilities in your life. It rules exuberance, enthusiasm, wisdom, knowledge, generosity, and all forms of expansion in general. It rules actors, statesmen, clerics, professional people, religion, publishing, and the distribution of many people over large areas.

Sometimes Jupiter makes you think you deserve everything, and you become sloppy, wasteful, careless and rude, prodigal and lawless, in the illusion that nothing can ever go wrong. Then there is the danger of overconfidence, exaggeration, undependability, and overindulgence.

Jupiter is the minimization of limitation and the emphasis on spirituality and potential. It is the thirst for knowledge and higher learning.

SATURN

Saturn circles our system in dark splendor with its mysterious rings, forcing us to be awakened to whatever we have neglected in the past. It will present real puzzles and problems to be solved, causing delays, obstacles, and hindrances. By doing so, Saturn stirs our own sensitivity to those areas where we are laziest.

Here we must patiently develop *method*, and only through painstaking effort can our ends be achieved. It brings order to a horoscope and imposes reason just where we are feeling least reasonable. By creating limitations and boundary, Saturn shows the consequences of being human and demands that we accept the changing cycles inevitable in human life. Saturn rules time, old age, and sobriety. It can bring depression, gloom, jealousy, and greed, or serious acceptance of responsibilities out of which success will develop. With Saturn there is nothing to do but face facts. It rules laborers, stones, granite, rocks, and crystals of all kinds.

THE OUTER PLANETS:
URANUS, NEPTUNE, PLUTO

Uranus, Neptune, Pluto are the outer planets. They liberate human beings from cultural conditioning, and in that sense are the lawbreakers. In early times it was thought that Saturn was the last planet of the system—the outer limit beyond which we could never go. The discovery of the next three planets ushered in new phases of human history, revolution, and technology.

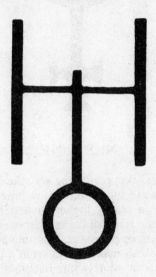

URANUS

Uranus rules unexpected change, upheaval, revolution. It is the symbol of total independence and asserts the freedom of an individual from all restriction and restraint. It is a breakthrough planet and indicates talent, originality, and genius in a horoscope. It usually causes last-minute reversals and changes of plan, unwanted separations, accidents, catastrophes, and eccentric behavior. It can add irrational rebelliousness and perverse bohemianism to a personality or a streak of unaffected brilliance in science and art. It rules technology, aviation, and all forms of electrical and electronic advancement. It governs great leaps forward and topsy-turvy situations, and *always* turns things around at the last minute. Its effects are difficult to predict, since it rules sudden last-minute decisions and events that come like lightning out of the blue.

NEPTUNE

Neptune dissolves existing reality the way the sea erodes the cliffs beside it. Its effects are subtle like the ringing of a buoy's bell in the fog. It suggests a reality higher than definition can usually describe. It awakens a sense of higher responsibility often causing guilt, worry, anxieties, or delusions. Neptune is associated with all forms of escape and can make things seem a certain way so convincingly that you are absolutely sure of something that eventually turns out to be quite different.

It is the planet of illusion and therefore governs the invisible realms that lie beyond our ordinary minds, beyond our simple factual ability to prove what is "real." Treachery, deceit, disillusionment, and disappointment are linked to Neptune. It describes a vague reality that promises eternity and the divine, yet in a manner so complex that we cannot really fathom it at all. At its worst Neptune is a cheap intoxicant; at its best it is the poetry, music, and inspiration of the higher planes of spiritual love. It has dominion over movies, photographs, and much of the arts.

PLUTO

Pluto lies at the outpost of our system and therefore rules finality in a horoscope—the final closing of chapters in your life, the passing of major milestones and points of development from which there is no return. It is a final wipeout, a closeout, an evacuation. It is a distant, subtle but powerful catalyst in all transformations that occur. It creates, destroys, then recreates. Sometimes Pluto starts its influence with a minor event or insignificant incident that might even go unnoticed. Slowly but surely, little by little, everything changes, until at last there has been a total transformation in the area of your life where Pluto has been operating. It rules mass thinking and the trends that society first rejects, then adopts, and finally outgrows.

Pluto rules the dead and the underworld—all the powerful forces of creation and destruction that go on all the time beneath, around, and above us. It can bring a lust for power with strong obsessions.

It is the planet that rules the metamorphosis of the caterpillar into a butterfly, for it symbolizes the capacity to change totally and forever a person's lifestyle, way of thought, and behavior.

THE MOON IN EACH SIGN

The Moon is the nearest planet to the Earth. It exerts more observable influence on us from day to day than any other planet. The effect is very personal, very intimate, and if we are not aware of how it works it can make us quite unstable in our ideas. And the annoying thing is that at these times we often see our own instability but can do nothing about it. A knowledge of what can be expected may help considerably. We can then be prepared to stand strong against the Moon's negative influences and use its positive ones to help us to get ahead. Who has not heard of going with the tide?

The Moon reflects, has no light of its own. It reflects the Sun—the life giver—in the form of vital movement. The Moon controls the tides, the blood rhythm, the movement of sap in trees and plants. Its nature is inconstancy and change so it signifies our moods, our superficial behavior—walking, talking, and especially thinking. Being a true reflector of other forces, the Moon is cold, watery like the surface of a still lake, brilliant and scintillating at times, but easily ruffled and disturbed by the winds of change.

The Moon takes about 27⅓ days to make a complete transit of the Zodiac. It spends just over 2¼ days in each sign. During that time it reflects the qualities, energies, and characteristics of the sign and, to a degree, the planet which rules the sign. When the Moon in its transit occupies a sign incompatible with our own birth sign, we can expect to feel a vague uneasiness, perhaps a touch of irritableness. We should not be discouraged nor let the feeling get us down, or, worse still, allow ourselves to take the discomfort out on others. Try to remember that the Moon has to change signs within 55 hours and, provided you are not physically ill, your mood will probably change with it. It is amazing how frequently depression lifts with the shift in the Moon's position. And, of course, when the Moon is transiting a sign compatible or sympathetic to yours, you will probably feel some sort of stimulation or just be plain happy to be alive.

In the horoscope, the Moon is such a powerful indicator that competent astrologers often use the sign it occupied at birth as the birth sign of the person. This is done particularly when the Sun is on the cusp, or edge, of two signs. Most experienced astrologers, however, coordinate both Sun and Moon signs by reading and confirming from one to the other and secure a far more accurate and personalized analysis.

For these reasons, the Moon tables which follow this section (see pages 86–92) are of great importance to the individual. They show the days and the exact times the Moon will enter each sign of the Zodiac for the year. Remember, you have to adjust the indicated times to local time. The corrections, already calculated for most of the main cities, are at the beginning of the tables. What follows now is a guide to the influences that will be reflected to the Earth by the Moon while it transits each of the twelve signs. The influence is at its peak about 26 hours after the Moon enters a sign. As you read the daily forecast, check the Moon sign for any given day and glance back at this guide.

MOON IN ARIES
This is a time for action, for reaching out beyond the usual self-imposed limitations and faint-hearted cautions. If you have plans in your head or on your desk, put them into practice. New ventures, applications, new jobs, new starts of any kind—all have a good chance of success. This is the period when original and dynamic impulses are being reflected onto Earth. Such energies are extremely vital and favor the pursuit of pleasure and adventure in practically every form. Sick people should feel an improvement. Those who are well will probably find themselves exuding confidence and optimism. People fond of physical exercise should find their bodies growing with tone and well-being. Boldness, strength, determination should characterize most of your activities with a readiness to face up to old challenges. Yesterday's problems may seem petty and exaggerated—so deal with them. Strike out alone. Self-reliance will attract others to you. This is a good time for making friends. Business and marriage partners are more likely to be impressed with the man and woman of action. Opposition will be overcome or thrown aside with much less effort than usual. CAUTION: Be dominant but not domineering.

MOON IN TAURUS
The spontaneous, action-packed person of yesterday gives way to the cautious, diligent, hardworking "thinker." In this period ideas will probably be concentrated on ways of improving finances. A great deal of time may be spent figuring out and going over schemes and plans. It is the right time to be careful with detail.

People will find themselves working longer than usual at their desks. Or devoting more time to serious thought about the future. A strong desire to put order into business and financial arrangements may cause extra work. Loved ones may complain of being neglected and may fail to appreciate that your efforts are for their ultimate benefit. Your desire for system may extend to criticism of arrangements in the home and lead to minor upsets. Health may be affected through overwork. Try to secure a reasonable amount of rest and relaxation, although the tendency will be to "keep going" despite good advice. Work done conscientiously in this period should result in a solid contribution to your future security. CAUTION: Try not to be as serious with people as the work you are engaged in.

MOON IN GEMINI
The humdrum of routine and too much work should suddenly end. You are likely to find yourself in an expansive, quicksilver world of change and self-expression. Urges to write, to paint, to experience the freedom of some sort of artistic outpouring, may be very strong. Take full advantage of them. You may find yourself finishing something you began and put aside long ago. Or embarking on something new which could easily be prompted by a chance meeting, a new acquaintance, or even an advertisement. There may be a yearning for a change of scenery, the feeling to visit another country (not too far away), or at least to get away for a few days. This may result in short, quick journeys. Or, if you are planning a single visit, there may be some unexpected changes or detours on the way. Familiar activities will seem to give little satisfaction unless they contain a fresh element of excitement or expectation. The inclination will be toward untried pursuits, particularly those that allow you to express your inner nature. The accent is on new faces, new places. CAUTION: Do not be too quick to commit yourself emotionally.

MOON IN CANCER
Feelings of uncertainty and vague insecurity are likely to cause problems while the Moon is in Cancer. Thoughts may turn frequently to the warmth of the home and the comfort of loved ones. Nostalgic impulses could cause you to bring out old photographs and letters and reflect on the days when your life seemed to be much more rewarding and less demanding. The love and understanding of parents and family may be important, and, if it is not forthcoming, you may have to fight against bouts of self-pity. The cordiality of friends and the thought of good times with them that are sure to be repeated will help to restore you to a happier frame

of mind. The desire to be alone may follow minor setbacks or rebuffs at this time, but solitude is unlikely to help. Better to get on the telephone or visit someone. This period often causes peculiar dreams and upsurges of imaginative thinking which can be helpful to authors of occult and mystical works. Preoccupation with the personal world of simple human needs can overshadow any material strivings. CAUTION: Do not spend too much time thinking—seek the company of loved ones or close friends.

MOON IN LEO

New horizons of exciting and rather extravagant activity open up. This is the time for exhilarating entertainment, glamorous and lavish parties, and expensive shopping sprees. Any merrymaking that relies upon your generosity as a host has every chance of being a spectacular success. You should find yourself right in the center of the fun, either as the life of the party or simply as a person whom happy people like to be with. Romance thrives in this heady atmosphere and friendships are likely to explode unexpectedly into serious attachments. Children and younger people should be attracted to you and you may find yourself organizing a picnic or a visit to a fun-fair, the movies, or the beach. The sunny company and vitality of youthful companions should help you to find some unsuspected energy. In career, you could find an opening for promotion or advancement. This should be the time to make a direct approach. The period favors those engaged in original research. CAUTION: Bask in popularity, not in flattery.

MOON IN VIRGO

Off comes the party cap and out steps the busy, practical worker. He wants to get his personal affairs straight, to rearrange them, if necessary, for more efficiency, so he will have more time for more work. He clears up his correspondence, pays outstanding bills, makes numerous phone calls. He is likely to make inquiries, or sign up for some new insurance and put money into gilt-edged investment. Thoughts probably revolve around the need for future security—to tie up loose ends and clear the decks. There may be a tendency to be "finicky," to interfere in the routine of others, particularly friends and family members. The motive may be a genuine desire to help with suggestions for updating or streamlining their affairs, but these will probably not be welcomed. Sympathy may be felt for less fortunate sections of the community and a flurry of some sort of voluntary service is likely. This may be accompanied by strong feelings of responsibility on several fronts and health may suffer from extra efforts made. CAUTION: Everyone may not want your help or advice.

MOON IN LIBRA

These are days of harmony and agreement and you should find yourself at peace with most others. Relationships tend to be smooth and sweet-flowing. Friends may become closer and bonds deepen in mutual understanding. Hopes will be shared. Progress by cooperation could be the secret of success in every sphere. In business, established partnerships may flourish and new ones get off to a good start. Acquaintances could discover similar interests that lead to congenial discussions and rewarding exchanges of some sort. Love, as a unifying force, reaches its optimum. Marriage partners should find accord. Those who wed at this time face the prospect of a happy union. Cooperation and tolerance are felt to be stronger than dissension and impatience. The argumentative are not quite so loud in their bellowings, nor as inflexible in their attitudes. In the home, there should be a greater recognition of the other point of view and a readiness to put the wishes of the group before selfish insistence. This is a favorable time to join an art group. CAUTION: Do not be too independent—let others help you if they want to.

MOON IN SCORPIO

Driving impulses to make money and to economize are likely to cause upsets all around. No area of expenditure is likely to be spared the ax, including the household budget. This is a time when the desire to cut down on extravagance can become near fanatical. Care must be exercised to try to keep the aim in reasonable perspective. Others may not feel the same urgent need to save and may retaliate. There is a danger that possessions of sentimental value will be sold to realize cash for investment. Buying and selling of stock for quick profit is also likely. The attention turns to organizing, reorganizing, tidying up at home and at work. Neglected jobs could suddenly be done with great bursts of energy. The desire for solitude may intervene. Self-searching thoughts could disturb. The sense of invisible and mysterious energies in play could cause some excitability. The reassurance of loves ones may help. CAUTION: Be kind to the people you love.

MOON IN SAGITTARIUS

These are days when you are likely to be stirred and elevated by discussions and reflections of a religious and philosophical nature. Ideas of faraway places may cause unusual response and excitement. A decision may be made to visit someone overseas, perhaps a person whose influence was important to your earlier character development. There could be a strong resolution to get away from present intellectual patterns, to learn new subjects, and to meet more interesting people. The superficial may be rejected in all its forms. An impatience with old ideas and unimaginative contacts could lead to a change of companions and interests. There may be an upsurge of religious feeling and metaphysical inquiry. Even a new insight into the significance of astrology and other occult studies is likely under the curious stimulus of the Moon in Sagittarius. Physically, you may express this need for fundamental change by spending more time outdoors: sports, gardening, long walks appeal. CAUTION: Try to channel any restlessness into worthwhile study.

MOON IN CAPRICORN
Life in these hours may seem to pivot around the importance of gaining prestige and honor in the career, as well as maintaining a spotless reputation. Ambitious urges may be excessive and could be accompanied by quite acquisitive drives for money. Effort should be directed along strictly ethical lines where there is no possibility of reproach or scandal. All endeavors are likely to be characterized by great earnestness, and an air of authority and purpose which should impress those who are looking for leadership or reliability. The desire to conform to accepted standards may extend to sharp criticism of family members. Frivolity and unconventional actions are unlikely to amuse while the Moon is in Capricorn. Moderation and seriousness are the orders of the day. Achievement and recognition in this period could come through community work or organizing for the benefit of some amateur group. CAUTION: Dignity and esteem are not always self-awarded.

MOON IN AQUARIUS
Moon in Aquarius is in the second last sign of the Zodiac where ideas can become disturbingly fine and subtle. The result is often a mental "no-man's land" where imagination cannot be trusted with the same certitude as other times. The dangers for the individual are the extremes of optimism and pessimism. Unless the imagination is held in check, situations are likely to be misread, and rosy conclusions drawn where they do not exist. Consequences for the unwary can be costly in career and business. Best to think twice and not speak or act until you think again. Pessimism can be a cruel self-inflicted penalty for delusion at this time. Between the two extremes are strange areas of self-deception which, for example, can make the selfish person think he is actually being generous. Eerie dreams which resemble the reality and even seem to continue into the waking state are also possible. CAUTION: Look for the fact and not just for the image in your mind.

MOON IN PISCES

Everything seems to come to the surface now. Memory may be crystal clear, throwing up long-forgotten information which could be valuable in the career or business. Flashes of clairvoyance and intuition are possible along with sudden realizations of one's own nature, which may be used for self-improvement. A talent, never before suspected, may be discovered. Qualities not evident before in friends and marriage partners are likely to be noticed. As this is a period in which the truth seems to emerge, the discovery of false characteristics is likely to lead to disenchantment or a shift in attachments. However, when qualities are accepted, it should lead to happiness and deeper feeling. Surprise solutions could bob up for old problems. There may be a public announcement of the solving of a crime or mystery. People with secrets may find someone has "guessed" correctly. The secrets of the soul or the inner self also tend to reveal themselves. Religious and philosophical groups may make some interesting discoveries. CAUTION: Not a time for activities that depend on secrecy.

NOTE: When you read your daily forecasts, use the Moon Sign Dates that are provided in the following section of Moon Tables. Then you may want to glance back here for the Moon's influence in a given sign.

MOON TABLES

CORRECTION FOR NEW YORK TIME, FIVE HOURS WEST OF GREENWICH

Atlanta, Boston, Detroit, Miami, Washington, Montreal,
Ottawa, Quebec, Bogota, Havana, Lima, Santiago .. Same time

Chicago, New Orleans, Houston, Winnipeg, Churchill,
Mexico City... Deduct 1 hour

Albuquerque, Denver, Phoenix, El Paso, Edmonton,
Helena .... Deduct 2 hours

Los Angeles, San Francisco, Reno, Portland,
Seattle, Vancouver .... Deduct 3 hours

Honolulu, Anchorage, Fairbanks, Kodiak .... Deduct 5 hours

Nome, Samoa, Tonga, Midway.................... Deduct 6 hours

Halifax, Bermuda, San Juan, Caracas, La Paz,
Barbados..Add 1 hour

St. John's, Brasilia, Rio de Janeiro, Sao Paulo,
Buenos Aires, Montevideo..........................Add 2 hours

Azores, Cape Verde Islands...........................Add 3 hours

Canary Islands, Madeira, Reykjavik ....Add 4 hours

London, Paris, Amsterdam, Madrid, Lisbon,
Gibraltar, Belfast, Rabat...........................Add 5 hours

Frankfurt, Rome, Oslo, Stockholm, Prague,
Belgrade...Add 6 hours

Bucharest, Beirut, Tel Aviv, Athens, Istanbul, Cairo,
Alexandria, Cape Town, Johannesburg ....Add 7 hours

Moscow, Leningrad, Baghdad, Dhahran,
Addis Ababa, Nairobi, Teheran, Zanzibar.........Add 8 hours

Bombay, Calcutta, Sri Lanka..................... Add 10 ½ hours

Hong Kong, Shanghai, Manila, Peking, Perth...... Add 13 hours

Tokyo, Okinawa, Darwin, Pusan.................... Add 14 hours

Sydney, Melbourne, Port Moresby, Guam.......... Add 15 hours

Auckland, Wellington, Suva, Wake................. Add 17 hours

1999 MOON SIGN DATES—
NEW YORK TIME

JANUARY		FEBRUARY		MARCH	
Day Moon Enters		**Day Moon Enters**		**Day Moon Enters**	
1. Cancer	3:16 am	1. Virgo	8:38 pm	1. Virgo	5:06 am
2. Cancer		2. Virgo		2. Virgo	
3. Leo	5:32 am	3. Virgo		3. Libra	1:35 pm
4. Leo		4. Libra	4:57 am	4. Libra	
5. Virgo	10:50 am	5. Libra		5. Libra	
6. Virgo		6. Scorp.	4:07 pm	6. Scorp.	0:23 am
7. Libra	7:54 pm	7. Scorp.		7. Scorp.	
8. Libra		8. Scorp.		8. Sagitt.	0:47 pm
9. Libra		9. Sagitt.	4:39 am	9. Sagitt.	
10. Scorp.	7:50 am	10. Sagitt.		10. Sagitt.	
11. Scorp.		11. Capric.	4:11 pm	11. Capric.	0:55 am
12. Sagitt.	8:24 pm	12. Capric.		12. Capric.	
13. Sagitt.		13. Capric.		13. Aquar.	10:33 am
14. Sagitt.		14. Aquar.	0:58 am	14. Aquar.	
15. Capric.	7:30 am	15. Aquar.		15. Pisces	4:31 pm
16. Capric.		16. Pisces	6:41 am	16. Pisces	
17. Aquar.	4:12 pm	17. Pisces		17. Aries	7:14 pm
18. Aquar.		18. Aries	10:07 am	18. Aries	
19. Pisces	10:41 pm	19. Aries		19. Taurus	8:10 pm
20. Pisces		20. Taurus	0:30 pm	20. Taurus	
21. Pisces		21. Taurus		21. Gemini	9:06 pm
22. Aries	3:26 am	22. Gemini	2:55 pm	22. Gemini	
23. Aries		23. Gemini		23. Cancer	11:34 pm
24. Taurus	6:53 am	24. Cancer	6:10 pm	24. Cancer	
25. Taurus		25. Cancer		25. Cancer	
26. Gemini	9:30 am	26. Leo	10:45 pm	26. Leo	4:23 am
27. Gemini		27. Leo		27. Leo	
28. Cancer	11:58 am	28. Leo		28. Virgo	11:35 am
29. Cancer				29. Virgo	
30. Leo	3:17 pm			30. Libra	8:50 pm
31. Leo				31. Libra	

Summer time to be considered where applicable.

1999 MOON SIGN DATES— NEW YORK TIME

APRIL Day Moon Enters		MAY Day Moon Enters		JUNE Day Moon Enters	
1. Libra		1. Scorp.		1. Capric.	
2. Scorp.	7:50 am	2. Sagitt.	2:37 am	2. Capric.	
3. Scorp.		3. Sagitt.		3. Aquar.	8:38 am
4. Sagitt.	8:08 pm	4. Capric.	3:13 pm	4. Aquar.	
5. Sagitt.		5. Capric.		5. Pisces	6:02 pm
6. Sagitt.		6. Capric.		6. Pisces	
7. Capric.	8:40 am	7. Aquar.	2:41 am	7. Pisces	
8. Capric.		8. Aquar.		8. Aries	0:09 am
9. Aquar.	7:25 pm	9. Pisces	11:17 am	9. Aries	
10. Aquar.		10. Pisces		10. Taurus	2:44 am
11. Aquar.		11. Aries	3:54 pm	11. Taurus	
12. Pisces	2:36 am	12. Aries		12. Gemini	2:49 am
13. Pisces		13. Taurus	4:57 pm	13. Gemini	
14. Aries	5:47 am	14. Taurus		14. Cancer	2:15 am
15. Aries		15. Gemini	4:08 pm	15. Cancer	
16. Taurus	6:08 am	16. Gemini		16. Leo	3:08 am
17. Taurus		17. Cancer	3:40 pm	17. Leo	
18. Gemini	5:40 am	18. Cancer		18. Virgo	7:13 am
19. Gemini		19. Leo	5:38 pm	19. Virgo	
20. Cancer	6:28 am	20. Leo		20. Libra	3:11 pm
21. Cancer		21. Virgo	11:16 pm	21. Libra	
22. Leo	10:07 am	22. Virgo		22. Libra	
23. Leo		23. Virgo		23. Scorp.	2:19 am
24. Virgo	5:05 pm	24. Libra	8:30 am	24. Scorp.	
25. Virgo		25. Libra		25. Sagitt.	2:52 pm
26. Virgo		26. Scorp.	8:06 pm	26. Sagitt.	
27. Libra	2:47 am	27. Scorp.		27. Sagitt.	
28. Libra		28. Scorp.		28. Capric.	3:13 am
29. Scorp.	2:14 pm	29. Sagitt.	8:38 am	29. Capric.	
30. Scorp.		30. Sagitt.		30. Aquar.	2:20 pm
		31. Capric.	9:07 pm		

Summer time to be considered where applicable.

1999 MOON SIGN DATES—
NEW YORK TIME

JULY
Day Moon Enters
1. Aquar.
2. Pisces 11:35 pm
3. Pisces
4. Pisces
5. Aries 6:22 am
6. Aries
7. Taurus 10:23 am
8. Taurus
9. Gemini 0:01 pm
10. Gemini
11. Cancer 0:28 pm
12. Cancer
13. Leo 1:27 pm
14. Leo
15. Virgo 4:40 pm
16. Virgo
17. Libra 11:20 pm
18. Libra
19. Libra
20. Scorp. 9:31 am
21. Scorp.
22. Sagitt. 9:49 pm
23. Sagitt.
24. Sagitt.
25. Capric. 10:09 am
26. Capric.
27. Aquar. 8:55 pm
28. Aquar.
29. Aquar.
30. Pisces 5:28 am
31. Pisces

AUGUST
Day Moon Enters
1. Aries 11:48 am
2. Aries
3. Taurus 4:10 pm
4. Taurus
5. Gemini 6:58 pm
6. Gemini
7. Cancer 8:54 pm
8. Cancer
9. Leo 10:57 pm
10. Leo
11. Leo
12. Virgo 2:23 am
13. Virgo
14. Libra 8:25 am
15. Libra
16. Scorp. 5:41 pm
17. Scorp.
18. Scorp.
19. Sagitt. 5:33 am
20. Sagitt.
21. Capric. 6:00 pm
22. Capric.
23. Capric.
24. Aquar. 4:50 am
25. Aquar.
26. Pisces 0:51 pm
27. Pisces
28. Aries 6:10 pm
29. Aries
30. Taurus 9:42 pm
31. Taurus

SEPTEMBER
Day Moon Enters
1. Taurus
2. Gemini 0:26 am
3. Gemini
4. Cancer 3:11 am
5. Cancer
6. Leo 6:30 am
7. Leo
8. Virgo 10:58 am
9. Virgo
10. Libra 5:17 pm
11. Libra
12. Libra
13. Scorp. 2:09 am
14. Scorp.
15. Sagitt. 1:36 pm
16. Sagitt.
17. Sagitt.
18. Capric. 2:14 am
19. Capric.
20. Aquar. 1:39 pm
21. Aquar.
22. Pisces 9:52 pm
23. Pisces
24. Pisces
25. Aries 2:35 am
26. Aries
27. Taurus 4:52 am
28. Taurus
29. Gemini 6:22 am
30. Gemini

Summer time to be considered where applicable.

1999 MOON SIGN DATES—
NEW YORK TIME

OCTOBER		NOVEMBER		DECEMBER	
Day Moon Enters		**Day Moon Enters**		**Day Moon Enters**	
1. Cancer	8:32 am	1. Virgo	11:08 pm	1. Libra	0:30 pm
2. Cancer		2. Virgo		2. Libra	
3. Leo	0:14 pm	3. Virgo		3. Scorp.	10:36 pm
4. Leo		4. Libra	6:58 am	4. Scorp.	
5. Virgo	5:41 pm	5. Libra		5. Scorp.	
6. Virgo		6. Scorp.	4:47 pm	6. Sagitt.	10:28 am
7. Virgo		7. Scorp.		7. Sagitt.	
8. Libra	0:53 am	8. Scorp.		8. Capric.	11:15 pm
9. Libra		9. Sagitt.	4:16 am	9. Capric.	
10. Scorp.	10:02 am	10. Sagitt.		10. Capric.	
11. Scorp.		11. Capric.	5:01 pm	11. Aquar.	12:00 pm
12. Sagitt.	9:20 pm	12. Capric.		12. Aquar.	
13. Sagitt.		13. Capric.		13. Pisces	11:19 pm
14. Sagitt.		14. Aquar.	5:47 am	14. Pisces	
15. Capric.	10:05 am	15. Aquar.		15. Pisces	
16. Capric.		16. Pisces	4:22 pm	16. Aries	7:31 am
17. Aquar.	10:18 pm	17. Pisces		17. Aries	
18. Aquar.		18. Aries	10:58 pm	18. Taurus	11:46 am
19. Aquar.		19. Aries		19. Taurus	
20. Pisces	7:34 am	20. Aries		20. Gemini	0:40 pm
21. Pisces		21. Taurus	1:27 am	21. Gemini	
22. Aries	0:42 pm	22. Taurus		22. Cancer	11:53 am
23. Aries		23. Gemini	1:15 am	23. Cancer	
24. Taurus	2:26 pm	24. Gemini		24. Leo	11:33 am
25. Taurus		25. Cancer	0:30 am	25. Leo	
26. Gemini	2:34 pm	26. Cancer		26. Virgo	1:35 pm
27. Gemini		27. Leo	1:20 am	27. Virgo	
28. Cancer	3:10 pm	28. Leo		28. Libra	7:15 pm
29. Cancer		29. Virgo	5:12 am	29. Libra	
30. Leo	5:48 pm	30. Virgo		30. Libra	
31. Leo				31. Scorp.	4:37 am

Summer time to be considered where applicable.

1999 PHASES OF THE MOON— NEW YORK TIME

New Moon	First Quarter	Full Moon	Last Quarter
Dec. 18 ('98)	Dec. 26 ('98)	Jan. 1	Jan. 9
Jan. 17	Jan. 24	Jan. 31	Feb. 8
Feb. 16	Feb. 22	March 2	March 10
March 17	March 24	March 31	April 8
April 15	April 22	April 30	May 8
May 15	May 22	May 30	June 6
June 13	June 20	June 28	July 6
July 12	July 20	July 28	Aug. 4
Aug. 11	Aug. 18	Aug. 26	Sept. 2
Sept. 9	Sept. 17	Sept. 25	Oct. 1
Oct. 9	Oct. 17	Oct. 24	Oct. 31
Nov. 7	Nov. 16	Nov. 23	Nov. 29
Dec. 7	Dec. 15	Dec. 22	Dec. 29

Each phase of the Moon lasts approximately seven to eight days, during which the Moon's shape gradually changes as it comes out of one phase and goes into the next.

There will be a partial solar eclipse during the New Moon phase on February 16 and August 11.

There will be a lunar eclipse during the Full Moon phase on July 28.

1999 FISHING GUIDE

	Good	Best
January	3-4-5-17-24-28-30-31	1-2-9-29
February	1-2-3-16-23-27-28	8
March	1-2-3-10-28-29-30	4-5-17-24-31
April	16-22	1-2-3-9-27-28-29-30
May	2-3-8-15-22-29-30-31	1-27-28
June	13-20-25-26-27-30	1-2-7-28-29
July	1-6-13-25-28-29-30	20-26-27-31
August	11-19-23-24-25-26-29	4-27-28
September	2-9-17-22-25-26	23-24-27-28
October	22-23-24-26-27-31	2-9-17-21-25
November	16-20-23-24-29	8-21-22-25-26
December	7-16-20-21-22-24-25	19-23

1999 PLANTING GUIDE

	Aboveground Crops	Root Crops
January	1-20-21-25-29	2-8-9-10-11-12-16
February	17-21-25-26	4-5-6-7-8-12-13
March	20-21-24-25-31	4-5-6-7-11-12-16
April	17-21-27-28-29	1-2-3-4-8-9-12-13
May	18-19-25-26-27-28	1-5-6-10-14
June	14-15-21-22-23-24	1-2-6-7-10-11-29
July	18-19-20-21-22-26-27	3-4-8-12-31
August	15-16-17-18-22-23	4-5-8-9-27-28-31
September	11-12-13-14-18-19-23-24	1-4-5-27-28
October	10-11-12-16-17-21	2-8-25-29-30
November	8-12-13-17-18-21-22	5-6-7-25-26
December	9-10-14-15-19	2-3-4-5-23-29-30-31

	Pruning	Weeds and Pests
January	2-11-12	4-5-6-7-13-14
February	7-8	1-2-3-9-10-14-15
March	6-7-16	2-9-10-14
April	3-4-12-13	5-6-10-11-15
May	1-10	2-3-7-8-12-30-31
June	6-7	4-5-8-9-12
July	3-4-12-31	1-2-6-10-29
August	8-9-27-28	2-6-7-10-29-30
September	4-5	2-3-7-8-9-26-30
October	2-29-30	4-5-6-7-27-31
November	7-25-26	1-2-3-23-24-27-28-29-30
December	4-5-23-31	7-25-26-27-28

MOON'S INFLUENCE OVER PLANTS

Centuries ago it was established that seeds planted when the Moon is in signs and phases called Fruitful will produce more growth than seeds planted when the Moon is in a Barren sign.

Fruitful Signs: Taurus, Cancer, Libra, Scorpio, Capricorn, Pisces
Barren Signs: Aries, Gemini, Leo, Virgo, Sagittarius, Aquarius
Dry Signs: Aries, Gemini, Sagittarius, Aquarius

Activity	Moon In
Mow lawn, trim plants	**Fruitful sign:** 1st & 2nd quarter
Plant flowers	**Fruitful sign:** 2nd quarter; best in Cancer and Libra
Prune	**Fruitful sign:** 3rd & 4th quarter
Destroy pests; spray	**Barren sign:** 4th quarter
Harvest potatoes, root crops	**Dry sign:** 3rd & 4th quarter; Taurus, Leo, and Aquarius

MOON'S INFLUENCE OVER YOUR HEALTH

ARIES	Head, brain, face, upper jaw
TAURUS	Throat, neck, lower jaw
GEMINI	Hands, arms, lungs, shoulders, nervous system
CANCER	Esophagus, stomach, breasts, womb, liver
LEO	Heart, spine
VIRGO	Intestines, liver
LIBRA	Kidneys, lower back
SCORPIO	Sex and eliminative organs
SAGITTARIUS	Hips, thighs, liver
CAPRICORN	Skin, bones, teeth, knees
AQUARIUS	Circulatory system, lower legs
PISCES	Feet, tone of being

Try to avoid work being done on that part of the body when the Moon is in the sign governing that part.

MOON'S INFLUENCE OVER DAILY AFFAIRS

The Moon makes a complete transit of the Zodiac every 27 days 7 hours and 43 minutes. In making this transit the Moon forms different aspects with the planets and consequently has favorable or unfavorable bearings on affairs and events for persons according to the sign of the Zodiac under which they were born.

When the Moon is in conjunction with the Sun it is called a New Moon; when the Moon and Sun are in opposition it is called a Full Moon. From New Moon to Full Moon, first and second quarter—which takes about two weeks—the Moon is increasing or waxing. From Full Moon to New Moon, third and fourth quarter, the Moon is decreasing or waning.

Activity	Moon In
Business: buying and selling new, requiring public support	Sagittarius, Aries, Gemini, Virgo 1st and 2nd quarter
meant to be kept quiet	3rd and 4th quarter
Investigation	3rd and 4th quarter
Signing documents	1st & 2nd quarter, Cancer, Scorpio, Pisces
Advertising	2nd quarter, Sagittarius
Journeys and trips	1st & 2nd quarter, Gemini, Virgo
Renting offices, etc.	Taurus, Leo, Scorpio, Aquarius
Painting of house/apartment	3rd & 4th quarter, Taurus, Scorpio, Aquarius
Decorating	Gemini, Libra, Aquarius
Buying clothes and accessories	Taurus, Virgo
Beauty salon or barber shop visit	1st & 2nd quarter, Taurus, Leo, Libra, Scorpio, Aquarius
Weddings	1st & 2nd quarter

CAPRICORN

CAPRICORN

Character Analysis

People born under Capricorn, the tenth sign of the Zodiac, are generally strong-willed and goal-directed. They seldom do anything without a purpose. They tend to be quite ambitious. They hammer away at something until they have made their point. Capricorns know what they want out of life. Through perseverance and patience, they generally achieve it. There is almost nothing they cannot attain once they make up their minds. They are interested in progress, in making things better. When Capricorns believe in something, they put themselves behind it totally. They do not believe in acting in a halfhearted fashion.

The Goat is the zodiacal symbol of Capricorn. The Goat climbs, always slowly and surely, keeping balance even under unstable circumstances and on difficult terrain. At times, in order to get ahead, Capricorn will make use of people. But these people are also likely to gain through such manipulation.

Capricorns, because of their steady nature, inspire confidence and trust. They do not sit idly by watching the action. And they openly admire qualities they lack. Overall, Capricorn is an excellent manager and very shrewd in their quiet way.

When Capricorns like or believe in someone, they will stick by that person for the rest of their life. They are loyal and constant. They seldom waver once they have committed themselves to an ideal or a person. They can always be depended on to speak up for something or someone they believe in. At times Capricorn is utterly charming, at other times aloof and proud.

Capricorn men and women are in possession of clear, uncluttered minds. They are not necessarily brilliant, but they are capable of concentrating on what interests them in an effective manner. They believe in doing things right, never halfway. Generally, Capricorns are exact and accurate. They pride themselves on doing their work correctly. They are conscientious and careful. They can always be counted on to hold up their end of a bargain. They tend to be stiff when it comes to making judgments. They are more interested in justice than forgiveness. In spite of this, one could never accuse them of not being fair-minded in most things. They make a point of it.

Capricorns could hardly be called softhearted. They can be quite harsh at times in the way they handle someone, especially if they think they're right. People are likely to find Capricorn cold and callous. Honor and pride are important, and Capricorn is bound to have some intellectual pretensions.

Capricorns who are weak in character are apt to feel they are a cut above others and will do what they can to let this be felt. Often they suffer from a feeling of inadequacy. They may not know how to rid themselves of this complex that has an adverse effect on their disposition. They are often depressed and insecure. For these reasons, people may find Capricorn difficult to get along with. If Capricorn men and women are too conscious of the qualities they lack, they may ruin their chances of attaining the ends they desire.

Some Capricorns of this caliber find it difficult to settle down. They roam from one thing to another, never satisfied. Their cleverness may become mean and cutting. They may be destructive rather than constructive and positive. They may be afraid to forge ahead. The future frightens them and increases their feelings of insecurity. The frightened Goat may strike out at people he suspects are laughing at him behind his back.

The weak Capricorn man or woman is not an easy person to get along with. Others may be afraid to be truthful with them. This Capricorn is likely to be narrow-minded and conservative. They cling desperately to the past, afraid of moving on. They think more of themselves than of others and may abuse friends and acquaintances.

Some Capricorns may be lacking in a healthy sense of humor. A harmless joke may make them suspicious and aggressive if they think it was secretly directed at them. They cannot easily laugh at themselves when they pull a boner.

Some Capricorns are exceedingly careful with their money. As a rule, however, they tend to be on the generous side. They would never refuse someone in need. They will, at times, go out of their way to help someone in trouble. They do not expect or insist that the favor be returned; a word of thanks is good enough for them.

Capricorn men and women are very grateful when someone offers to lend them a helping hand. They never forget a favor. Although they may find it difficult to express thanks at times, they do appreciate any help that is given to them.

Health

During childhood, Capricorns may not be too strong or sturdy. Often they are subject to a series of childhood diseases. As they grow older, however, they become stronger. An adult Capricorn often has a strong resistance to diseases. The Goat is a fighter. They never want to lose in anything, not even illness. Many people born under this sign live a long life. They are generally very active people and have a store of energy at their disposal.

The weak areas of a Capricorn person's body are the knees and joints. When they have an accident, these areas are often involved. Some Capricorns have poor teeth; this may be the result of insufficient calcium in the system. Skin troubles often plague them. In later life they may become the victim of an arthritic disease.

Being a practical sort of person, Capricorn generally sees to it that they eat sensibly. A balanced diet is essential. They need plenty of fresh fruits and vegetables in order to remain fit. Hard work and exercise help them to maintain their good constitution. As they mature, Capricorns become stronger and their strength is seldom undermined.

Moods, however, may have an unsettling effect on the health in general. Capricorn is given to dark, somber moods. Gloomy thoughts and depressed feelings can be hard to dispel. Melancholy can persist longer than is wise or desirable. Capricorn men and women can easily fall into the bad habit of worrying about small things. Such worries can drain them of energy and may make them prey to a variety of illnesses.

Plenty of fresh air, sunshine, and exercise will help Capricorn keep a healthy disposition and a happy frame of mind. Companions and associates will also play a great role in Capricorn's health. They get along best with people who are youthful, positive, and energetic.

Occupation

The Capricorn man or woman is very much interested in being successful in life. They will work hard to win at whatever it is they do. Reputation means a lot to them. They will fight to advance and to hold their position. They like a job that carries a bit of prestige with it. Having people respect them is very important. Capricorn enjoys being in a position of authority.

Money, of course, has a great attraction for the man or woman born under the sign of the Goat. When accepting a job, salary usually plays an important part. They would not take a job just for the glory or prestige alone. It has to have its financial advantages.

There are Capricorns who believe that the only way to win is to stick to something that is regular, or routine. They don't mind plodding along if they are sure that they will get that pot of gold at the end of the rainbow. Still and all, the strong Capricorn, while seeing the advantages of routine work, will never become a robot or slave to a humdrum work schedule. Capricorn men and women try to move along with the times. They keep abreast of new developments in the field, applying new techniques to their work wherever they see fit.

Hard work does not frighten Capricorn. They are willing to put in long and hard hours, if they feel the benefits they are to receive are indeed worth their efforts. They are usually conscientious and loyal in their work. Many of them start at the bottom and slowly work their way up.

There are seldom any complaints about Capricorn's work. These men and women are very good at what they do. They are determined, methodical, thorough. They have a fine grasp of details while keeping sight of the big idea. They are supremely focused and fixed in their purpose—to do an excellent job. Any employer of Capricorn men and women are usually satisfied with their job performance because they are accurate and professional.

Although they are interested in being successful, some Capricorns tend to become a bit depressed if it seems to take them longer than it does for other people. But Capricorns are willing to bide their time. They hold no rosy view of the future. They know that they will really have to apply themselves to their tasks in order to attain their goals.

It is the idea of winning that keeps Capricorn on the go. They never falter once they have made up their mind to get ahead in the world. Some of them never attain what they're after until very late in life. But they are not afraid of pushing ahead, making small gains here and there, as long as they seem to be on the right road.

Once on the road to any fame or fortune, the success-oriented Capricorn man or woman is sure to steer steadily ahead. He or she will let no one stand in the way. At times, Capricorn can be quite brutal and heartless in their methods for getting to the top. So the climb to the summit can be agonizing indeed—at least for the person who the Goat is pushing out of the way.

Needless to say, the pushy sort of Goat has no trouble becoming unpopular with teammates and associates. Obsessed with success, he or she is always on the lookout for an opportunity to get ahead. If necessary, they will step on another's toes in order to make a gain, no matter how small it is.

Politics is an area where someone born under the sign of the Goat usually excels. Capricorn has a diplomatic way and a tactful demeanor. They are interested in justice and being fair. Some Capricorns make good researchers. They are not afraid to put in long hours when involved in investigation. They are reliable and steady. In a position that gives them a chance to organize or arrange things, they could do very well.

Authoritarian positions hold a particular attraction for Capricorn men and women. They enjoy the challenge of this sort of position, also the respect it generally commands. Having people under their control sometimes makes them respect themselves more. It makes them more sure of their own worth. In crafts and sciences, they often do well, too.

Money is important to the Capricorn man and woman. They'll work hard to build up their financial resources. If they wind up rich, it's not because of luck, generally, but because they have earned it. Capricorn is an open opportunist, and will not try to disguise this. He or she is no hypocrite. They are direct in actions, even if they do not talk about them.

Of all the signs, Capricorn is the most interested in gain and profit. Security is something the Goat must have. It drives them on; it motivates them. During difficult moments, they may feel a bit discouraged or depressed. Still, there is that interest in the ultimate goal that keeps Capricorn going.

Capricorn individuals are generally thrifty. They believe in saving. Waste disgusts them. For the most part they are quite conservative in the way they handle their finances. Although they may be given to moods in which they feel very expansive or generous, on the whole they manage to keep tight control of their money. They can be trusted with other people's money, too.

During their youth, Capricorn may impress others as being rather penny-pinching. They are cautious in the way they manage finances. Generally, they can account for every cent they spend.

With an eye always on the future, they think about that inevitable rainy day, and prepare themselves for it. However, once they have gained quite a bit and feel financially secure, their attitudes are likely to change. They become generous and charitable. They are very helpful to those in need, especially if a person's background is similar to their own.

Home and Family

The average Capricorn enjoys the security of home life. Still, it generally does not appeal to them in the same way as it does others. They may not marry for love or companionship alone. They may think of marriage and domesticity as a practical means for realizing their material goals.

The person born under this sign sometimes marries for position or money. Not that they are all that coldhearted and calculating. But Capricorn finds it just as easy to fall in love with a socially prominent and wealthy person as it is to become romantically involved with a poor person.

The occupation or career of a Capricorn man or woman is apt to play the central role in their life. Family comes in second, playing a supporting role. Many Capricorns are not fond of large families, that is, one with many children.

Parenthood can be something of a burden for the average Capricorn. They take their responsibilities toward the family very seriously. Family ties are strong, but the Goat may seem a bit distant even to loved ones. Capricorn is capable of great affection, but is apt to be more demonstrative when managing or organizing household affairs. The goal is that everything connected with home life should run smoothly.

Capricorns sometimes feel lacking in some quality or characteristic. It is this feeling of inadequacy that drives them in romance. They want to find someone who has what they lack. A loving mate and a harmonious family give Capricorn the feeling of being needed, of being a complete person. Once settled, then he or she is interested in improving or expanding home life in various ways.

The Capricorn husband or wife will often do what he or she can to make the home harmonious and tasteful. They generally have a great interest in all that is beautiful and cultural. Some Capricorns are fond of music, and a piano in the home is a must. The home of a Capricorn person generally radiates good taste and beauty. It may be a bit on the luxurious side—if they can afford it—but never in an ostentatious way.

The home is usually peaceful and harmonious. Capricorn feels that everything in the household should run on some regular basis: a special time for meals, for sleeping, for entertaining. The home is a comfortable place, and it is usually easy for someone to feel at ease while visiting a Capricorn friend.

Capricorns are proud of their home and property. They are responsible members of the community and will do what is necessary to fulfill their duties as a neighbor. However, they like to keep their home life to themselves. They value their privacy.

Capricorn's home is usually well kept and attractive. They like to be respected and highly thought of because of their possessions. Prestige in the community is important to them. A materialistic duel with the Joneses is not beneath the Goat. They will always try to do the neighbors one better if they can afford it.

Children bring joy into the Goat's life. Still, Capricorn men and women may not be very fond of a large family. But they will give the necessary love and attention to the few children they do have. Capricorn parents are interested in the youngsters as distinct individuals and enjoy seeing them grow up. The hope, of course, is that the children will be a credit to the parents and will reflect the good upbringing Capricorn has given them.

At times, the Capricorn parent may seem a bit unsympathetic, especially if the youngsters misbehave. But as they mature, they will respect and love their Capricorn parent for the security he or she has given them while they were growing up.

Social Relationships

The Capricorn personality projected onto the social scene is marked by reserve and dignity. At first it may appear that these men and women are hanging back, waiting to be drawn into the thick of things. Capricorns may seem unapproachable and cold to someone newly introduced. But the one who does win a Goat's friendship is rewarded by kindness, loyalty, and fidelity.

Capricorns have many acquaintainces but true few friends. Among strangers the Goat may feel scrutinized and judged, so there is a tendency to wait in the wings, to hide from imagined harsh criticism. The fear of criticism also gives rise to a tendency to be secretive. Capricorns are unwilling to broadcast their intentions, except to the chosen few.

Capricorn men and women seldom, if ever, gossip or talk behind someone's back. Friends can always count on them to guard a confidence. Even though the Goat is wary of revealing his or her own secrets, the secrets of other people are kept under wraps.

Capricorn sometimes picks the wrong people as companions. In youth and early adulthood the Goat may be tempted to run with a bad crowd, and unfortunately is likely to gain a bad reputation because of it. The troublemakers and freeloaders take advantage and often blame the innocent Goat. Such disappointments and betrayals are all too common. But Capricorns learn from their mistakes. For that reason, as they mature they become more cautious and discriminating in their choice of friends.

Capricorn men and women are prominent in the life of their community. They play an active role in neighborhood groups and civic organizations. Where there is a club or association formed to promote the general good, you will find a Capricorn and often in a leadership position.

To true friends, Capricorn is a pillar of strength, a rock. He or she is capable of making great sacrifices in order to help a friend. That is why solid friendships last a lifetime and provide much support and comfort all around.

Love and Marriage

The Capricorn man or woman is not what one could accurately describe as being romantic. But they are emotional, and their feelings run deep. Their respect for intellect and convention may prevent them from expressing themselves in a demonstrative way, vigorously exhibiting their love and affection.

Capricorn is a considerate lover, a well-mannered dating partner. Their approach to courtship and romance is conventional. They would never do anything that might injure the feelings or sensibilities of their mate or date. Doing the right thing at the right time is important.

Capricorns do not let their affections run rampant. Their mind reigns over their emotions. Flirting has little or no appeal. When in love, the Goat is serious. Even if a love relationship does not end in a permanent union, the Goat takes it seriously. Capricorn men and women will not run from one love affair to another—or enjoy several romances at the same time. Capricorn is constant.

Still, Capricorn will not give his or her heart away immediately. They like to begin a romance by being friends. If the love interest is encouraging and indicates reciprocal feelings, Capricorn will then allow the relationship to enter a more intimate phase. He or she does not want to be deceived or made a fool of. Ever protective, the Goat will take steps to guard against betrayal.

Driven by ambition, Capricorn in love is apt to direct his or her affections toward someone who can help them get ahead in their career. In love, they do not totally lose their heads. They know what they want. That does not mean Capricorn is insincere in love—just practical.

The person who falls under Capricorn's charm—and there is plenty of it—may find it difficult to understand the dark and pessimistic moods that emerge from nowhere. The inhibition and hesitation and secretiveness seem to be without reason. Although Capricorns build a love affair slowly, they will end it quickly if they feel it is a waste of time. When disappointed, they are direct and to the point.

The cultivated, strong Capricorn tries to be open in love so that the relationship will be a lasting one. They admit their faults readily and do what they can to more affectionate and demonstrative. An exciting, impulsive person is sometimes the ideal mate for a Capricorn man or woman.

Romance and the Capricorn Woman

The Capricorn woman is very serious when it comes to love and courtship. She is correct. When her loved one offends her sensibilities, she lets him know in short order. She can be quite affectionate with the right man. On the whole, however, she is rather inhibited. A warm and understanding man can teach her how to be more demonstrative in her affection.

She is not fond of flirting. A man who tries to win her with his charm may not have much of a chance. She is interested in someone who is serious on whom she can depend. Respect also plays an important part when she selects a lover or partner. A man who abuses her affections is quickly dismissed. She will never take the lead in a love affair, yet she is not fond of people who move fast. She likes to take her time getting to know someone. Whirlwind romance has very little appeal to a Capricorn woman.

She is a perfectionist to some extent. She wants a man she can look up to and respect. Someone who is in a position to provide a good home and the necessary security is more important and interesting to her than someone who is amorous and charming.

The Capricorn woman needs someone who is warm and affectionate even though she may not show or indicate it. She needs someone who is what she is not. She may spend a great deal of time looking for the right person. She is not someone who will settle for something short of her ideals. Some female Goats marry late in life as a result. The cultivated Capricorn woman, however, knows how to take the bitter with the sweet. If she meets someone who basically lines up with her ideals but is not perfect, she will settle for him and try to make the most of it.

The Capricorn wife runs her home in a very efficient manner. She is faithful and systematic. She enjoys taking care of her family and sees to it that everything runs smoothly. She may not be very romantic, even after marriage. However, the right man can help her to develop a deeper interest in love and companionship as the marriage grows.

She is a correct mother. Her children never want. She may not be too loving or sympathetic, but she is responsible and protective. Children's love for her grows as they grow older.

Romance and the Capricorn Man

The Capricorn man is no Lothario. He will never be swept off his feet by romance. He's more intellectual than romantic. He is fond of affection but may find it difficult to express affection toward the one he is interested in.

He is capable of great passion—yet passion that is lacking in affection. His loved one is apt to find him difficult to understand at times. He is honest in his love relationships. He would never lead a woman astray. Flirting has no interest for him. He believes in steady, gradual relationships. He likes to know his partner well as a person before going on to romance or love. He may seem casual at first in the way he demonstrates his interest. As he wins the woman's trust, however, he will begin to unwind and reveal his feelings for what they are.

A woman who can help him gain those things in life that interest him holds a great attraction for him. He is not a fortune hunter. But if the woman he is interested in has some money or social background, so much the better. He can be practical, even when in love.

He is an idealist. He has a dream woman running around in his head, and he won't give up his search until he has found her—or someone like her. He is faithful in marriage. He does what he can to provide well for his family. He can be depended on to fulfill his role as father and husband to the letter.

He always tries to do what is best for his children. He may not be the most affectionate father, but he is dutiful and responsible. The feelings a Capricorn father has for his youngsters generally intensify as they grow up.

Woman—Man

CAPRICORN WOMAN
ARIES MAN

In some ways, the Aries man is the black sheep in the family, always seeking adventure. He has an insatiable thirst for knowledge. He's ambitious and is apt to have his finger in many pies. He can do with a woman like you—someone attractive, quick-witted, and smart.

He is not interested in a clinging vine kind of wife. He wants someone who is there when he needs her, someone who can give advice if he should ever need it, which is not likely to be often. The Aries man wants a woman who will look good on his arm without hanging on it too heavily. He is looking for a woman who has both feet on the ground and yet is mysterious and enticing, a kind of domestic Helen of Troy whose face can launch a thousand business deals if need be.

That woman he's in search of sounds a little like you, doesn't she? If the shoe fits, put it on. You won't regret it. The Aries man makes a good husband. He is faithful and attentive. He is an affectionate man. He'll make you feel needed and loved.

Love is a serious matter for the Aries man. He does not believe in flirting or playing the field—especially after he's found the woman of his dreams. He'll expect you to be as constant in your affection as he is in his. He'll expect you to be one hundred percent his. He won't put up with any nonsense while romancing you.

The Aries man may be pretty progressive and modern about

many things. However, when it comes to pants wearing, he's the boss and that's that. Once you have learned to accept that, you'll find the going easy.

The Aries man, with his endless energy and drive, likes to relax in the comfort of his home at the end of the day. The good home-maker can be sure of holding his love. He likes to watch the news from his favorite chair. If you see to it that everything in the house is where he expects to find it, you'll have no difficulty keeping the relationship on an even keel.

Life and love with an Aries man may be just the medicine you need. He'll be a good provider. He'll spoil you if he's financially able.

The Aries father is young at heart and will spoil the children every chance he gets. His quick mind and energetic behavior ap-peal to the young. His ability to jump from one thing to another keeps the kids hopping. You must introduce some focus into the children's activities. Always emphasize the practical in order to prepare the kids for success.

CAPRICORN WOMAN
TAURUS MAN

Some Taurus men are strong and silent. They do all they can to protect and provide for the women they love. The Taurus man will never let you down. He's steady, sturdy, and reliable. He's pretty honest and practical, too. He says what he means and means what he says. He never indulges in deceit and will always put his cards on the table.

Taurus is affectionate. Being loved, appreciated, understood is important for his well-being. Like you, he is also looking for peace and security in his life. If you both work toward these goals to-gether, you'll find that they are easily attained.

If you should marry a Taurus man, you can be sure that the wolf will never darken your door. Bulls are notoriously good pro-viders and do everything they can to make their families com-fortable and happy.

He'll appreciate the way you have of making a home warm and inviting. Soft lights and the evening papers are essential ingredi-ents in making your Taurus husband happy at the end of the workday. Although he may be a big lug of a guy, you'll find that he's fond of gentleness and soft things. If you puff up his pillow and tuck him in at night, he'll eat it up and ask for more.

You probably won't complain about his friends. Taurus tends to seek out friends who are successful or prominent. You admire people, too, who work hard and achieve what they set out for.

The Taurus man doesn't care too much for change. He's the

original stay-at-home. Chances are that the house you move into after you're married will be the house you'll live in for the rest of your life.

You'll find that the man born under the sign of the Bull is easy to get along with. It's unlikely that you'll have many quarrels or arguments that last more than a short time.

Although he'll be gentle and tender with you, your Taurus man is far from being a sensitive type. He's a man's man. Chances are he loves sports from fishing to football. He can be earthy as well as down to earth.

Taurus, born under an earth sign as you are, has much affection for the children and has no trouble demonstrating his love and warmth. Yet the Taurus father does not believe in spoiling the kids, so you and he will share the challenge of disciplining them. Both of you want your youngsters to succeed in the world. The Taurus father especially sees to it they grow up knowing their place in society.

CAPRICORN WOMAN
GEMINI MAN

Gemini men, in spite of their charm and dashing manner, may leave you cold. They seem to lack the sort of common sense you set so much store in. Their tendency to start something, then out of boredom never finish it, may exasperate you.

You may interpret a Gemini's jumping around from here to there as childish, if not downright neurotic. A man born under the sign of the Twins will seldom stay put. If you should take it upon yourself to try and make him sit still, he will resent it strongly.

On the other hand, the Gemini man may think you're a slow-poke—someone far too interested in security and material things. He's attracted to things that sparkle and dazzle. You, with your practical way of looking at things most of the time, are likely to seem a little dull and uninteresting to this gadabout. If you're looking for a life of security and permanence, you'd better look elsewhere for your Mr. Right.

Chances are you'll be taken by his charming ways and facile wit. Few women can resist Gemini magic. But after you've seen through his live-for-today, gossamer facade, you'll most likely be very happy to turn your attention to someone more stable, even if he is not as interesting.

You want a man who is there when you need him. You need someone on whom you can fully rely. Keeping track of a Gemini's movements will make you dizzy. Still, if you are patient, you should be able to put up with someone contrary—especially if you feel the experience is worth the effort.

A successful and serious Gemini could make you a very happy woman, if you gave him half a chance. He generally has a good brain and can make good use of it when he wants. Some Geminis who have learned the importance of being consistent have risen to great heights professionally. Once you can convince yourself that not all people born under the sign of the Twins are witless grasshoppers, you'll find that you've come a long way in trying to understand them.

Life with a Gemini man can be more fun than a barrel of clowns. You'll never have a chance to experience a dull moment. He's always the life of the party. He's a little scatterbrained when it comes to handling money most of the time. You'd better handle the budgeting and bookkeeping.

The Gemini father is in some ways like a child himself, and perhaps that is why he gets along so well with the younger generation. He usually lets the children do what they want until they are running the household. You will put a stop to this nonsense without suppressing the sense of humor the youngsters have picked up from their Gemini father.

CAPRICORN WOMAN
CANCER MAN

The Cancer-Capricorn combination is astrologically linked. You two are zodiacal mates, as well as zodiacal opposites, so chances are you will hit if off in love. But Cancer is very sensitive—thin-skinned and moody. You've got to keep on your toes not to step on his.

Cancer may be lacking in some of the qualities you seek in a man. But when it comes to being faithful and being a good provider, he's hard to beat.

True to his sign, the Crab can be fairly cranky and crabby when handled the wrong way. If you want to catch him and keep him, you will learn to understand and flow with his moods.

The perceptive woman will not mistake the Crab's quietness for sullenness or his thriftiness for penny-pinching. In some respects, he is like that wise old owl out on a limb. He may look like he's dozing, but actually he hasn't missed a thing.

Cancers often possess a well of knowledge about human behavior. They can come up with helpful advice to those in trouble or in need. He can certainly guide you in making investments both in time and money. He may not say much, but he's always got his wits about him.

If you're smarter than your Cancer friend, be smart enough not to let him know. Never give him the idea that you think he's a little short on brainpower. It would send him scurrying back into his shell, and all that lost ground will never be recovered.

The Crab is most comfortable at home. Settled down for the night or the weekend, wild horses couldn't drag him any further than the gatepost, unless those wild horses were dispatched by his mother. The Crab is sometimes a Mama's boy. If his mate does not put her foot down, he will see to it that his mother always comes first.

No self-respecting Capricorn wife would ever allow herself to play second fiddle to her mother-in-law. With a little bit of tact, you'll slip into that number-one position as easy as pie.

Cancers make proud, patient, and protective fathers. But they can be a little too protective. Their sheltering instincts can interfere with a youngster's natural inclination to test the waters outside the home. Still, the Cancer father doesn't want to see his kids learning about life the hard way from the streets. The fact that you are Cancer's zodiacal opposite, as well as mate, helps to balance how your children will view life and cope with a variety of challenging situations.

CAPRICORN WOMAN
LEO MAN

To know a man born under the sign of the Lion is not necessarily to love him—even though the temptation may be great. When he fixes most girls with his leonine double-whammy, it causes their hearts to pitter-pat and their minds to cloud over.

You are a little too sensible to allow yourself to be bowled over by a regal strut and a roar. Still, there's no denying that Leo has a way with women—even sensible women like yourself. Once he's swept a woman off her feet, it may be hard for her to scramble upright again. Still, you are no pushover for romantic charm—especially if you feel it's all show.

He'll wine you and dine you in the fanciest places. He'll croon to you under the moon and shower you with diamonds if he can get a hold of them. Still, it would be wise to find out just how long that shower is going to last before consenting to be his wife.

Lions in love are hard to ignore, let alone brush off. Your reserve will have a way of nudging him on until he feels he has you completely under his spell. Once mesmerized by this romantic powerhouse, you will most likely find yourself doing things you never dreamed of.

Leos can be vain pussycats when involved romantically. They like to be cuddled and petted. This may not be your cup of tea exactly. Still, you'll do everything to make him purr.

Although he may be big and magnanimous while trying to win

you, he'll whine if he thinks he's not getting the tender love and care he feels is his due. If you keep him well supplied with affection, you can be sure his eyes will never look for someone else and his heart will never wander.

Leo men often tend to be authoritarian. They are bound to lord it over others in one way or another it seems. If he is the top banana at his firm, he'll most likely do everything he can to stay on top. If he's not number one, he's most likely working on it and will be sitting on the throne before long.

You'll have more security than you can use if he is in a position to support you in the manner to which he feels you should be accustomed. He is apt to be too lavish, though, at least by your standards.

You'll always have plenty of friends when you have a Leo for a mate. He's a natural-born friend-maker and entertainer. He loves parties, and he will help you let your hair down and have a good time.

Leo fathers have a tendency to spoil the children—up to a point. That point is reached when the children become the center of attention, and Leo feels neglected. Then he becomes strict and insists that his rules be followed. You will have your hands full pampering both your Leo mate and the children. As long as he comes first in your affections, the family will be happy.

CAPRICORN WOMAN
VIRGO MAN

Although the Virgo man may be a bit of a fussbudget at times, his seriousness and dedication to common sense may help you to overlook his tendency to sometimes be overcritical about minor things.

Virgo men are often quiet, respectable types who set great store in conservative behavior and levelheadedness. He'll admire you for your practicality and tenacity, perhaps even more than for your good looks. He's seldom bowled over by a glamor-puss.

When he gets his courage up, he turns to a serious and reliable woman for romance. He'll be far from a Valentino while dating. In fact, you may wind up making all the passes. Once he does get his motor running, however, he can be a warm and wonderful fellow—to the right woman.

He's gradual about love. Chances are your romance with him will most likely start out looking like an ordinary friendship. Once he's sure you're no fly-by-night flirt and have no plans of taking him for a ride, he'll open up and rain sunshine all over your heart.

Virgo men tend to marry late in life. He believes in holding out until he's met the right partner. He may not have many names in his little black book. In fact, he may not even have a black book. He's not interested in playing the field; leave that to men of the more flamboyant signs. The Virgo man is so particular that he may remain romantically inactive for a long period. His lover has to be perfect or it's no go.

If you find yourself feeling weak-kneed for a Virgo, do your best to convince him that perfect is not so important when it comes to love. Help him realize that he's missing out on a great deal by not considering the near-perfect or whatever it is you consider yourself to be. With your surefire perseverance, you will make him listen to reason and he'll wind up reciprocating your romantic interests.

The Virgo man is no block of ice. He'll respond to what he feels to be the right flame. Once your love life with a Virgo man starts to bubble, don't give it a chance to fall flat. You may never have a second chance at winning his heart.

If you should ever break up with him, forget about patching up. He'd prefer to let the pieces lie scattered. Once married, though, he'll stay that way—even if it hurts. He's too conscientious to try to back out of a legal deal of any sort.

The Virgo man is as neat as a pin. He's thumbs down on sloppy housekeeping. Keep everything bright, neat, and shiny. And that goes for the children, too, at least by the time he gets home.

The Virgo father appreciates courtesy, good manners, and family honor as much as you do. He will instill a sense of order in the household, and he expects the children to respect his wishes. He is very concerned with the health and hygiene of the youngsters, so he may try to restrict their freedom, especially at play. Although you are an earth sign like your Virgo mate, you will be less fearful and will prepare the children always to be poised and practical.

CAPRICORN WOMAN
LIBRA MAN

If there's a Libra in your life, you are most likely a very happy woman. Men born under this sign have a way with women. You'll always feel at ease in a Libra's company. You can be yourself when you're with him.

The Libra man can be moody at times. His moodiness is often puzzling. One moment he comes on hard and strong with declarations of his love. The next moment you find that he's left you like yesterday's mashed potatoes. He'll come back, though; don't worry. Libras are like that. Deep down inside he really knows what he wants even though he may not appear to.

You'll appreciate his admiration of beauty and harmony. If you're dressed to the teeth and never looked lovelier, you'll get a ready compliment—and one that's really deserved. Libras don't indulge in idle flattery. If they don't like something, however, they are tactful enough to remain silent.

Libras will go to great lengths to preserve peace and harmony, even tell a fat lie if necessary. They don't like showdowns or disagreeable confrontations. The frank woman is all for getting whatever is bothering her off her chest and out into the open, even if it comes out all wrong. To Libra, making a clean breast of everything seems like sheer folly sometimes.

You may lose your patience while waiting for your Libra friend to make up his mind. It takes him ages sometimes to make a decision. He weighs both sides carefully before committing himself to anything. You seldom dillydally—at least about small things—and so it's likely that you will find it difficult to see eye-to-eye with a hesitating Libra when it comes to decision-making methods.

All in all, though, he is kind, considerate, and fair. He is interested in the real truth. He'll try to balance everything out until he has all the correct answers. It's not difficult for him to see both sides of a story.

Libras are not show-offs. Generally, they are well-balanced, modest people. Honest, wholesome, and affectionate, they are serious about every love encounter they have. If he should find that the woman he's dating is not really suited to him, he will end the relationship in such a tactful manner that no hard feelings will come about.

The Libra father is patient and fair. He can be firm without exercising undue strictness or discipline. Although he can be a harsh judge at times, he will radiate sweetness and light with the youngsters in the hope that they will grow up to follow his gentle, charming manner.

CAPRICORN WOMAN
SCORPIO MAN

Some people have a hard time understanding the man born under the sign of Scorpio. Few, however, are able to resist his fiery charm. When angered, he can act like an overturned wasps' nest. His sting can leave an almost permanent mark. If you find yourself interested in the Scorpio man, you'd better learn how to keep on his good side.

Scorpio men are straight to the point. They can be as sharp as a razor blade and just as cutting to anyone who crosses them. In fact, Scorpio prides himself on his bluntness. But at times he may seem rather hard-hearted. He can be touchy every now and then, which is apt to get on your nerves after a while. When you feel like you can't take it anymore, you'd better tiptoe away from the scene rather than chance an explosive confrontation.

If he finds fault with you, he'll let you know. He might misinterpret your patience as indifference. Still, you can adapt to almost any sort of relationship or circumstance if you put your heart and mind to it.

Scorpio men are all quite perceptive and intelligent. In some respects, they know how to use their brains more effectively than most. They believe in winning at whatever they do. Second place holds no interest for them. In business, they usually achieve the position they want through drive and use of intellect.

Your interest in home life is not likely to be shared by him. No matter how comfortable you've managed to make the house, it will have very little influence on him or make him aware of his family responsibilities. He does not like to be tied down, and would rather be out on the battlefield of life, belting away at some just and worthy cause. Don't try to keep the home fires burning too brightly while you wait for him to come home.

The Scorpio man is passionate in all things—including love. Most women are easily attracted to him, and you are perhaps no exception. Those who allow themselves to be swept off their feet by a Scorpio man soon find that they're dealing with a carton of romantic fireworks. The Scorpio man is passionate with a capital P, make no mistake about that. Some women may find that he's too intensely sexual and too intent on sex.

Scorpio likes fathering large families. That may not suit your desire to have a small, close-knit family, especially as Scorpio often fails to live up to his responsibilities as a parent. But when he takes his fatherly duties seriously, he is a proud and patient parent. He is wonderful with difficult youngsters because he knows how to tap the best in each child. Like you, he believes in preparing the children for the hard knocks life sometimes delivers.

CAPRICORN WOMAN
SAGITTARIUS MAN

Sagittarius men are not easy to catch. They get cold feet whenever visions of the altar enter the romance. You'll most likely be attracted to Sagittarius because of his sunny nature. He's lots of laughs and easy to get along with. But as soon as the relationship begins to take on a serious hue, you may find yourself a little let down.

Sagittarius are full of bounce, perhaps too much bounce to suit you. They are often hard to pin down; they dislike staying put. If he ever has a chance to be on the move, he'll latch onto it without so much as a how-do-you-do. Sagittarius are quick people both in mind and spirit. If ever they do make mistakes, it's because of their zip. They leap before they look.

If you offer him good advice, he most likely won't follow it. Sagittarius like to rely on their own wits and ways whenever possible.

His up-and-at-'em manner about most things is likely to drive you up the wall at times. He's likely to find you a little too slow and deliberate. He may tease and nudge you when you're accompanying him on a stroll or jogging through the park. He can't abide a slowpoke.

At times you'll find him too much like a kid—too breezy and casual. Don't mistake his youthful zest for premature senility. Sagittarius are equipped with first-class brainpower and know how to use it. They are often full of good ideas and drive. Generally, they are very broad-minded people and very much concerned with fair play and equality.

In romance he's quite capable of loving you wholeheartedly while treating you like a good pal. His hail-fellow-well-met manner in the arena of love is likely to scare off a dainty damsel. However, a woman who knows that his heart is in the right place won't mind it too much if backpatting takes the place of a gentle embrace.

He's not much of a homebody. He's got ants in his pants and enjoys being on the move. Humdrum routine, especially at home, bores him silly. At the drop of a hat, he may ask you to travel away for a night out. He's a past master in the instant surprise department. He'll love to keep you guessing. His friendly, candid nature will win him many friends. He'll expect his friends to be yours, and vice versa.

The Sagittarius father can be all thumbs when it comes to tiny tots. He will dote on any infant son or daughter from a distance. As soon as the children are old enough to walk and talk, Sagittarius feels comfortable enough to play with them. He will encourage all their talents and skills, and he will see to it that they get a well-rounded education.

CAPRICORN WOMAN
CAPRICORN MAN

The Capricorn man may be more inhibited and cautious than the Capricorn woman. So it may be up to you to thaw his romantic reserve and warm his sensual interest in you. He is capable of giving his heart completely once he has found the right lover. As you know, Capricorn is thorough and deliberate in all that he does. He is slow and steady and sure.

He doesn't believe in flirting and would never lead a heart on a merry chase just for the game. If you win his trust, he'll give you his heart on a platter. Quite often, the woman has to take the lead when romance is in the air. As long as he knows you're making the advances in earnest, he won't mind—in fact, he'll probably be grateful.

Although some Capricorns are indeed quite capable of expressing passion, others often have difficulty in trying to display affection. He should have no trouble in this area, however, as long as you are patient and understanding.

The Capricorn man is very interested in getting ahead. He's quite ambitious and usually knows how to apply himself well to whatever task he undertakes. He's far from being a spendthrift. Like you, he knows how to handle money with extreme care. Both of you have a knack for putting away pennies for that rainy day. The Capricorn man thinks in terms of future security. He wants to make sure that he and his wife have something to fall back on when they reach retirement age. There's nothing wrong with that; in fact, it's a plus quality.

The Capricorn man will want to handle household matters efficiently. Most Capricorn women will have no trouble in doing this. If he should check up on you from time to time, don't let it irritate you. Once you assure him that you can handle it all to his liking, he'll leave you alone.

Although he's a hard man to catch when it comes to marriage, once he's made that serious step, he's quite likely to become possessive. Capricorns need to know that they have the support of their wives in whatever they do—every step of the way.

The Capricorn man needs to be liked. He may seem dull to some, but underneath his reserve there is sometimes an adventurous streak that has never had a chance to express itself. He may be a real daredevil in his heart of hearts. The right woman— the affectionate, adoring woman—can bring out that hidden zest in his nature.

A Capricorn father is dutiful and steady, although he may not understand the children as well as you do. He can be cold and aloof at times, and the youngsters may confide to you that they secretly dislike him. However, as they get older and wiser, they realize that the Capricorn father always acted in their best interests.

CAPRICORN WOMAN
AQUARIUS MAN

You will find the Aquarius man the most broad-minded man you have ever met. On the other hand, you will find him the most impractical. Oftentimes, he's more of a dreamer than a doer. If you don't mind putting up with a man whose heart and mind are as wide as the universe but whose head is almost always up in the clouds, then start dating that Aquarius who has somehow captured your fancy. Maybe you, with your good sense, can bring him back down to earth when he gets too starry-eyed.

He can be busy making some very complicated and idealistic plans when he's got that out-to-lunch look in his eyes. But more than likely he'll never execute them. After he's shared one or two of his progressive ideas with you, you may think he's crazy. But don't go jumping to conclusions. There's a saying that Aquarius are a half-century ahead of everybody else in the thinking department.

If you decide to marry him, you'll find out how right his zany whims are on or about your 50th anniversary. Maybe the wait will be worth it. Could be that you have an Einstein on your hands— and heart.

Life with an Aquarius won't be one of total despair if you can learn to temper his airiness with your down-to-earth practicality. He won't gripe if you do. Aquarius always maintains an open mind. He'll entertain the ideas and opinions of everybody. He may not agree with all of them.

Don't go tearing your hair out when you find that it's almost impossible to hold a normal conversation with your Aquarius friend at times. No matter what he says, keep in mind that he means well.

His broad-mindedness doesn't stop when it comes to you and your personal freedom. You won't have to give up any of your hobbies or projects after you're married. He'll encourage you to continue in your interests.

He'll be a kind and generous husband. He'll never quibble over petty things. Keep track of the money you both spend. He can't. Money burns a hole in his pocket.

At times, you may feel like calling it quits. Chances are, though, that you'll always give him another chance.

The Aquarius father is a good family man. He understands children as much as he loves them. He sees them as individuals in their own right. Aquarius can talk to the kids on a variety of subjects, and his knowledge can be awe-inspiring. You will often have to bring the youngsters back down to earth.

CAPRICORN WOMAN
PISCES MAN

Pisces could be the man you've looked for high and low and thought never existed. He's terribly sensitive and terribly romantic. Still, he has a very strong individual character and is well aware that the moon is not made of green cheese. He'll be very considerate of your every wish and will do his best to see to it that your relationship is a happy one.

The Pisces man is great for showering the object of his affection with all kinds of little gifts and tokens of his love.

He's just the right mixture of dreamer and realist; he's capable of pleasing most women. When it comes to earning bread and butter, the strong Pisces will do all right in the world. Quite often they are capable of rising to the very top. Some do extremely well as writers or psychiatrists.

He'll be as patient and understanding with you as you undoubtedly will be with him. One thing a Pisces man dislikes is pettiness. Anyone who delights in running another into the ground is almost immediately crossed off his list of possible mates. If you have any small grievances with your friends, don't tell him. He couldn't care less and will think less of you if you do.

If you fall in love with a weak kind of Pisces, don't give up your job at the office before you get married. Better hang onto it until a good time after the honeymoon; you may still need it. A Pisces man can be content almost anywhere. This is perhaps because he is quite inner-directed and places little value on material things. In a shack or a palace, the Pisces man is capable of making the best of all possible adjustments. He won't kick up a fuss if the roof leaks and if the fence is in sad need of repair.

At this point, you'll most likely feel like giving him a piece of your mind. Still and all, the Pisces man is not shiftless or aimless. It is important to understand that material gain is never a direct goal for someone born under this sign.

Pisces men have a way with the sick and troubled. He can listen to one hard-luck story after another without seeming to tire. He often knows what's bothering someone before that someone knows it himself.

As a lover, he'll be quite attentive. You'll never have cause to doubt his intentions or sincerity. Everything will be aboveboard in his romantic dealings with you.

The Pisces father, always permissive and understanding, is immensely popular with children. He plays the double role of confidant and playmate for the kids. It will never enter his mind to discpline a child, no matter how spoiled or incorrigible that youngster becomes.

Man—Woman

CAPRICORN MAN
ARIES WOMAN

The Aries woman may be a little too bossy and busy for you. Generally, Aries are ambitious creatures. They tend to lose their patience with thorough and deliberate people who take a lot of time to complete something. The Aries woman is a fast worker. Sometimes she's so fast she forgets to look where she's going.

When she stumbles or falls, it would be nice if you were there to grab her. But Aries are proud. They don't like to be chided when they err. Scolding can turn them into blocks of ice. However, don't begin to think that the Aries woman frequently gets tripped up in her plans. Quite often she is capable of taking aim and hitting the bull's-eye. You'll be flabbergasted at times by her accuracy as well as by her ambition.

You are perhaps somewhat slower than Aries in attaining your goals. Still, you are not apt to make mistakes along the way; you're seldom ill-prepared.

The Aries woman is quite sensitive at times. She likes to be handled with gentleness and respect. Let her know that you love her for her brains as well as for her good looks. Never give her cause to become jealous. When your Aries woman sees green, you'd better forget about sharing a rosy future together. Handle her with tender love and care and she's yours.

The Aries woman can be giving if she feels her partner is deserving. She is no iceberg; she responds to the proper masculine flame. She needs a man she can look up to and feel proud of. If the shoe fits, put it on. If not, better put your sneakers back on and quietly tiptoe out of her sight. She can cause you plenty of heartache if you've made up your mind about her and she hasn't made up hers about you.

Aries women are very demanding at times. Some of them tend to be high-strung. They can be difficult if they feel their independence is being hampered.

The cultivated Aries woman makes a wonderful homemaker and hostess. You'll find that she's very clever in decorating; she knows how to use colors. Your house will be tastefully furnished. She'll see to it that it radiates harmony. Friends and acquaintances will love your Aries wife. She knows how to make everyone feel at home and welcome.

The Aries woman makes a fine, affectionate mother. Because she is not keen on burdensome responsibilities, like you she prefers a small family with a few children. She is skilled at juggling both career and motherhood, so the kids will never feel she is an absentee parent. You can help prepare the youngsters for their roles as young adults.

CAPRICORN MAN
TAURUS WOMAN

A Taurus woman, an earth sign like you, could perhaps understand you better than most women. She is very considerate and loving. She is thorough and methodical in whatever she does. She knows how to take her time in doing things; she is anxious to avoid mistakes. She is a careful person. She never skips over things that may seem unimportant; she goes over everything with a fine-tooth comb.

Home is very important to the Taurus woman. She is an excellent homemaker. Although your home may not be a palace, it will become, under her care, a comfortable and happy abode. She'll love it when friends drop by for the evening. She is a good cook and enjoys feeding people well. No one will ever go away from your house with an empty stomach.

The Taurus woman is serious about love and affection. When she has taken a tumble for someone, she'll stay by him—for good, if possible. She will try to be practical in romance, to some extent. When she sets her cap for a man, she keeps after him until he's won her. The Taurus woman is a passionate lover, even though she may appear otherwise at first glance. She is on the lookout for someone who can return her affection fully. Taurus are sometimes given to fits of jealousy and possessiveness. They expect fair play in the area of marriage. When it doesn't come about, they can be bitingly sarcastic and mean.

But the Taurus woman is generally easygoing. She's fond of keeping peace. She won't argue unless she has to. She'll do her best to maintain your love relationship on an even keel.

Marriage is generally a one-time thing for Taurus. Once they've made the serious step, they seldom try to back out of it. Marriage is for keeps. They are fond of love and warmth. With the right man, they turn out to be ideal wives.

The Taurus woman will respect you for your steady ways. She'll have confidence in your common sense.

The Taurus mother will share with you the joys, the burdens, and the challenges of parenthood. She seldom puts up with any nonsense from the youngsters. She can wield an iron fist in a velvet glove. She may have some difficult times when they reach adolescence. But in later life the teenagers are often thankful they were brought up in such a conscientious fashion.

CAPRICORN MAN
GEMINI WOMAN

The Gemini woman may be too much of a flirt for you. Then again, it depends on what kind of mood she's in. Gemini women can change from hot to cold quicker than a cat can wink its eye. Chances are her fluctuations will tire you after a time, and you'll pick up your heart—if it's not already broken into small pieces—and go elsewhere. Women born under the sign of the Twins have the talent of being able to change their moods and attitudes as frequently as they change their party dresses.

Sometimes, Gemini gals like to whoop it up. Some of them are good-time gals who love burning the candle to the wick. You'll see them at parties and gatherings, surrounded by men of all types, laughing gaily or kicking up their heels at every opportunity. The next day you may bump into this creature at the neighborhood library and you'll hardly recognize her for her sensible attire. She'll probably have five or six books under her arm—on five or six different subjects. In fact, she may even work there.

You'll probably find her a dazzling and fascinating creature—for a time, at any rate. Most men do. But when it comes to being serious about love you may find that this sparkling Eve leaves quite a bit to be desired. It's not that she has anything against being serious, it's just that she might find it difficult trying to be serious with you.

At one moment, she'll be capable of praising you for your steadfast and patient ways. The next moment she'll tell you in a cutting way that you're an impossible stick in the mud.

Don't even begin to fathom the depths of her mercurial soul—it's full of false bottoms. She'll resent close investigation, anyway, and will make you rue the day you ever took it into your head to try to learn more about her than she feels is necessary. Better keep the relationship full of fun and fancy-free until she gives you the go-ahead sign. Take as much of her as she is willing to give; don't ask for more until she takes a serious interest in you.

There will come a time when the Gemini woman will realize that she can't spend her entire life at the ball. The security and warmth you have to offer is just what she needs to be a happy, complete woman.

A Gemini mother, like her children, is often restless, adventurous, and easily bored. She will never complain about their fleeting interests because she understands the changes they will go through as they mature. She has a youthful streak that guides her in bringing up the kids through the various stages of infancy through young adulthood. Better make sure she doesn't spoil the children.

CAPRICORN MAN
CANCER WOMAN

A Capricorn-Cancer union can be a match made in heaven, at least in the astrological scheme of things. You are, after all, zodiacal opposites as well as zodiacal mates. If you fall in love with a Cancer woman, though, be prepared for anything. In one hour she can unravel a whole gamut of emotions; it will leave you in a tizzy. She'll always keep you guessing, that's for sure.

You may find her a little too uncertain and sensitive for your liking. You'll most likely spend a good deal of time encouraging her—helping her to erase her foolish fears.

Don't chide her about her personal interests, or her family. If you do, you'll most likely reduce her to tears. She can't stand being made fun of. It will take bushels of roses and tons of chocolates—not to mention the apologies—to get her to come back out of her shell.

In matters of money managing, she may not be as generous as you are. You may get the notion that your Cancer sweetheart or mate is a direct descendant of Scrooge. If she has her way, she'll hang onto that first dollar you earned. She's not only that way with money, but with everything right on up from bakery string to jelly jars. She's a saver; she never throws anything away, no matter how trivial.

Once she loves you, she will be an affectionate, self-sacrificing, and devoted woman. Her love for you will never alter unless you want it to. She'll put you up on a high pedestal and will do everything—even if it's against your will—to keep you there.

Cancer women love home life. For them, marriage is an easy step to make. They're domestic with a capital D. She'll do her best to make your home comfortable and cozy. The Cancer woman is happiest in her own home. She makes an excellent hostess. The best in her comes out when she's in her own environment, one in which she can be a nurturer and caregiver.

Of all the signs of the Zodiac, Cancer women make the best mothers. She'll treat every complaint of her child as a major catastrophe. With her, children come first. If you're lucky, you'll run a close second. You may think she's too devoted to the children. You may have a hard time convincing her to cut her apron strings. Still, the Cancer-Capricorn parent combination is one of the best in terms of devotion and discipline for the youngsters.

CAPRICORN MAN
LEO WOMAN

The Leo woman can make most men roar like lions. If any woman in the Zodiac has that indefinable something that can make men lose their heads and find their hearts, it's the Leo woman.

She's got more than a fair share of charm and glamour. And she knows how to make the most of her assets, especially when she's in the company of the opposite sex. Jealous men are apt to lose their cool or their sanity when trying to woo a woman born under the sign of the Lion.

She likes to kick up her heels quite often and doesn't care who knows it. She often makes heads turn and tongues wag. You don't necessarily have to believe any of what you hear—it's most likely jealous gossip or wishful thinking. Needless to say, other women in her vicinity turn green with envy and will try anything to put her out of the running.

This Leo vamp makes the blood rush to your head and makes you momentarily forget all the things you thought were important and necessary in your life. You may feel differently when you come back down to earth and the stars are out of your eyes.

You may feel that she isn't the kind of woman you planned to bring home to Mother. Not that your mother might disapprove of your choice—but you might after the shoes and rice are a thing of the past. Although the Leo woman may do her best to be a good wife for you, chances are she'll fall short of your idea of what a good wife should be like.

If you're planning on not going as far as the altar with that Leo woman who has you flipping your lid, you'd better be financially equipped for some very expensive dating. Be prepared to shower her with expensive gifts and to take her dining and dancing in the smartest spots in town. Promise her the moon if you're in a position to deliver. Luxury and glamour are two things that are bound to lower a Leo's resistance. She's got expensive tastes, and you'd better cater to them if you expect to get to first base with this lady.

If you've got an important business deal to clinch and you have doubts as to whether you can swing it or not, bring your Leo partner along to the luncheon. Chances are that with her on your arm, you'll be able to win any business battle. She won't have to say or do anything—just be there at your side. The grouchiest oil magnate can be transformed into a gushing, obedient schoolboy if there's a charming Leo woman in the room.

A Leo mother can be so proud of her children that she is sometimes blind to their faults. Yet when she wants them to learn and take their rightful place in the social scheme of things, the Leo mother can be strict. She is a patient teacher, lovingly explaining the rules the youngsters are expected to follow. Easygoing and friendly, she loves to pal around with the kids and show them off on every occasion.

CAPRICORN MAN
VIRGO WOMAN

The Virgo woman may be a little too difficult for you to understand at first. Her waters run deep. Even when you think you know her, don't take any bets on it. She's capable of keeping things hidden in the deep recesses of her womanly soul—things she'll only release when she's sure that you're the man she's been looking for.

It may take her some time to come around to this decision. Virgo women are finicky about almost everything. Everything has to be letter-perfect before they're satisfied. Many of them have the idea that the only people who can do things right are Virgos.

Nothing offends a Virgo woman more than slovenly dress, sloppy character, or a careless display of affection. Make sure your tie is not crooked and your shoes sport a bright shine before you go calling on this lady. Take her arm when crossing the street.

Don't rush the romance. Trying to corner her in the back of a cab may be the one way of striking out. Never criticize the way she looks. In fact, the best policy would be to agree with her as much as possible. Still, there's just so much a man can take; all those dos and don'ts you'll have to observe if you want to get to first base with a Virgo may be just a little too much to ask of you.

After a few dates, you may come to the conclusion that she just isn't worth all that trouble. However, the Virgo woman is mysterious enough generally speaking to keep her men running back for more. Chances are you'll be intrigued by her airs and graces.

If lovemaking means a lot to you, you'll be disappointed at first in the cool ways of your Virgo friend. However, under her glacial facade there lies a hot cauldron of seething excitement. If you're patient and artful in your romantic approach, you'll find that all that caution was well worth the trouble. When Virgos love, they don't stint. It's all or nothing as far as they're concerned. Once they're convinced that they love you, they toss all cares to the wind.

One thing a Virgo woman can't stand in love is hypocrisy. They don't give a hoot about what the neighbors say if their hearts tell them to go ahead. They're very concerned with human truths. So if their hearts stumble upon another fancy, they will be true to the new heartthrob and leave you standing in the rain. She's honest to her heart and will be as true to you as you are with her. Do her wrong once, however, and it's farewell.

The Virgo mother has high expectations for her children, and she will strive to bring out the very best in them. The children usually turn out just as she hoped, despite her anxiety about their health and hygiene, their safety and good sense. Like her, you are an earth sign and can understand her fears for the children both in school and at play. Both of you will see the need for discipline. But the Virgo mother is more tender than strict.

CAPRICORN MAN
LIBRA WOMAN

The Libra woman's changeability, in spite of its undeniable charm, could actually drive even a man of your patience up the wall. She's capable of smothering you with love and kisses one day, and on the next avoid you like the plague. If you're a man of steel nerves, then perhaps you can tolerate her sometime-ness without suffering too much. However, if you're only a mere mortal who can only take so much, then you'd better fasten your attention on a partner who's somewhat more constant.

But don't get the wrong idea. A love affair with a Libra is not bad at all. In fact, it can have an awful lot of pluses to it. Libra women are soft, very feminine, and warm. She doesn't have to vamp all over the place in order to gain a man's attention. Her delicate presence is enough to warm any man's heart. One smile and you're a piece of putty in the palm of her hand.

She can be fluffy and affectionate, which you like. On the other hand, her indecision about which dress to wear, what to cook for dinner, or what to decorate could make you tear your hair out. What will perhaps be more exasperating is her flat denial of the accusation that she cannot make even the simplest decision. The trouble is that she wants to be fair or just in all matters. She'll spend hours weighing pros and cons. Don't make her rush into a decision; that will only irritate her.

The Libra woman likes to be surrounded by beautiful things. Money is no object when beauty is concerned. There will always be plenty of flowers in the house. She'll know how to arrange them tastefully, too. Libras adore beautiful clothes and furnishings. These women will run up bills without batting an eye—if given the chance.

Once she's cottoned to you, the Libra woman will do everything in her power to make you happy. She'll wait on you hand and foot when you're sick and bring you breakfast in bed Sundays. She'll be very thoughtful and devoted. If anyone dares suggest you're not the grandest man in the world, your Libra wife will tell that person where to get off in no uncertain terms.

The Libra mother is moderate and even-tempered, like you, so together you will create a balanced family life in which the children can grow up to be equal partners in terms of responsibilities and privileges. She knows that youngsters need both guidance and encouragement in a harmonious environment. The children will never lack for anything that could make their lives easier and richer.

CAPRICORN MAN
SCORPIO WOMAN

When the Scorpio woman chooses to be sweet, she's apt to give the impression that butter wouldn't melt in her mouth. But, of course, it would. When her temper flies, so will everything else that isn't bolted down. She can be as hot as a tamale or as cool as a cucumber when she wants. Whatever mood she's in, you can be sure it's for real. She doesn't believe in poses or hypocrisy.

The Scorpio woman is often seductive and sultry. Her femme fatale charm can pierce the hardest heart like a laser beam. She doesn't have to look like Mata Hari (many of them resemble the tomboy next door). But once you've looked into those tantalizing eyes, you're a goner.

The Scorpio woman can be a whirlwind of passion. Life with her will not be all smiles and smooth sailing. If you think you can handle her tempestuous moods, then try your luck.

The stable and steady Capricorn man will most likely have a calming effect on her. You're the kind of man she can trust and rely on. But never cross her—even in the smallest things. If you do, you'd better tell Fido to make room for you in the doghouse; you'll be his guest for the next couple of days.

The Scorpio woman will keep family battles within the walls of your home. When company visits, she'll give the impression that married life with you is one big joyride. It's just her way of expressing her loyalty to you, at least in front of others. She believes that family matters are and should stay private. She'll certainly see to it that others have a high opinion of you both. She'll be right behind you in whatever it is you want to do.

Although she's an individualist, after she has married, she'll put her own interests aside for those of the man she loves. With a woman like this backing you up, you can't help but go far. She'll never try to take over your role as boss of the family. She'll give you all the support you need in order to fulfill that role. She won't complain if the going gets rough. She is a courageous woman. She's as anxious as you to find that place in the sun for you both. She's as determined a person as you are.

Although the Scorpio mother loves her children, she will not put them on a pedestal. She is devoted to developing her youngsters' talents. The Scorpio mother is protective yet encouraging. Under her skillful guidance, the children will learn how to cope with extremes. She will teach her young ones to be courageous and steadfast.

CAPRICORN MAN
SAGITTARIUS WOMAN

The Sagittarius woman is hard to keep track of. First she's here, then she's there. She's a woman with a severe case of itchy feet. She's got to keep on the move.

People generally like her because of her hail-fellow-well-met manner and breezy charm. She is constantly good-natured and almost never cross. She is the kind of gal you're likely to strike up a palsy-walsy relationship with. You might not be interested in letting it go any farther. She probably won't sulk if you leave it on a friendly basis, either. Treat her like a kid sister and she'll eat it up like candy.

She'll probably be attracted to you because of your steady self-assured manner. She'll need a friend like you to help her over the rough spots in her life. She'll most likely turn to you for advice on money and investments.

There is nothing malicious about the female Archer. She is full of bounce and good cheer. Her sunshiny disposition can be relied upon even on the rainiest of days. No matter what she says or does, you'll always know that she means well.

Sagittarius are sometimes short on tact. Some of them say anything that comes into their heads no matter what the occasion. Sometimes the words that tumble out of their mouths seem cutting and cruel. They mean well, but often everything they say comes out wrong. She's quite capable of losing her friends—and perhaps even yours—through a careless slip of the lip. Always remember that she is full of good intentions. Stick with her if you like her and try to help her mend her ways.

She's not a woman you'd most likely be interested in marrying, but she'll certainly be lots of fun to pal around with. Quite often, Sagittarius women are outdoor types. They're crazy about hiking, fishing, camping, and mountain climbing. They love the wide open spaces. They are fond of all kinds of animals. Make no mistake about it—this busy little lady is no slouch. She's full of get-up-and-go.

She's great company most of the time. She's more fun than a three-ring circus when she's in the right company. You'll like her for her candid and direct manner. On the whole, Sagittarius are very kind and sympathetic women.

If you do wind up marrying this girl-next-door type, you'd better see to it that you handle all of the financial matters. Sagittarius often let money run through their fingers like sand.

The Sagittarius mother is a wonderful friend to her children. She'll shower them with love and give them all the freedom they think they need. She is not afraid if a youngster learns some street smarts. But she might preach too much for the kids. You must switch the focus to the practical in order to prepare the youngsters for wordly success.

CAPRICORN MAN
CAPRICORN WOMAN

The Capricorn woman shares with you the same approach to romance. A Capricorn mate may be the right man for her. She believes in true love. She doesn't appreciate getting involved in flings. To her, they're just a waste of time.

She's looking for a man who means business—in life as well as in love. Although she can be very affectionate with her boyfriend or mate, she tends to let her head govern her heart. That is not to say she is cool or calculating. On the contrary, she just feels she can be more honest about love if she consults her brains first. She wants to size up the situation before throwing her heart in the ring. She wants to make sure it won't get stepped on.

The Capricorn woman is faithful, dependable, and systematic in just about everything she undertakes. She is quite concerned with security and sees to it that every penny she spends is spent wisely. She is very economical about using her time, too. She does not believe in whittling away her energy on a scheme that is bound not to pay off.

Ambitious themselves, they are quite often attracted to ambitious men—men who are interested in getting somewhere in life. If you win her heart, she'll stick by you and do all she can to help you get to the top.

The Capricorn woman is almost always diplomatic. She makes an excellent hostess. She can be very influential when your business acquaintances come to dinner.

The Capricorn woman is very concerned, if not downright proud, about her family tree. Relatives are important to her, particularly if they're socially prominent.

She's generally thorough in whatever she does. Capricorn women are well-mannered and gracious, no matter what their backgrounds. They seem to have it in their natures to always behave properly.

If you should marry a a female Goat, you need never worry about her going on a wild shopping spree. She understands the value of money better than most women. If you turn over your paycheck to her at the end of the week, you can be sure that a good hunk of it will wind up in the bank.

The Capricorn mother is very ambitious for her children, just as you are. She wants them to have every advantage and to benefit from things she perhaps lacked as a child. She will train the youngsters to be polite and kind, and to honor traditional codes of conduct. Together, Capricorn parents can be correct to a fault. But the children will have an edge in the world.

CAPRICORN MAN
AQUARIUS WOMAN

If you find that you've fallen head over heels for a woman born under the sign of the Water Bearer, you'd better fasten your safety belt. It may take you quite a while to actually discover what this woman is like. Even then you may have nothing to go on but a string of vague hunches.

Aquarius is like a rainbow, full of bright and shining hues. She's like no other female you've ever known. There is something elusive about her, something difficult to put your finger on.

The Aquarius woman can be odd and eccentric at times. Some say this is the source of her mysterious charm. You may think she's just a plain screwball, and you may be half right.

Aquarius women often have their heads full of dreams. By nature, they're unconventional. They have their own ideas about how the world should be run. Sometimes their ideas may seem pretty weird. Chances are they're just a little bit too progressive. They say that Aquarius is about fifty years ahead of the rest of the world in her thinking. She'll most likely be the most tolerant and open-minded woman you've ever encountered.

If you find that she's too much mystery and charm for you to handle, just talk it out with her and say that you think it would be better to call it quits. She'll most likely want to remain friends. Aquarius women are like that. Perhaps you'll both find it easier to get along in a friendship than in a romance.

It is not difficult for her to remain buddy-buddy with an ex-lover. For many Aquarius, the line between friendship and romance is a fuzzy one.

She is not a jealous person. And while you're romancing her, she won't expect you to be, either. You'll find her a free spirit most of the time. Just when you think you know her inside out, you'll discover that you don't really know her at all.

She's a very sympathetic and warm person. She is often helpful to those in need of assistance and advice.

She'll seldom be suspicious even when she has every right to be. If the man she loves makes a little slip, she's will forgive and forget up to a point. Don't test her limits.

The Aquarius mother is generous and seldom refuses her children anything. You may feel the youngsters need a bit more discipline and practicality. But you will appreciate your Aquarius mate's worldly views, which prepares the youngsters to get along in life. They will grow up to be tolerant young people who fit in and feel at ease in any situation.

CAPRICORN MAN
PISCES WOMAN

The Pisces woman places great value on love and romance. She's gentle, kind, and receptive. She has very high ideals. She will only give her heart to a man who she feels can live up to her expectations.

Many a man dreams of an alluring Pisces woman. You're perhaps no exception. She's soft and cuddly and very domestic. She'll let you be the brains of the family; she's contented to play a behind-the-scenes role in order to help you achieve your goals. The illusion that you are the master of the household is the kind of magic that the Pisces woman is adept at creating.

She can be very ladylike and proper. Your business associates and friends will be dazzled by her warmth and femininity. Although she's a charmer, there is a lot more to her than just a pretty exterior. There is a brain ticking away behind that soft, womanly facade. You may never become aware of it—that is, until you're married to her. It's no cause for alarm, however; she'll most likely never use it against you, only to help you and possibly set you on a more successful path.

If she feels you're botching up your married life through careless behavior or if she feels you could be earning more money than you do, she'll tell you about it. But any wife would, really. She will never try to usurp your position as head and breadwinner of the family.

She can do wonders with a house. She is very fond of dramatic and beautiful things. There will always be plenty of fresh-cut flowers around the house. She will choose charming artwork and antiques, if they are affordable. She'll see to it that the house is decorated in a dazzling yet welcoming style.

She'll have an extra special dinner prepared for you when you come home from an important business meeting. Don't dwell on the boring details of the meeting, though. But if you need that grand vision, the big idea, to seal a contract or make a conquest, your Pisces woman is sure to confide a secret that will guarantee your success. She is canny and shrewd with money, and once you are on her wavelength you can manage the intricacies on your own.

If you are patient and kind, you can keep a Pisces woman happy for a lifetime. She is not without her faults. Her sensitivity may get on your nerves. You may find her lacking in practicality and good old-fashioned stoicism. You may even feel that she uses her tears as a method of getting her own way.

The Pisces mother has a strong bond with her children. Self-sacrificing, she can deny herself in order to fulfill their needs. She will teach her youngsters the value of service to the community while not letting them lose their individuality. She will see to it that her children earn honors.

CAPRICORN
LUCKY NUMBERS 1999

Lucky numbers and astrology can be linked through the movements of the Moon. Each phase of the thirteen Moon cycles vibrates with a sequence of numbers for your Sign of the Zodiac over the course of the year. Using your lucky numbers is a fun system that connects you with tradition.

New Moon	First Quarter	Full Moon	Last Quarter
Dec. 18 ('98)	Dec. 26 ('98)	Jan. 1	Jan. 9
9 3 2 7	1 8 4 9	1 6 1 0	1 3 5 8
Jan. 17	Jan. 24	Jan. 31	Feb. 8
0 2 3 6	6 4 9 5	7 6 6 8	8 1 0 7
Feb. 16	Feb. 22	March 2	March 10
7 3 9 7	3 8 5 9	2 9 2 4	4 0 1 6
March 17	March 24	March 31	April 8
6 9 5 1	0 7 2 2	2 4 6 0	9 3 8 2
April 15	April 22	April 30	May 8
2 9 5 7	4 8 8 0	4 3 0 9	9 5 8 6
May 15	May 22	May 30	June 6
6 2 7 3	7 7 9 2	6 0 8 4	4 7 5 1
June 13	June 20	June 28	July 6
0 6 3 7	7 4 6 8	0 5 1 0	4 2 7 3
July 12	July 20	July 28	August 4
3 9 4 4	6 7 0 4	3 9 3 1	0 6 2 8
August 11	August 18	August 26	Sept. 2
8 3 3 5	5 7 0 8	8 7 5 1	0 6 3 7
Sept. 9	Sept. 17	Sept. 25	Oct. 1
7 7 9 2	2 0 8 5	2 6 2 7	7 4 8 8
Oct. 9	Oct. 17	Oct. 24	Oct. 31
8 1 3 0	6 9 5 2	9 5 1 7	7 2 2 4
Nov. 7	Nov. 16	Nov. 23	Nov. 29
4 6 0 3	3 8 2 3	5 4 1 0	5 5 7 9
Dec. 7	Dec. 15	Dec. 22	Dec. 29
9 3 6 2	2 5 3 4	1 9 6 0	1 0 3 5

CAPRICORN
YEARLY FORECAST 1999

*Forecast for 1999 Concerning Business
and Financial Affairs, Job Prospects,
Travel, Health, Romance and Marriage
for Those Born with the Sun
in the Zodiacal Sign of Capricorn.
December 21–January 19*

For those born under the influence of the Sun in the zodiacal sign of Capricorn, ruled by Saturn, planet of structure and discipline, this promises to be a year of creativity and achievement. An increase in travel opportunities is likely to lead to new business and social options. There should be good chances this year to develop and strengthen your creative talents. A change in perspective and priorities may lead to a major move. Leisure activities have a chance of becoming more serious business this year. Although time may be at a premium, you are likely to want a real vacation far from your usual base of operations. A break from long-term connections is likely to allow you to establish new and profitable associations. Unusual opportunities for creative expansion may arise when you least expect them. A business partnership could represent a burden during the first quarter of the year, although solid returns are foreseen throughout the remaining months. In handling tricky money matters, prepare for unexpected fluctuations in your income. Fortunately, profits from a property interest are likely to remain stable, something you can fall back on during any tight period. Creative interests may cause considerable expenditure, but you can view this as an investment for the future. Routine occupational affairs are apt to be hectic. It is vital not to overcommit yourself. A schedule which is too packed could make you feel constantly stressed out and overloaded. Travel opportunities are likely to increase during the early months of the year. That is a starred time to explore new horizons. Domestic travel may take priority over trips far from home. Your own health should not be a serious problem at any time this year. However, concern over a partner's health and happiness may take its toll on you emotionally, and this can be reflected in your own physical well-being. If there is a genuine medical condition to contend with, try to develop a strategy which enables you to be supportive without worrying constantly. Capricorn singles have the opportunity this year to establish a definite liaison. There may be an emotional cost, however, in a relationship which you are not free to reveal by virtue of the circumstances involved.

For professional Capricorn men and women, strong ties with a certain business partner could restrict your ability to move into new areas at the start of the year. Nevertheless, creativity is the overall theme in your life this year regardless of any confining structure you have to work within. There is a possibility of breaking away from one particular associate because you have achieved all that you can do together. An increase in travel could open up new business possibilities for you, bringing you into contact with people at or from a distance. Chance options to expand in a new direction may fall into your lap. Gradual development is the key to long-term success this year. Your ability to build up a wider network of contacts should increase options both socially and in your business life. Your creative talents are likely to play an important role in strengthening the financial side of business. It may be worth investing in training which allows you to develop your latent abilities or at least to explore them. Investment in business areas which involving supplying goods could be profitable, although you may not see a substantial return on your investment for some time. Nevertheless, when the rewards eventually come they should be worth the wait. If business is slow during the first few months of the year, it may be necessary to restructure your budget for the remaining months. Lean toward being cautious and conservative all year, as is your Capricorn nature. Business profits should thrive over the summer months, particularly during the period from June 29 to August 24. However, this may not balance out problems concerning older debts, which could take more than the summer to clear up entirely.

Financially, this is apt to be an unstable year, partly because you do not have all your eggs in one highly profitable basket. However, this strategy may also provide a safety net. If one source of income suddenly ceases, there is something else to fall back on providing you are diversified. Renting out property promises to be a prosperous and stable source of income throughout the next twelve months. A strong desire this year to develop your creative and leisure interests is likely to be expensive. Social networking and investment in talents which can be put to lucrative business use should turn out to be highly profitable at a later date. As a Capricorn you tend to be cautious, and it is well to maintain that stance where money is concerned. Anticipate fluctuations in your income due to circumstances beyond your direct control. You probably will not be the only person to suffer a downturn for a temporary period. It is a question of developing the right strategy to cope rather than being concerned about what other people are doing or how they think of you. Pinning yourself down to extra major financial commitments is not wise if you know that your situation could potentially change. Errors in accounting and general financial dealings tend to work both for and against you. Keep close track of your expenses and of money owed to you. Also keep a diligent eye on your statements. The value of investments made in the distant past may increase this year, perhaps bringing an added bonus at a time you need it most. Utility costs may be higher, and a greater need to maintain frequent contact with people at a distance could result in a more costly telephone bill. It is vital to maintain strict control over general spending during the period between March 18 and May 5, particularly if you are planning on taking a summer vacation or on making a major purchase.

Routine occupational affairs could produce quite a strenuous twelve months. You may feel that it is your duty to do more, perhaps because your mate or partner is not in a position to take on permanent, full-time work. However, there could be a price to pay for overcommitting yourself. Although your Earth sign logic and practicality, together with your Capricorn perseverance, allows you to persist with a tough schedule, it could leave you somewhat overwhelmed with responsibility. Therefore it is especially important this year to ensure that you have a get-away-from-it-all vacation. Make travel arrangements and reserve your vacation dates well ahead of time. Overall, you are coming to the end of one particular way of handling your affairs. Your personal circumstances, or those of the company you work for, are slowly but surely evolving into something different from the present.

Short trips are likely to take up more of your time during the early months of the year. Socially and in your business, do not hesitate to explore new horizons, which will probably involve intense networking in your local community. Your busy daily schedule may make you yearn for a complete break and change of scene. Getting away on weekends can be the ideal solution. Being close to nature can be a real tonic for you, countering feelings of being hemmed in by your daily routine. The period between June 29 and August 24 is ideal for a summer vacation.

With regard to health matters, it may be the medical condition of a person close to you that you are most concerned about, perhaps because they have been working intensely over a long period of time and badly need a break. Look for a practical solution; you may become increasingly worried if the situation does not change. This year there is a strong correlation between psychological factors and your own physical health. It is wise to try to reduce mental and emotional stress whenever and wherever possible. If situations that create stress cannot be avoided, a class in yoga, meditation, or relaxation techniques can help you learn to cope.

Single Capricorn men and women are unlikely to be interested in casual romances this year. Your patience with a relationship which has been on again, off again may run out in the spring or summer, leading to issuing an ultimatum. This tends to be a make-or-break period, signifying either the end of the affair or a shift to a long-term understanding. Either way you are likely to feel happier than if you simply persist in waiting to see where the relationship will go. Capricorn people who are already attached should try to avoid too much of a set routine. Travel experiences shared together may prevent you from getting into a rut, adding greater interest and excitement to the relationship. The summer months are likely to be highly romantic because together you have more opportunities to indulge in the finer things of life.

CAPRICORN
DAILY FORECAST

January–December 1999

JANUARY

1. FRIDAY. Mixed. If you are recovering from the New Year festivities, spend a quiet day relaxing at home. Visiting or entertaining may leave you feeling a little frayed at the edges. Restrict yourself to the house. Tackling a major project right now is likely to take more energy than you can spare. A telephone call from a close relative could upset or annoy you, but giving them the benefit of the doubt can avoid an unpleasant scene. Try not to take rumor or gossip too seriously; it is probably exaggerated. All the signs are that you will stick to your resolutions, at least for today. You have the willpower to give up a habit you know is bad for you.

2. SATURDAY. Stressful. Lingering quarrels with loved ones are likely to crop up again today. Far from wanting to resolve the matter, you are apt to be charging at it like a bull at a gate. Consider swallowing your pride and backing down. Work worries could crowd in on you even though it is the weekend. Plan strategy to handle a thorny problem. Being away from the distractions of the office gives you a greater chance of making a breakthrough. Guard against becoming drawn into a public scene if you go out. Protect your wallet. Lock your car, and watch your step. A social gathering could be marred by a tactless remark or an embarrassing incident involving a child.

3. SUNDAY. Frustrating. Although the sparks may have been flying yesterday, relationships are apt to be frosty today. Any efforts on your part to charm family members out of their chilly mood is likely to be ignored. You may be needed to step in as a peacemaker for estranged relatives. Be careful to walk a tightrope between keeping your emotional distance while not appearing to be aloof or uncaring. This is not a good time to review your budget; you are likely to soon face an important expenditure that has not occurred to you. Part of the day may be spent frantically searching for a mislaid wallet, checkbook, or keys. A walk can be a good way of unwinding from the day's tensions.

4. MONDAY. Useful. This is a favorable time for all kinds of research. Sifting through facts and figures as well as historical data can bring some important new facts to light. Disquieting developments received by telephone or fax could lead to a misunderstanding regarding a financial transaction. You may not have as much money to spare as you think for an investment or credit card payment. However, a brainstorm later in the day could provide just the solution you are looking for. Your concentration is good. Combining this with the chance to work alone this afternoon means that you get through the day's activities in double-quick time. Set the tone for this evening by staging a romantic dinner with your loved one.

5. TUESDAY. Confusing. This is a much better day for any and all financial transactions. However, be sure to read the small print of a contract carefully before signing on the dotted line. There is a risk of confusion over repayment terms. Delving into the causes of a current stressful situation can be an eye-opener. What you learn from this could provide the solid foundation you need to build on in the future. Someone who has been quietly working behind the scenes on your behalf is likely to make their efforts known to you. You can trust what they have to say, especially when it comes to planning for your own future security. Guard against impulse buying; a luxury item could turn into a white elephant.

6. WEDNESDAY. Rewarding. People around you may be up in arms over a proposed move or other change. You may be the only one who can sort out the situation and calm their fears. It is important to keep a sense of fair play; looking for a scapegoat can be counterproductive. Those who matter are sure to be impressed by the way you are able to turn things around. Unforeseen circumstances may force you to cancel a long-distance trip. Good news from someone at a distance means that you can relax about a situation close to your heart. You can expect to reap the rewards from an advertising campaign or special offer if you are quick to take advantage of it.

7. THURSDAY. Unsettling. Your unwillingness to say no to certain people can cause you to overstretch your schedule. Try to reschedule meetings at a distance and obtain a deadline extension for an important project. Sticking to local venues means you will not waste valuable time traveling. A well-timed long-distance telephone conversation can keep things ticking over. Control your Capricorn tendency to blow things out of proportion or you could be accused of making a mountain out of a molehill. Keeping a sense of humor about your circumstances can help maintain the right perspective. You could be in the mood to play a practical joke, or you could become the victim of one. Either way, keep it lighthearted.

8. FRIDAY. Favorable. Capricorn employees who earn a weekly salary may receive an unexpected pay boost, possibly in the form of a tax rebate or reduced insurance premium. By all means let your superiors know what a good job you are doing for them, but guard against a tendency to overstate your own contributions to group effort. A thoughtless remark to an older person can lead to a quarrel. This is an excellent time to invest spare cash; even a short-term purchase could yield high rewards. Keep abreast of all that is going on in the background of your routine activities. There is a risk of a backlog building up. A surprising announcement is likely to provide you with the opportunity to climb one more rung up the ladder of success.

9. SATURDAY. Disconcerting. There may not be much opportunity to relax this weekend. You could be forced to respond to a challenge or serious difference of opinion, especially when it comes to matters concerning an older relative. You could have no option but to correct whatever is going wrong, no matter how many people you annoy in the process. However, against becoming embroiled in a confrontation with an old rival or competitor. Unless you are ready for a long-term fight, chances are that you will not win in a battle of words. If you are making plans for yourself, do not think twice about saying goodbye to someone who has been holding you back by their actions or lack of action.

10. SUNDAY. Demanding. The demands of home life may seem very restrictive to you, especially if you have definite career plans you hope to fulfill. If you usually work on the weekend, you may have to deal with an urgent problem. If you are normally off, you may be called in to work. Loved ones left behind at home may feel a little neglected as a result. Few things are more hurtful than a disloyal friend, but what you learn about a certain person today means that you know who to trust in the future. An unguarded remark could lead you to spill the beans about a certain secret matter. Double-check your social arrangements for later on; you could have the wrong time or place.

11. MONDAY. Variable. Capricorns who are involved in a community project or local politics can expect to be hear good news. This is a favorable day for delivering a speech, or you may be asked to make one in the near future. This is also a good time to freely express your personal opinions on a particular subject.

Chances are your views will be taken seriously by those who matter. Refusing a friend a favor can be difficult. If you must do so, let them down gently, especially if they are asking for a loan. Pooling your resources with a friend or family member is not favored right now. A surprising new development about a joint venture later in the day is likely to change your views. Consider replacing a broken appliance rather than having it fixed; repairs may not last very long.

12. TUESDAY. Excellent. This is an excellent day if you are in sales or in any way deal directly with the public. There are plenty of opportunities, especially among your friends and the groups with which you are involved. A hard-sell technique is probably not required. Just let them know what is being offered; it should be enough to generate a good deal of interest. You have an instinct for the best deal. This, coupled with your famous Capricorn head for business, can lead to making a financial killing. Mixing business with pleasure is favored. Woo prospective clients by inviting them to lunch or dinner at a restaurant or, better yet, at your home. Taking part in a business fair is also favored.

13. WEDNESDAY. Mixed. The pressure that you were under to get ahead earlier in the week may mean that you now have a backlog of paperwork. This is a good day for catching up. Looking through past records can reveal a surprising new pattern. However, cross-check your findings before acting on them. Choose who you take into your confidence with extra care. Otherwise you may give an important advantage to someone who does not have your best interests at heart. Keep a confidence to yourself, even with those you would normally trust. Jot down payments you make by credit or charge card. There is a possibility of exceeding your card limit and embarrassing yourself in front of a group.

14. THURSDAY. Changeable. Opt for a change in your everyday routine. The time is right to look ahead and to change those aspects of your life that you know are wrong or misguided in some way. Help is close at hand if you need some support in achieving your objectives. Be sure to take the opinions of your loved ones seriously. It is all too easy to dismiss what they have to say because it does not agree with your own plans. Even the most casual remark made to you in passing could be useful. Creating a private space for yourself at home is very important and could turn out to be a motivating factor. You need peace and quiet in order to come up with new plans.

15. FRIDAY. Manageable. Both your personal and professional schedule is likely to go as expected. However, you may need to put in extra effort in order to resolve a problem from the past. Your desire to get ahead is obvious, so there is little point in trying to hide it. Just keep in mind that everything is relative, especially if you start to think that other people have it much easier than you. Go along with any changes that are taking place at work. The weekend lull may get in the way of progress. Focus on the world beyond your own door. Events at a distance are having a strong impact on you. Work and play to go hand in hand this evening.

16. SATURDAY. Cautious. Avoid giving tasks to other people that you know you can do better yourself. Nobody knows the ropes of your own world better than you do. No matter how much others try to put themselves in your shoes, they cannot be expected to work to your consistently high standard. This is a good day for getting to the root of difficulties that have surrounded you for some time, but use caution and diplomacy in your investigations. Conversation is apt to be intriguing, even when you know that it is more rumor than fact. News you receive from a distance may make you realize that your expectations are too high. Handling several different tasks at the same time is a fact of life at present.

17. SUNDAY. Difficult. Your mate, partner, or a very close friend may sense that you are trying to test them in some way. Once you stop to think about the facts of the situation, you may see why they feel this way despite your other intentions. Avoid a tendency to get involved in matters that do not directly concern you. Curb a tendency to lord your inside knowledge over others. Creating a good atmosphere at home should not be as difficult as you might think. However, a certain amount of extra effort on your part is necessary if you want to set matters straight. Spend an hour or two mulling over facts and figures. This preparatory work should stand you in good stead during the week ahead.

18. MONDAY. Deceptive. A negative approach to a certain situation could be undermining your efforts. It may seem that everyone but you is making good progress. Fortunately, these adverse influences are going to be short-lived. You can actually use them to your advantage by taking a back seat for a while. Because you are in a very receptive mood right now, you can accept the ideas of other people much more readily than you normally do. What you learn is likely to put you in a good position when conditions allow you to spring into action. A social encounter at a party or some other function can be very rewarding. Do not hold back on a personal discussion of any sort, especially one that can clear up a misunderstanding.

19. TUESDAY. Rewarding. This is an excellent day for all kinds of money transactions. If you recently made a long-term purchase, you can be confident that you have invested wisely. If you now are thinking of making a new investment, do not hesitate to strike while the iron is hot. Your Capricorn instincts can be trusted when it comes to future security for yourself and your family providing you proceed with that sense of caution you are famous for. This approach offsets any tendency to impulsiveness when making long-term commitments. There is a risk of trouble brewing in domestic matters. A disagreement between relatives could put you directly in the line of fire. However, you may be asked to act as the peacemaker and arbitrator.

20. WEDNESDAY. Tricky. A letter or important document could turn up missing, delaying your day's schedule as a result. Do not twiddle your thumbs while you are waiting for news or developments. This could be the perfect opportunity to catch up with neglected tasks. Take care of routine paperwork and chores you have been putting aside. Computer e-mails and fax machines are likely to be troublesome; you may have to wait until tomorrow to send or receive an all-important message. Make backups if you regularly work with computers, especially those connected to a network. There is a possibility that a bug or virus could contaminate your recent efforts.

21. THURSDAY. Useful. This is a much better day for all of your communications. Face-to-face meetings are the best way to speak your mind. This is no time to be backward in coming forward to express your opinion. Other people are likely to listen to you and appreciate your honesty and forthrightness. This is a starred day if you work in sales or advertising, especially to dream up a new campaign for a product. Public relations efforts are likely to draw in lucrative new contracts. On a personal note, this is a favored time for healing any rift that may have developed with your neighbors. At a minimum, you should be able to agree to disagree.

22. FRIDAY. Productive. The day begins on a bright note with some good news likely by phone. It could be an invitation to a party or family news that you have been waiting to receive. Later in the day the emphasis switches to domestic concerns. This is a good time to clarify any misunderstanding or confusion over the family budget. Review recent expenditure or you could find yourself overdrawn before next payday. A domestic crisis such as a plumbing problem or leaky roof may force you to withdraw money from special savings in order to get it fixed. Try not to let unfounded fears regarding your future security cloud your judgment about your financial situation.

23. SATURDAY. Easygoing. A routine shopping trip can be memorable. There is a good chance of coming across an item you have long wanted to own. Even if it seems a little out of your price range, you can find a way to buy it by putting down a deposit and arranging to pay in installments. A legacy or other financial windfall may come at just the right time for you. As a Capricorn you are not known to blow your own horn. However, little harm can be done by letting others know how much you have achieved. If you are job hunting, this is a good time for sprucing up your resume. You should be able to turn it into an attention grabber with very little effort.

24. SUNDAY. Changeable. Capricorns cannot be accused of being extravagant, although a certain family member may be exceeding the budget. Disputes over money can be tricky. You need to tread a fine line between condoning or condemning their expenditures. A deep insecurity may be at the root of a loved one's fears. Although money matters continue to be of concern, the emphasis shifts to children later in the day. A child may make unreasonable demands for designer clothes or shoes, or they may ask for extra money without wanting to tell you why they want it. Use this as an opportunity to show that you trust them rather than trying to lay down the law.

25. MONDAY. Cautious. Routine matters are likely to run smoothly. However, do not be surprised if your social plans change at the last moment. For Capricorn parents and those who work with children, this is not a favored day to go on an outing. If you must be out and about with youngsters, strive to keep an extra close eye on them; there is an increased possibility that they will wander off. Children are likely to be unruly and troublesome because they are all too easily bored. Try to plan a special activity for them by way of a change. Capricorn singles are in for a disappointment as a new romantic interest ends just as quickly as it began or runs into serious problems that at first seem insurmountable.

26. TUESDAY. Fair. Consider becoming a penpal with someone who lives far away. This correspondence is apt to be interesting on both sides and long lasting. Money matters involving children continue to be problematic. Expecting them to work for their pocket money can be a good compromise and can also teach them the importance of earning their way. A hasty or thoughtless remark that you blurt out is likely to cause offense. Choose your words carefully, especially when talking with a relative or close friend. On the work front, this is a day to proceed carefully and cautiously. Be sure you pay your bills on time. This is also a good time to contact people who owe you money. Check invoices before they are mailed; chances are one contains an error that is not in your favor.

27. WEDNESDAY. Unpredictable. Unexpected news could come as a bolt out of the blue. However, there is no need to look on the negative side. Someone working quietly behind the scenes is ready to come to your aid. Before the day is out, there is a good chance that the tables will turn once again. Keep a level head at all times; put off making any major decision until you are sure of the way forward. Do not believe everything you hear, especially if the source is a known gossiper. It is likely that they are deliberately trying to muddy the waters. Make sure you get all the facts straight before passing on information to others. Communicating by letter can be especially tricky because of possible double meanings of your words.

28. THURSDAY. Excellent. Get an early start this morning. By all means put your heart into whatever you hope to achieve, but guard against spreading yourself too thin or overextending yourself. Your sense of optimism about the future coupled with your famous Capricorn capacity for realistic thinking indicates that your plans and aspirations are on a sure course to success. Later, your thoughts are likely to turn to the weekend and how you want to spend it. Consider reserving a table at your favorite restaurant for Saturday night, or booking seats at a movie premiere or for a hit play. Any social plans you have for tonight are likely to be especially successful if you include a mixture of workmates and friends.

29. FRIDAY. Happy. This is an especially wonderful time for Capricorns who are in love. Consider putting your feelings in a love letter. Capricorn singles could develop a romantic interest with someone who has previously only been a friend. You should be happy to learn that your feelings are mutual. If you are in a long-term relationship, your partner's attentions are apt to be fully focused on pleasing you. Take some time out to be alone together and you could find yourselves falling in love all over again. Generally, you are in tune with friends as well as loved ones. Expecting the best from others and from life is the way to make it happen; your optimism is contagious.

30. SATURDAY. Changeable. If you were on cloud nine as far as relationships were concerned yesterday, today's bump back to earth is likely to be painful. Loved ones may be rather preoccupied with their own concerns, even if this amounts to nothing more than shopping. The sooner you get the day's chores done, the sooner you can go out to enjoy the rest of the weekend. Capricorn parents should consider asking in-laws or a neighbor to babysit so that you can go out and enjoy adult companionship. Chances are you will receive some disturbing news about a friend or acquaintance; the matter is apt to be out of your hands and beyond your control. Later, someone close to you is likely to confide in you about a personal financial matter.

31. SUNDAY. Disquieting. Increased tension at home could result in a sudden eruption of emotions. It is better to face the music now rather than trying to sweep everything under the rug. Do not let someone's outward appearance cloud your judgment about their abilities. If you go out, keep your checkbook separate from your credit card. Take along cash money only if you think you will need it. Guard against pushing through any idea by sheer force of your will. Other people need time to catch up with your advance thinking. Your mate or partner may not be ready to tell you about something that is bothering them. Do not pry; let them pick the moment to bring up the matter. Be especially kind to an older relative.

FEBRUARY

1. MONDAY. Fair. This is a good day for reviewing insurance policies and long-term investments. Check your home insurance policy in particular; there is a possibility that it has lapsed or that the coverage is no longer adequate. Someone who is older and wiser than you is in a good position to give sound advice about a confidential matter. Guard against fair-weather friends, especially those who are asking for money or another favor. Think carefully about sinking personal funds into a group venture; what looks good on paper may not turn out so well in reality. Information that happens to come your way could turn out to be of great value to you in making an important decision, but do not rely on hearsay.

2. TUESDAY. Unsettling. A long-distance call could lead you to take a trip at short notice. Someone you know well is likely to turn up on your doorstep and shock you into realizing that you both have some unfinished business to deal with. You may struggle with a difficult assignment or new responsibility. Be sure to take regular breaks. If you try to plow ahead without stopping, you could wind up becoming groggy and irritable. Machines are prone to break down. Consider replacing an old model rather than trying to have it fixed; all the signs are that this would be a false economy. Be honest enough not to deceive yourself.

3. WEDNESDAY. Successful. Tokens of generosity are likely from an unexpected direction. These could be gifts or practical offers of help. Accept with good grace. It is unwise to refuse other people's offers of help just because you want to show how independent you can be. Your desire for overnight success may have to be curbed a little. Although it is important to keep an open mind, a little careful advance planning and patience can ensure that you make the most of today's trends. A strange coincidence may help you see the funny side of life. It is a mistake to take minor irritations too seriously. Laughter can be the best way to reduce tension.

4. THURSDAY. Variable. Today could be a little tiresome, mainly because you have to work so hard to make even minimum headway. However, as a Capricorn you are not usually hesitant to exert some extra effort when necessary. Your can-do attitude should help you come out on top. If something has been puzzling you for a while, this is a good time to give the problem another airing. Your concentration is good and your analytical skills are razor sharp. Answers that have been eluding you are likely to come more easily. Professionally, too, you can make good progress by jumping at a chance to talk to a person of influence. Voice your opinions forcefully but tactfully.

5. FRIDAY. Sensitive. Work and the practical aspects of your life are assuming renewed importance. As a Capricorn you tend to be highly ambitious, willing to labor long and hard to reap rewards. However, do not let your eagerness to climb the ladder of success make you forget your obligations to the ones you love. Putting yourself out for a family member or friend can reward you in unexpected ways. Continue to keep an open mind, especially when it comes to promotion or an increase in salary. What looks at first to be a second best option could turn out to be just right for you. Finances are strengthening, allowing you to confidently do some forward planning and new budgeting.

6. SATURDAY. Inactive. The pace of your life is slowing down a little. This is not bad if it allows you to spend more time reflecting rather than in frantic activity. Let your mate or partner take over for today while you take a back seat. Guard against living in the past; there is little to be gained by raking over old ground. Do not be taken in by a sob story. The best way to help others can be to show them how they can help themselves. Do not allow a minor disappointment with a loved one or friend to prevent you from following your chosen path. Take minor setbacks for what they are, rather than turning them into major obstacles that freeze you in place.

7. SUNDAY. Deceptive. Even the smallest details need to be looked at with total honesty and objectivity. Protect your own financial interests at all levels. In particular, if you go out with friends, avoid being unnecessarily generous with your hard-earned money. Matters of friendship and loyalty can present some ticklish problems. As a Capricorn you have a strong sense of what is right and wrong, which should stand you in good stead. However, guard against hasty judgment, especially if you hear only one side of a story. The behavior of a loved one can be difficult to understand, especially if you try to figure everything out by strict logic. Your mate or partner needs your support in public even if you disagree in private.

8. MONDAY. Frustrating. Keep a friend's secret for a while longer. Although you may be bursting to tell someone, you can take away your friend's element of surprise by doing so. A good first impression is vital. However, try to strike the right balance between what is expected of you and what you really want to do. Taking a chance can pay off financially, but do not risk your shirt on a wild gamble. Lack of help from one area of your life may be compensated by a new understanding with someone else. Guard against being taken in by a fast talker. This is not a good day for shopping for an expensive item you have not researched thoroughly. You could wind up paying too much.

9. TUESDAY. Fortunate. If you entertain, you are likely to be at your most efficient and are bound to make a favorable and lasting impression. Paperwork can be signed in the confidence that you are doing the right thing. However, avoid rushing headlong into a commitment that you know in your heart you probably cannot meet. Fixed opinions are subject to outside influence. You may well find yourself changing your mind about a certain acquaintance or co-worker. Work interests may be beginning to make you neglect your family. Nevertheless, consider accepting an invitation from a work colleague to attend a social event with business overtones. Your hunch about a new person on the scene is probably correct.

10. WEDNESDAY. Disquieting. Ongoing work could be stalled because of lack of supplies or resources. As a result, you are likely to have some extra time on your hands. Turn to a project you had to put aside. Give people who rigidly refuse to modify their ideas a wide berth. Guard against getting caught up in an argument that does not involve you directly. Even though the combatants try to drag you into it, keep a safe distance. If you do step in, you could be accused of interfering. Younger members of the family need to learn the fine art of give-and-take. Reply immediately to an offer or suggestion you receive by mail; delay could prove costly. Avoid doing anything you would not want to talk about.

11. THURSDAY. Satisfactory. This is a good day for going public with confidential information. Capricorns in research can now announce findings; if you are in business, you may unveil new company plans. You may be in the mood to change your appearance. Do so on a small scale at first to see what reaction you get. New eyeglass frames, or switching to contact lenses, can give you a whole new demeanor. Capricorns who are active in the community may be asked to organize a group outing. You can have a significant influence in group activities without raising your voice. However, guard against putting your own interests above the will of the majority.

12. FRIDAY. Successful. Your confidence is beginning to soar again, but avoid a tendency to correct people, especially when you do not really know much more than they do. This is the ideal time to be traveling, or at least to start thinking about your vacation plans. Encounters with one or two disagreeable people are likely. Try not to react verbally to the situation; the stern look that you are famous for delivering could be all it takes. You can afford to take a well-calculated risk, but do not make a hasty decision even if the pressure is on to do exactly that. This evening, a workout or a swim can help you burn off excess energy and clear your mind. Give loved ones your full attention rather than watching TV tonight.

13. SATURDAY. Enjoyable. A day out with your friends is sure to be fun. Whiling away happy hours in congenial company, with interesting conversation, is today's favored activity. Your diplomatic abilities are heightened, which could be useful if you are called upon to settle an argument between friends. Consider an informal gathering at your home where everyone brings something to eat or to drink. In that way you do not have the hassle of having to make all the preparations. By all means enjoy yourself, putting the emphasis on relaxing rather than burning the candle at both ends. Joint creative effort can be very rewarding, especially making something as a fund-raiser.

14. SUNDAY. Confusing. Loved ones are apt to demand your time and attention even though you would rather be alone. A spur-of-the-moment decision to get away from it all can be right for you, but make sure that those closest to you do not take it the wrong way. Use part of the day to attend to routine financial matters. A cash-flow crisis may make you think twice about buying a luxury item you really want. Reconsider it for a few days; if you come back a little later in the week and it is still available, at least you will know that it is probably meant for you. A blockbuster novel is likely to be completely absorbing; you may even stay up very late to finish reading it.

15. MONDAY. Variable. This is a time for taking action on financial advice you received earlier in the month. However, guard against investing too large a sum up front in your eagerness to make a profit. Even if you only put in a small amount, it is likely to produce excellent returns. You could be asked to pay an outstanding debt in full. Make sure you call in money owed to you at the same time. The obligations that you feel to help others could leave you feeling restless and neglected when it comes to your own wants and needs. It is up to you to do something about this situation. You may be amazed at the support and encouragement you get from your friends and loved ones.

16. TUESDAY. Fortunate. Money and security are very important for Capricorns. You are now entering a phase where making money is more important than investing. Explore new avenues and opportunities that are opening up for you. New technology and the latest communication equipment may play a major role in your financial success. Dressing to impress while maintaining your Capricorn air of authority can be an irresistible combination when it comes to dealing with people in positions of authority. You are likely to get a boost for your current work from an important person, probably an elected official. An enthusiastic friend or co-worker may have some inspired ideas to share. Talking with people in person can be more effective than telephoning or writing letters.

17. WEDNESDAY. Mixed. All it takes to improve your abilities is an extra measure of discipline on your part. Consider signing up for a course that offers a certificate of achievement upon completion of it. Learning more about computer software or hardware is also favored. Improving your study skills can be a financial lifesaver at a later date. Cultivate your connections with a social group or political organization. Be an example to others through what you do rather than what you say. You are apt to be on a short fuse. However, you should come out on top in a fight, unless it is with another Capricorn. You may have trouble putting up with foolish people or be angered to realize that someone has been trying to take you for a fool. Your words may be taken out of context and your ideas misstated.

18. THURSDAY. Fair. If you are a Capricorn in love, this is an excellent time to put your feelings in writing. Also consider sending an extravagant bouquet of flowers to your loved one. If you cannot be with the one you love, a long-distance telephone call can help bridge the gap. Later in the day, your thoughts are likely to be on career matters. You have the Midas touch today, with a nose for the best money-making deal. However, guard against becoming too confident. People are less likely to trust you if you let your dreams carry you far from reality. You may have to work hard to maintain your normal income level. Delays are possible in payments due to you. Watch your spending; an unnecessary purchase could leave you strapped for ready cash.

19. FRIDAY. Exciting. Focus most of your attention on immediate necessities. There are tasks that need to be done in order to clear away the cobwebs and get yourself better organized. Coming to grips with this is likely to be very satisfying. Help is available from family members and close colleagues, who can easily be won over by your enthusiasm. You can get the best out of them because you are able to coordinate their efforts without being bossy. Because you understand one another, problems can be readily solved as they arise. A phone call from someone you met earlier in the week may lead to an invitation to an event that turns out to be a lot of fun. Keep romance on a light note; resist coming on strong with an expression of your intense feelings.

20. SATURDAY. Tricky. The changes taking place in one special relationship are apt to conflict with your need for a peaceful and relaxing time. Misunderstandings could arise even as you try to improve communications between you. Domestic harmony may be threatened. The outcome of a certain course you chose at the start of the year is now becoming apparent. This is the time to consolidate your position or cut loose if things are not working out as you had hoped. As a Capricorn you have a good sense of discipline and self-control, but knowing where to draw the line as far as children are concerned is likely to be difficult. Single Capricorns can look forward to an intriguing encounter that leads to an extra-special romance.

21. SUNDAY. Stressful. Do not pay too much attention to gossip and rumors. Malicious talk may be based on pure imagination and envy. Try not to be drawn into any conversation where someone's reputation is being tarnished. Word is likely to get back to them, which could leave you in an embarrassing position. Continual interruptions from phone calls or drop-in visitors may keep you from making much headway with your routine chores. Saying no to social invitations is the simplest solution if you have matters to attend to that will not wait. A disconcerting message from a distant family member may give the impression that things are worse that they really are. Get the full story before you react.

22. MONDAY. Buoyant. You should have no worries as far as your physical well-being is concerned. This, coupled with a sense that all is well with the world, means that you are walking on air. Follow your intuition, especially when it comes to saying just what is on your mind. Even routine chores are apt to be rewarding; you can clear the decks in double-quick time. If you belong to a spiritual or charitable organization, you may be asked to take a position of responsibility, perhaps as secretary or treasurer. A dream you had last night is worth investigating to discover its hidden meaning. This is a good time to search for ways to work smarter rather than just harder. The benefits of increased efficiency are likely to be felt very quickly.

23. TUESDAY. Enjoyable. If you are considering buying or adopting a pet, today is the day. Consider whether you want a pedigree which you can enter in competition or just a family pet. A change in business policy could produce improvements quicker than even you anticipate. Expansion is the key. Take advantage of a higher-up's availability to press your cause. This is a good time for signing a contract or other document involving your family's future security. Make sure that any computer-based information or data is up to date; basing your arguments on outmoded facts could backfire. Wind up the day with loved ones and close family members. Treat them and yourself to dinner at a favorite family restaurant.

24. WEDNESDAY. Useful. Work you delegated to someone else or skimped on in the past is likely to require your urgent attention now. Do not allow current pressures to tempt you to rush through your schedule. Even if it means working longer hours, doing a thorough job is likely to pay big dividends in the future. Take advantage of informal contacts with influential people. Catch up on what's being whispered about on the grapevine. Networking can put you in a good position for handling future developments.

A journey undertaken today is subject to delays. If you intend to drive, find out if there are any major road repairs going on. It might be better to use public transportation rather than sitting and stewing in a traffic jam.

25. THURSDAY. Changeable. If circumstances permit, this is a good day to get away for an early and extended weekend. Time spent with loved ones is likely to prove especially enjoyable. If you feel sociable, accept an invitation to visit friends this evening, or take the initiative and invite them to be your guests. At work, keep new ideas to yourself for a while longer. If you share them before they have matured in your mind, people are likely to regard them as half-baked schemes. There is also a risk that someone will steal your ideas and claim them as their own at a later date. Confidential messages could fall into the wrong hands. Communicating with foreigners can be especially difficult because of the language barrier.

26. FRIDAY. Rewarding. A family member may make you very proud. Give them every possible encouragement in their work. They need your support and approval more than they may be willing to admit. Keep in mind that even small achievements are something to be celebrated. The skills of your business partners and associates can be adapted in handling a new project or venture, especially if it requires good communication or teaching skills. Submit a report or designs to influential people for approval. Not only are you likely to gain their verbal support, you could also get some financial backing. Apply for a scholarship or free tuition if you hope to return to school in order to enhance your employment possibilities.

27. SATURDAY. Exciting. A certain excitement in the air makes you feel adventurous. You could end up being three steps ahead of yourself as everything falls into place magically. Do not waste valuable time and energy in gossip and idle chat. Be on guard against people who puff themselves up and are full of pretentions. Fact is often stranger than fiction, and more interesting. Being able to talk with loved ones about philosophical or religious matters can raise your relationship to a higher plane. Do all that you can to enhance your public image. For self-employed Capricorns, there is a greater chance of increased profitability, especially when it comes to investing on someone else's behalf.

28. SUNDAY. Disconcerting. Be alert for sudden surprises, some of which might come as a real shock. Check out insurance policies to make sure you are adequately covered. Making progress in a professional sense during the weekend can be difficult, but you can do much to help things along. Bring an old resume up to date; turning it into a document that really emphasizes your training and experience can help make you stand out from others. Do not take on more commitments than you know you can comfortably handle, even though others might try very hard to press you into service. Joint finances may need close attention, especially if you are saving for a special purchase.

MARCH

1. MONDAY. Exciting. There may be an encounter with an attractive stranger, or with someone from out of town who you have not seen for quite some time. Either way, you are sure to delight in the company that surrounds you and can gain socially from the many and varied contacts that can be made. A letdown by a certain friend or associate is likely, however; do not take it too much to heart. Your energy level may be a little low, but your desire to get ahead is not. Try to stay within your own limits rather than pushing yourself too hard. Current trends are moving matters in your direction. Good news has a way of coming to you as it is. Be sure to return a long-distance phone message.

2. TUESDAY. Excellent. If you want any favor done for you, there is hardly a better time to ask than now. Bringing others around to your point of view should be easy, although you need to bear their interests in mind as much as your own. Do not put off any major decisions until a later date. They will require diligent effort and will not get any easier if shelved for a while. Legal matters, in particular, should be attended to as soon as possible. When it comes to practical matters, trust what you see with your own eyes rather than listening to other people's explanations or rationalizations. Promise yourself a peaceful few moments alone at some point in the day.

3. WEDNESDAY. Demanding. All work and no play can make even hardworking Capricorns a bit dull. Although your keen sense of duty and ambition may keep you burning the midnight oil, your efforts today are unlikely to bear much fruit. This is a time to retreat a little in order to reflect on your situation rather than trying to forge blindly ahead. Regard this as an opportunity to recharge your batteries, not as a waste of valuable time. A dispute could arise at home because of the hours you are putting in. If loved ones are beginning to feel neglected, they are almost sure to voice their opinions. Taking time out to be with them can do much to smooth ruffled feathers and restore home harmony.

4. THURSDAY. Variable. Some powerful emotions are likely to rise to the surface, possibly linked to feelings of insecurity about the future. However, such fears are probably unfounded. Rather than dwelling on them, concentrate on practical, everyday concerns. You are likely to find yourself invited to just the right social gathering. Even if it is a short event, or even a lunch, making an appearance can do much to raise your personal profile. A family member is in a position to do you a good turn. They could surprise you by their determination to help you out. At work, too, you may be able to take advantage of a colleague's goodwill. Arrange a quiet evening for you and that special person in your life.

5. FRIDAY. Buoyant. The pace of life is picking up. There is much exciting new information available if you listen for it. A surprise turn of events in the romantic area of your life could leave your head spinning. The signs are favorable for Capricorn singles to embark on an exciting new liaison. Although other aspects of your life may not come up to your expectations, a rare opportunity to show what you are capable of doing artistically is likely. You should be in just the right frame of mind to exploit it to the fullest. The attitudes of both younger and older family members may surprise you. Be especially tactful when dealing with those who are sensitive and vulnerable to criticism.

6. SATURDAY. Disconcerting. This is not the luckiest day of the month for you. It would be wise not to take any gamble or make any risky decision while current conditions prevail. Although as a Capricorn you cannot normally be accused of being foolhardy, exercise extra caution in all of your dealings today. In particular, guard against being drawn into someone else's fantasy world. You may find yourself being emotionally blackmailed by someone who is trying to manipulate you. Keeping firm boundaries and refusing to enter into their games can help you overcome any difficulties they pose. Relaxing with a novel will not get the chores done, but at least you are less likely to be frustrated by lack of progress in that area.

7. SUNDAY. Sensitive. Take another look at certain social issues in the light of changing circumstances. Nothing is as straightforward as it may seem at first. Rethink aspects of a problem that has been a source of confusion for you. Avoid getting so upset and uptight about a cause dear to your heart; other people may only see you as argumentative or provocative. A can-do approach is more likely to inspire them to help. A friend could drop in unexpectedly, leaving you feeling a little grumpy, even irritated. However, you are likely to benefit from a little light relief. Plan a quiet dinner at home or at a cozy restaurant. Restoring your positive attitude can prove that there is light at the end of a particular emotional tunnel.

8. MONDAY. Quiet. This is a good day to devote time to community activity. Your contribution may help bring about a much needed change. You may be asked to sign a petition for a local cause. People may ask for your opinion on a local political issue, or a local politician may seek your support. Some people are apt to challenge your opinions but try to understand both sides of the argument. You may prefer to stay in the company of friends and acquaintances because people who are less familiar to you could leave you feeling a little uncertain. Devote some time to activities that are close to your heart, even if this means postponing one or two practical matters until another day.

9. TUESDAY. Fair. This is a good day for being extra thorough when handling important deals. Be sure you read and understand the small print before signing on the dotted line. It is not that anyone is trying to con you, more likely that you may misinterpret some wording. You may prefer your own company as many people clamor for your help in one way or another. Although keeping them at arm's length could be difficult, you can manage it somehow without hurting anyone's feelings. A minor inspiration is likely to come to you by simply taking time out to reflect. The vulnerable side of your nature is unusually sensitive at this time, which can lead to untypical reactions on your part in reacting to other people.

10. WEDNESDAY. Mixed. You would be better off doing things basically on your own if you have the chance. This is not a time to be following the lead of others because they may not have quite the same good common sense you are showing. It is important to look at news you receive today in a realistic light. Do not become pessimistic or gloomy about negative news, nor too elated if it is positive. Also try not to react too strongly to small problems; they will probably sort themselves out in due course. Avoid becoming discouraged by slow progress. The time will come soon enough when you can begin to pep things up once more.

11. THURSDAY. Slow. The mood continues to be slow but steady. By the end of today you should have a sense of real accomplishment. Obstacles in your path can be overcome with a few deft moves. Any restrictions only make you more determined to plan and act carefully. An opportunity may come along to improve your financial position, although it may hinge on an idea that you cannot put into practice just yet. Family members need sensitive handling in order to keep a minor disagreement from escalating into a major argument. Give loved ones the space they need; placing your trust in them now should put you in a better position later on to compromise.

12. FRIDAY. Fortunate. You may have a greater need to feel important. If this desire goes unfulfilled, you risk becoming a little irritable and emotional. Today you have to make your own luck. Consider roping in a friend to help you with a new venture or project, but do not involve them in any financial aspects of the deal. There is a chance that the friendship could be compromised down the line if money changes hands now. You could be in the mood to change your appearance in some striking way, but think about it for a day or two before making a final decision. You may be asked to arbitrate in a private discussion with friends, but do not try to impose your will or point of view on them.

13. SATURDAY. Stressful. A certain anxiety may exist regarding money matters, particularly those which are above and beyond your control. Adopt a wait-and-see attitude. What may make matters worse is someone close to you asking for a loan. Heed the wise advice of an older relative, even if it is not too welcome. This is not a good time for risky ventures in general. Take steps to protect your own interests. You should be able to make minor improvements to everyday affairs. This is a good day for sorting out personal difficulties between other people; try to remain impartial or you could wind up arguing with one of the antagonists.

14. SUNDAY. Frustrating. Your enthusiasm for a new project may begin to wane as minor setbacks continue to be troublesome. In the personal areas of your life, it may be futile to try to tackle important issues without the help of other people. Do all that you can to put such concerns aside and try to enjoy relaxing leisure pursuits. Loved ones may request special favors. If these involve money, it would be best to hold off for a couple of days while you think things over. Conforming socially could be difficult for you because of your Capricorn insight. Others may tend to view your behavior or opinions as mildly eccentric. Stay away from argumentative types.

15. MONDAY. Rewarding. The start of this workweek should find the restrictions, disruptions, and confusions of the last few days beginning to lift. You can now move forward with confidence. Do not reveal all that you know to fellow players in the game of life. There are distinct advantages to keeping a few tricks up your sleeve. A broad approach to life should work best at this time, particularly when you are in the company of professionals.

An easing of money concerns should put you in a more relaxed and secure frame of mind, while socially you enjoy increased popularity. Even your rapport with influential people is getting better day by day. The world should look bright as you formulate plans for an exciting new undertaking.

16. TUESDAY. Tricky. Although you might not agree with all that is being said in a work or family situation, make yourself heard rather than remaining quiet. This is especially true when it comes to the ticklish matter of discipline and responsibility. As a Capricorn your sound sense of justice puts you in an ideal position to make sure that any punishment or deprivation of privileges is done fairly and squarely. Do more to get better organized. A planned approach to an important activity can save time and energy down the line. Take what might sound like personal criticism with a grain of salt; wait until you have calmed down before deciding on what action to take.

17. WEDNESDAY. Uncertain. People you see on a daily basis may appear edgy or restless, probably because they are entering a new phase of their own. Give them the space they need to adjust to their new circumstances, but remain available for practical assistance if they ask for it. If you are looking for new work, this is an excellent time to scour the help-wanted pages. Get a feel for what you are worth in the marketplace. You may find that you have just the skills and experience to name your own salary. Be open to new ideas and propositions, even though they might seem too good to be true. New relationships may develop as the result of a short journey or a social event.

18. THURSDAY. Manageable. Any dark clouds that have been hanging over you should be fully dispersed now. Luck and high optimism are on your side, enabling you to make big strides forward. Recent misunderstandings between family members are likely to clear up. An after-dinner chat with someone close to you can be the perfect opportunity to clear the air. Common sense prevails in your life, making this a good day for getting together with someone of an equally practical nature. If starting any new project do not let your imagination run away with you. Remain as calm and in control as possible.

19. FRIDAY. Demanding. People may demand your attention, just at a time when extended discussions and negotiations are particularly stressful and important. Although you are busy dealing with the world, take care not to neglect your nearest and dearest. Despite your Capricorn vigor and energy, this is not a good time to burn the candle at both ends. Short bursts of activity followed by a recuperating break are favored. Beware of behaving arrogantly and of showing impatience in the face of necessary restrictions. Although it might be hard to own up to a past mistake, it should not be difficult to put things right. People are ready to help you if you are prepared to eat a little humble pie.

20. SATURDAY. Unsettling. If verbal confrontations come your way, you may be unwilling to back down. If you enjoy a good argument, by all means do not shy away. However, you may prefer to avoid potential flashpoints. Your wallet, keys, or eyeglasses may get lost or mislaid. There is also a possibility you are mistaken about the facts of a certain situation. When it comes to leisure pursuits, sporting activity can be an enjoyable challenge. Rushing to meet your goals is unlikely to produce desired results. Listen closely to the advice of someone who has been in a similar situation to the one you now are trying to cope with. Gambling or risk taking is not favored. Do not ever risk your hard-earned cash on a so-called safe bet.

21. SUNDAY. Disquieting. Leisure pursuits can cause unpredictable or unsettling events. It might seem that other people are being deliberately aloof. A cooler atmosphere in an intimate relationship is also foreseen. It is important to maintain a down-to-earth approach to all situations. Where feelings are concerned, you need to be thoughtful and tactful in order to get your points across. This is a time for putting your loved one's needs ahead of your own, but this is not to say that you should let them use you as a doormat. Do not burden yourself with new responsibilities; keep your life as uncomplicated and straightforward as possible. Concentrate on immediate issues and do not worry about the what-if's.

22. MONDAY. Fair. A dispute with a subordinate can easily be settled if you give in a little and also accept an apology. Discussing the problem in private, perhaps over lunch, should clear the air completely. This is a good time for finalizing budgets and forecasts. Encourage someone younger than you to come up with ideas of their own, then be ready to help implement them. Handle routine matters yourself, especially those you usually delegate to someone else. If you have recently been placed in a position of greater responsibility, seek the advice of a more experienced person. The way ahead appears clear to start the detailed aspects of a new project. Enjoy the evening with someone who makes you laugh.

23. TUESDAY. Variable. Your mate or partner may be in an argumentative mood, so you would be wise to skirt around sensitive subjects. Their reaction even to casual conversation could shock you. A disagreement is likely to erupt between you and an associate, probably requiring the help of someone in authority to resolve the differences between you. You need a new challenge. Offering to do a job others seem to be avoiding could be a chance to test yourself. If you get drawn into an unpleasant public scene, guard against overreacting. A dream you share with your loved one has a chance of coming true if you work on it together. Also consider joining a local organization that holds an interest for both of you.

24. WEDNESDAY. Challenging. You are apt to be unusually determined to get your own way. Consider switching strategies in order to win other people to your way of thinking. Your driving ambition coupled with a chance to fill in for a higher-up may ensure the promotion and recognition you deserve. Good news is foreseen for Capricorns who have applied for a scholarship or loan. Consider increasing your insurance to cover new family acquisitions. Single Capricorns may learn of a romantic rival. A declaration of your passion combined with an extravagant gift should win the day for you. Capricorn business people can benefit from accepting an associate's invitation to dinner, even if it is made at the last minute.

25. THURSDAY. Profitable. Any and all types of selling are favored today. If you recently volunteered your services to a good cause, you may be asked to distribute leaflets or collect signatures for a petition. You are likely to learn of some gossip from a work colleague or neighbor, but do not pass on anything negative and potentially hurtful. This is a good time to catch up on writing letters to relatives. Guard against the possibility of having your pocket picked. If you are planning a short trip, check the route by consulting an up-to-date map; a new road could save you many miles. Information you have been waiting for is apt to arrive in today's mail. Plan a quiet evening at home with a blockbuster movie or novel that lets you escape into fantasyland.

26. FRIDAY. Sensitive. A special person in your life may not be revealing everything you need to know. Despite this, turn a deaf ear to rumors that are circulating. Before long you will find out what is going on and will probably be relieved to realize that your fears were unfounded. Getting the whole truth from someone in a position of power or influence is unlikely. They are apt to give you the party line without providing any concrete information. You have to do your own digging to get at the truth, especially if negotiations are underway for a merger or takeover. Control how you react publicly, even though inwardly you may be anxious and nervous. Let off steam this evening by getting some physical exercise.

27. SATURDAY. Stressful. You can all too easily get carried away with a plan and miss out on what is going on at the same time. Try to be flexible and open to change. This is not a day when you can expect to make money, although there is a lot you would like to buy. Temper your urge to shop according to the money currently in your wallet. Conditions do not favor buying anything on credit. High interest charges can make even a sale item very expensive in the long run. Do not rely solely on your memory for key dates and times. If a new acquaintance seems vaguely familiar, you may be surprised to discover that you have a shared memory from childhood or your early school days.

28. SUNDAY. Exciting. Your good spirits and overriding optimism make this an ideal time to deal directly with the public. People will believe what you say and go along with what you suggest. Pick and choose among the many options available. There is little doubt about your sincerity. A serious matter should be brought out into the open and discussed in a public forum. Seek input from people representing every walk of life. If you surround yourself only with those who think and believe like you, new opportunities or ideas may pass you by. You can expect to be welcomed by an exclusive group and also by those who feel oppressed and deserted. If put to a vote, you are likely to be the one who comes out on top.

29. MONDAY. Manageable. Find a different approach to handle necessary chores. You may want to offer yourself a reward for completing all you have to do within a certain time. Accept whatever help is available in order to achieve your objectives. Even small children can do simple tasks. Encourage all family members to be an active part of the household team, doing whatever needs to be done. This can be a more flexible and fair approach than division of labor along gender lines. A newspaper article or book may stimulate you to find out more about a particular craft or skill. Your Capricorn creativity needs an outlet where you can give yourself free rein and also gain recognition.

30. TUESDAY. Cautious. Before the day is out you may encounter some petty-minded people. However, you are in far too generous a frame of mind to get drawn into inconsequential wranglings. This is an excellent time to plan ahead for a summer vacation. Making definite reservations now gives you something to look forward to for the next few months. Long-term projects are beginning to take on a different shape, which is all to the good. Use your excellent Capricorn intuition to the full to get the most out of the possibilities that crop up. If you are eager to broaden your horizons, encounters with people from an ethnic background different from yours can open your eyes to their way of thinking. Guard against jumping to conclusions based on your preconceptions.

31. WEDNESDAY. Challenging. Times are changing fast, forcing you to respond quickly to altering circumstances. Capricorns are a cardinal sign, which makes you excel taking the initiative at critical junctures. This is a day where you can show off that particular talent to the fullest. You are likely to receive a pat on the back from superiors; they are apt to be watching your moves with keen interest. At home, consider making some changes to add comfort to your life. This is a good time to start a home improvement project or to put your property up for sale. Before making a significant purchase for your home, do some price comparisons. An advertised deal may not actually be a bargain.

APRIL

1. THURSDAY. Lucky. As a Capricorn you strive for the top even if you have to begin at the bottom and work hard to succeed. A surprise development at work or a strange twist of fate is likely to help you move up a rung or two on the career ladder. It is also possible that you soon will be calling the shots at your place of work. You can create your own conditions to succeed and are unlikely to be held back by other people's lack of enthusiasm for your plans. Home life should be happy. The beneficial conditions of the past few days continue to inspire you. If you are planning a family get-together or celebration, you can expect the festivities to be a huge success.

2. FRIDAY. Confusing. Because difficult and confusing conditions prevail today, you can be forgiven for thinking that these situations are designed to test you. Friends, in particular, can be a source of frustration. There is a possibility that your feelings will be hurt by one of them, leaving you wondering. Your tendency toward muddled thinking will do little to alleviate matters. Under such circumstances, it is probably best to beat a retreat. You can always plead a headache or exhaustion, which is probably not far from the truth. At all costs, avoid making snap decisions or judgments. Give yourself extra time to consider various alternatives.

3. SATURDAY. Unsettling. Bottled-up tension may dog your steps. If you personally are not operating on a short fuse, those around you may be. The slightest provocation could be all that it takes to provoke a heated exchange. This is likely to wear heavily on your nerves; as a Capricorn you prefer a calm, controlled lifestyle. Your tendency is to keep others at bay emotionally, even at the risk of seeming aloof or cold. An unexpected event is likely to make you rethink a certain plan or intention. However, if you have already made up your mind, do not allow other people to talk you out of it. Burn off excess energy by getting some strenuous outdoor exercise this evening.

4. SUNDAY. Variable. Children are likely to be a problem. For Capricorn parents, there is a chance children are trying to play you off against your partner. They may be asking for money to buy an item you do not approve of for their age. A sense of perspective is required. A friend who has a child of the same age could be the best one to offer some practical advice. This is a good day for going out with your friends. Spend the afternoon in good conversation. An old acquaintance may phone or drop by with an interesting social or business proposition. However, you would be wise not to commit yourself unless you are sure you can devote the necessary time and energy. Keep in mind your prior commitments even if they are less exciting.

5. MONDAY. Sensitive. You may suffer from a bout of Monday morning blues, making life seem nothing but a chore. However, it is important to stay alert. Other people are relying on your sound judgment in both practical and financial matters. You should feel more at ease as the emotional turmoil of the past few days diminishes. Focus on the backlog of work left over from last week. Keep the lid on your ambitions for the moment; this is not a good time for pressing ahead too aggressively. The best course of action is to spoil yourself a little and relax whenever you get the opportunity.

6. TUESDAY. Mixed. News of someone who has been quietly working behind the scenes on your behalf is likely to be a real morale booster. An unexpected or forgotten bill may need to be paid immediately, leaving you a little strapped for cash. There is a chance of overdrawing your checking account if you do not keep your purchases to necessities only. This is a good day for puttering around and taking it easy. You are likely to enjoy your own company the most. You may have to go to the inconvenience of picking up a package at the post office, or you may receive one that got damaged in the mail. A family member may spring a happy surprise on you, but a child's behavior can lead you to believe they are not as innocent as they seem.

7. WEDNESDAY. Successful. You should be in a much more positive frame of mind today than earlier in the week. This can be a tremendous incentive to get motivated and could be a large part of the reason why you are so much in demand right now. Do not allow yourself to be thwarted regarding an issue you feel really strongly about. This is a good day for arranging a finance deal or a long-term loan. Business matters in general require extra attention. Your concentration is so good that you can expect to zip through any formalities. However, be sure you do not overlook minor but important points of detail in your determination to get ahead as quickly as possible.

8. THURSDAY. Good. Your powers of attraction are evident to everyone around you at the moment. Take care, however, that you do not land in hot water. A susceptibility to flattery and praise can make you overconfident, but consider the possibility that someone is only trying to sway you. Guard against a tendency to be a little impatient with other people, especially friends and acquaintances. What you intend as a humorous remark can sound like a putdown. Maintain your famous Capricorn authoritative air and others are likely to be impressed. Your self-confidence is high, and your own efforts can do much to help you succeed. This winning combination allows you to easily remove or overcome any obstacles in your path.

9. FRIDAY. Useful. Favorable results are now likely from efforts made in the past, particularly in terms of professional or personal plans. Significant news may come to your attention regarding the steps you should now take. Keep alert, however, or you could miss a golden opportunity. Expect the unexpected in romantic matters. A stimulating encounter is likely, especially in a crowded place of entertainment. You are apt to be at your best in a large gathering rather than a small one. If your attitude is the more the merrier, consider hosting a party tonight. In your private life there is still a serious matter to be dealt with, although you can put it off for a day or two.

10. SATURDAY. Demanding. A conflict with a family member over conduct is likely. Make certain that any discussion of this occurs in private. Consider withdrawing money from a reserve fund in order to help out a friend in need. They are sure to appreciate your gesture and are unlikely to be offended if you ask for a small amount of interest. News of a friend's love life could take you by surprise. It may be time to face the fact that a relationship of your own is unlikely to stand the test of time. An angry encounter with a friend is possible, especially if you have become overly dependent. This could be an ideal opportunity to break loose, or to put the friendship on a new basis.

11. SUNDAY. Changeable. Concentrate on low-key, low-energy activity. You are likely to be most effective with tasks that do not require much physical exertion. Browsing a computer bulletin board can prove useful. New ideas need to be considered and thought through carefully. There is a risk of blowing your budget because of an impulse buy. Do not purchase any expensive item today; think about it for a few days. If it is still available then, you can be sure it is meant for you. A family member may be economical with the truth, forcing you to issue a veiled threat in order to get at the truth. Check out directions you have been given to get to a particular meeting place; chances are they are wrong or too vague.

12. MONDAY. Rewarding. You are apt to be preoccupied with cash and all matters involving the security and comfort of yourself and your family. Someone you have been counting on has had long enough to honor commitments. This is an ideal time for making a final demand of your own. Look for ways of limiting incidental expenditure; consider revamping your budget for the little luxuries of life and sticking to it. Becoming a more discerning shopper can also be an effective way of cutting down on expenses. In your professional dealings, a combination of Capricorn charm with tried-and-tested methods is favored. Beware of committing a minor misdemeanor that could force you to pay a fine and possibly increase your insurance costs.

13. TUESDAY. Disquieting. Cooperative team effort is favored. A brainstorming session could produce some genuine inspiration, although some ideas may be very eccentric. Either you or a close associate could be the right person to sort out a problem and resolve it immediately. Friends and acquaintances are likely to seek you out. You may be invited to a social event connected with work. Chances are that the invitation is actually a command performance. Turn it down at your own peril. Expect some practical jokes, with one or two at your expense. Play it cool in negotiations. As a Capricorn you excel at keeping your options open and timing your moves to perfection.

14. WEDNESDAY. Buoyant. You are likely to find yourself in the right place at the right time, especially if you are involved in acquiring new business. Friendly introductions and conversations can do far more for your prospects than squirming through normal channels, although you should not ignore officials. Someone in an important position of power is apt to be happy to simply wave you on without too much fuss. Let your own light shine; there is no need to hide behind someone else's glory in the hope that it will rub off on you. Do not hesitate to ask for someone's credentials if they are unknown to you. This evening, spend some time pondering your future moves and how to achieve a dream.

15. THURSDAY. Good. A growing sense of purpose and self-direction can help you make the right decisions rather than hesitating at the crucial moment. Other people recognize that you have a clear idea about what you want. Loved ones are willing to go along with your plans, especially when they realize that you mean business. However, do not force others to agree with you; even pleading or cajoling is not favored. Instead, let them come around to your thinking in their own way and their own time. Although as a Capricorn you like to plan everything in advance, there are definite advantages in being more adventurous. Anything intended to improve your health and stamina is well worth the investment.

16. FRIDAY. Tricky. New developments that must be dealt with immediately could force you to burn the midnight oil. It is important to attend to essentials only; postpone anything that can keep until next week. In this way you can ease your workload and your conscience. Keep quiet about the more sensitive areas of your personal life. If someone close to you is determined to delve into your private affairs, tact and diplomacy are important despite their intrusion. Try to find ways to lighten the situation. New projects require careful handling. Family members are likely to promise more than they can deliver, so do not take them too seriously.

17. SATURDAY. Difficult. One or two minor upsets in your romantic life are apt to be intensified by today's conditions. Go with the flow, no matter how surprising or disconcerting the twists and turns may be. Enjoy the social possibilities that come your way. Consider accepting a last-minute invitation, even if it means canceling or postponing a previous engagement. The new people you meet can have a significant impact on your life in the future. If you have something important to reveal, it is best to speak out at once. However, guard against extremes. Other people are likely to give you a wide berth if your opinions appear too outlandish. They key today is to remain flexible.

18. SUNDAY. Pleasant. The emphasis is on getting things done around the house, although not everyone is in the same frame of mind as you. Dredge up some extra patience in order to cope with their reluctance. Concern for relatives who are having difficulties should be sorted out soon, in part because of your valuable practical assistance. Romance is in the air for single Capricorns. You are likely to attract congenial company even though you are in an unusually boisterous mood. This is definitely a day for letting go and having fun. Avoid any situation that you feel is restrictive or limiting. Freedom to do what you want is very important.

19. MONDAY. Fair. Take advantage of today's opportunity to catch up on chores. Pay outstanding bills; attend to minor repairs around the home. Tried-and-tested methods should work best for you. Making something with your own hands should be very satisfying. Health matters are highlighted. As a Capricorn you are conservative by nature, but a new kind of diet is likely to be intriguing. If you want reassurance about it, discuss it with your doctor. Take extra care in preparing any locally produced food. Look into a relaxation technique such as yoga or meditation that can keep you on an even keel.

20. TUESDAY. Stressful. Unresolved dilemmas in a personal relationship are likely to come to a head. Guard against starting an argument over breakfast; it could leave you in a grouchy mood for the rest of the day and could also make you late for work. Promise yourself some time in your busy schedule to deal with the problem as soon as possible. Brushing it under the carpet is likely to make matters worse in the long run. Tensions at work may erupt, too. Try to use these to your advantage to galvanize co-workers into decisive action. If some of your ideas or incentives have been blocked or delayed recently, this is a good time to become more aggressive but without alienating higher-ups by pushing too hard.

21. WEDNESDAY. Variable. You may wake up feeling tired and listless. Do all that you can to force yourself out of this mood. Avoid putting a damper on the generally buoyant atmosphere at work. Set your sights low so that you can gain from the small benefits of the day. Interruptions are indicated. Stick to simple tasks so that you can cope with the unexpected. Socializing may not be your cup of tea; turn down any invitation you receive. If you are viewing the world as a slightly threatening place, rely on your nearest and dearest to give you the reassurance and confidence you need.

22. THURSDAY. Frustrating. The day's events should move at a slow pace. If you are eager to get ahead, you are likely to encounter occasional setbacks and frustration. Conditions are not right for trying to produce change through sheer force of your will. The harder you try, the more frustrated you are apt to become. This is a much better time for consolidating your position and for bringing to a close matters which have been unrewarding or dissatisfying. Although as a Capricorn you are often quite reluctant to get involved in other people's business, you may nevertheless get drawn in. Neighbors, in particular, are likely to ask for your support or help with solving a problem.

23. FRIDAY. Exciting. You are able to get along well with other people and to find a common thread in your associations with them. This includes people you may not have seen eye-to-eye with in the past. Today marks the start of a phase that allows friendship to develop in directions you did not think were possible. This is an excellent time for healing old rifts and building bridges of understanding. A sense of excitement about the future could make you a little impatient with those who are not so eager to forge ahead, but try not to let your irritation show. It is likely your friends are a little amused by your uncharacteristic behavior. Work and play go hand in hand today. You can have a good time while getting a lot done.

24. SATURDAY. Disconcerting. You may be your own worst enemy. Other people are likely to see the progress you are making in a more positive light. There is no need to keep trying so hard. All it takes is self-confidence and the satisfaction of knowing that you can effectively resolve just about any situation that arises. You have to keep on your toes. Planning a minute-by-minute schedule for the day is pointless. Flexibility and quick thinking are needed to respond to fast-changing situations. Follow your good Capricorn instincts and you will not go far wrong. Group discussions and meetings are favored; the attention is apt to be focused on you. Loved ones, in particular, will be depending on you to get results.

25. SUNDAY. Fair. Although you may wish to spoil someone close to you with an expensive gift, be sure that your generosity does not lead to embarrassment. If you are looking for ways to make money, do not blindly believe the promises of a slick advertisement; indications are that it is a scam. Single Capricorns should not try to buy into someone's heart. An apparent injustice is bound to make you indignant, but control a tendency to overdramatize; emotionally charged reactions are unlikely to accomplish much. Guard against a tendency to treat other people with suspicion. Fears that someone is spreading rumors about you are probably unfounded. Highly spiced food could make it hard for you to get to sleep tonight.

26. MONDAY. Confusing. Avoid boasting about your achievements or exaggerating them. Keep in mind that good results speak for themselves. Work may be coming in faster than you can cope with it, but resist the urge to work late into the night in an effort to catch up. What you do in a rush when you are exhausted is likely to be of poor quality. Any attempt on your part to coerce others into your way of thinking is apt to provoke a strong reaction. Obsessing over a problem that refuses to be solved can result in nervous exhaustion. Safeguard any important documents connected with foreigners; otherwise there is a risk that one of them will turn up missing. You may receive duplicate bills; be wary of paying twice.

27. TUESDAY. Mixed. Your plans are likely to be disrupted when your mate or partner makes unexpected demands. Take advantage of any chance to break away from domestic routine. Something you have recently said or done is likely to come back to haunt you because it was twisted in the retelling. However, there is probably no need for regret once you set the record straight. Important changes in your social life are taking place. Although the transition could be difficult, important friendships are likely to endure. Wind up the day in the company of good friends. Inviting your loved to go along should ensure a successful evening, but do not stay out too late.

28. WEDNESDAY. Variable. If someone comes up with an interesting proposition, look at it carefully but without going overboard in any way. Whatever you decide, it would be a good idea to consult with your mate or partner beforehand. Mix-ups are almost certain unless you keep focused when dealing with professional matters. Although you might be in a partying mood, this is no time to relax while others do the work. A minor accident is possible if you let your concentration wander. Advance preparation is vital when it comes to trying to get others to go along with your ideas. Friends appear to be ideally placed to do you a good turn, but you have to ask for the favor.

29. THURSDAY. Demanding. Tread carefully. Your hasty remarks or actions could lead to misunderstandings, even upsets later on. Speak your mind, but choose diplomatic words. There may be a chance to seize a previously missed opportunity, especially one involving local politics or other community activity. Even an apparently insignificant encounter can lead to new possibilities. Remain as open-minded as possible to other people's points of view. You may witness a disturbance in a public place, but do not take the law into your own hands no matter how incensed you feel about what is happening. There is a possibility of an awkward moment with a friend which requires extra tact to remedy.

30. FRIDAY. Changeable. New acquaintances and attachments have a good chance of blossoming under the current stellar influences. Do not refuse friendship when it is offered. Help is available close to home. Support from loved ones in dealing with an ongoing problem should be welcomed. It will not be long before the world at large sees that your ideas have merit. In the meantime, keep faith with yourself. If there is a deadline to meet, spend a couple of extra hours clearing up the job before the weekend begins. Abide by the motto of not putting off until tomorrow what can be done today. The way is open for practical advancement of all your plans and dreams.

MAY

1. SATURDAY. Confusing. Try to read body language while listening to what your friends and family members have to say for themselves. Do not try to keep them quiet; their habit of speaking out can be a distinct advantage to you. Friendship is the key to better times, although you may not realize it just yet. Someone who knows you well can offer the best perspective on what is going on in your life. However, you are unlikely to take too kindly to interference from any source. In addition, family ties are becoming even more important. Far from being restrictive, you may find that their support offers you incentives you had not even considered previously. Surprising news can lead to a lucrative new agreement.

2. SUNDAY. Easygoing. Allow yourself as much freedom of expression as possible. On this easygoing day you have the time to do exactly as you please. Even so, try to spare some time for your nearest and dearest at some point in the day. If certain difficulties seem so overwhelming that you feel you cannot deal with them, put them out of your mind for a while. Later, a solution to your difficulties is likely to become obvious. You can move mountains if you allow yourself to consider all possibilities from all angles. Outstanding chores should be cleared up; attend to anything routine so that it does not nag at your Capricorn conscience. Get to bed early tonight.

3. MONDAY. Demanding. Really demanding people who are around just now are the sort of individuals you should avoid if possible. There is plenty going on in your own life without getting bogged down in a situation that is not of your own making or in your best interests. You may be suffering from a bout of restlessness, which is probably an indication of some worrisome issues you can neither ignore nor resolve right now. Any desire for overnight success has to be curbed. Consider new opportunities carefully and thoughtfully before taking action. Carry on in your own way. There is not enough time to take on extra commitments; you may even have to turn down a special invitation.

4. TUESDAY. Variable. A carefree, easygoing approach to life should work best for the moment, even in the face of some rather worrisome news. Take heart, however; even this can be turned to your advantage in time. New answers to old problems may come to you as a result of startling intuition. People from the past are apt to make their presence felt. Avoid becoming emotionally influenced by what is done and gone. Postpone testing out new ideas until this afternoon, when conditions begin to favor new beginnings. The morning favors finalizing details of your plans. Do not be swayed by the negative attitude of people who should know better than to dampen your spirits but may try anyway.

5. WEDNESDAY. Useful. This promises to be an easier day for you. Tasks which you feared would never get done can now be dispatched quickly. If you have some spare time on your hands, put your desk and files in order and catch up on telephone calls. Administrative odds and ends may also need your attention. This can be a good day for shopping; consider inviting a friend along for the ride. You may be asked to sign a petition for a community cause. This is a good time to arrange to see a celebrity at a charity gala or a premiere. For Capricorn singles, this can be the perfect time for a new romance with someone from work or school.

6. THURSDAY. Successful. If you rely on your creative skills in your work, inspiration can come to you just when you need it most. Although you may come up with one or two brilliant ideas, not all of them are likely to be workable; some will be too costly to implement or too complicated. Working with children can be especially rewarding. An innocent remark they make or their simplified outlook can put a worry of yours into true perspective. This is not a good day for speculative ventures of any kind. Even if you back what looks like a safe bet, you are likely to finish up the loser in the long run. A night out should be great fun, although it could cost a lot more than you anticipate.

7. FRIDAY. Disappointing. If you were hoping for an easy time today, you are likely to be disappointed. Upsets could be due to having to sort out a difficulty that has made your boss or another higher-up see red. You may even have to fire someone over a disciplinary matter or put up a strong defense on your own behalf. Check that the company has gone through all the required warnings. If you are dissatisfied with your own work, the temptation may be to simply walk out in anger. However, it is in your own best interests to get a new job lined up for yourself if you genuinely cannot improve your current situation. A neighbor may make unreasonable complaints; losing your cool only gives them more ammunition.

8. SATURDAY. Rewarding. Be sure to read the small print if you are planning to enter into any contractual agreement or if you go out bargain hunting. Someone may try to pull the wool over your eyes. The best policy is to defer your decision until you have thought about it for a day or two, especially if it involves a home improvement project or other domestic concerns. Offer advice only when asked; otherwise there is a chance you will be resented or rebuffed. A small-minded person may try to provoke you into an argument over trivialities. Allow plenty of time if you are traveling, even if it is just a short journey. If an unwelcome visitor turns up uninvited, you do not have to be hospitable.

9. SUNDAY. Enjoyable. A family outing should be very successful. Be sure to take along enough cash to cover incidents. If you are planning to stay at home, a traditional Sunday roast can be a lovely treat. There is a chance of bickering among family members probably because of general boredom. They may look to you for entertainment suggestions. A younger person's enthusiasm may have to be curbed. Time spent gardening or walking in the park can do much to relieve the past week's tensions. Working Capricorns may have to devote part of the evening to preparing for important meetings scheduled for the coming workweek. You should reap the benefits of putting in the time now.

10. MONDAY. Cautious. Check any invoice carefully before paying it or sending it out. There could be an error that leads to future embarrassment. If you are currently unemployed, make sure that you are receiving all the benefits due you, including retraining. There is a possibility that you are entitled to more than you realize or can take advantage of a new program. A windfall may be coming your way. Buying something beautiful for yourself can give you a much needed lift. Looking through fashion or home magazines is likely to give you some inspired ideas. If someone shares a secret with you, keep in mind that secrets are meant to be kept;

staying mum about this one can avoid an awkward situation later on. Be especially alert if driving during rush hour.

11. TUESDAY. Disquieting. There is an unusually heavy workload to get through today, but do not be tempted to delegate it to someone who does not have the necessary experience. They are likely to make mistakes and cause you more work in the long term. If possible, set aside some time to volunteer for a task that no one else seems to want to handle. However, do not appear too eager; this might arouse suspicion. A former colleague who has your best interests at heart may have the news you have been waiting for. Home life could turn into a battleground unless you ignore a pointed remark or criticism. Avoid overindulging in caffeine or alcohol; you may be particularly sensitive to its effects.

12. WEDNESDAY. Fair. The emphasis is on emotions and family ties. Because you are apt to feel somewhat insecure, you may overcompensate by being aloof and evasive. Focus on your loved ones and try to ignore their flaws, faults, and quirks. Keep in mind that no one is perfect. What took place in your personal life a while ago may have hurt your pride, but now you have the perfect chance to bring a long-standing grudge out into the open. Instead of feeling negative and somewhat sorry for yourself, show just how adaptable and self-protective you can be. In this way you are likely to learn something of lasting value from an emotional conflict or misunderstanding.

13. THURSDAY. Cautious. You may not exactly agree with the way a close relative is leading their life. Although for some time you may have wanted to express your feelings to them, restraint is called for. If you feel you must speak out make sure you deliver any criticism with a good dose of tact and charm. In this way they are more likely to seriously consider what you have to say. If you are dealing with a child's problem, you may have no choice but to dole out some advice and guidance and perhaps a threat of punishment as well. Take care with older children that you do not interfere but just set ground rules. If you are entertaining at home, you will probably play the part of host or hostess to perfection.

14. FRIDAY. Deceptive. While you may be expected to take on more responsibility, you are likely to be well rewarded for your efforts. However, avoid any kind of financial risk. Take extra care of your personal possessions while you are out. There is a chance of losing your wallet or credit card or of falling prey to a pickpocket. You are just the right person to talk calmly to a family member about a cash problem. Do not hesitate to ask for what you want, even if this means not telling the whole truth. It is not always necessary to lay all your cards on the table. Guard against self-indulgence when it comes to food and drink; eat light and right throughout the day.

15. SATURDAY. Sensitive. Children are apt to be boisterous and difficult to control. Take the opportunity to let go of adult concerns by entering into the spirit of their fun rather than getting wound up over their behavior. Consider getting some outdoor exercise with your mate or with a friend. Single Capricorns should not wait to be asked out tonight. A new romance is about to begin, but you may have to take the initiative. Deal with a forgotten financial matter even if you are not in the mood for it. Do what is necessary and the rest can wait. Avoid making a bad joke at someone else's expense; they could be genuinely annoyed as a result. Splurge on tonight's entertainment; you deserve a treat.

16. SUNDAY. Satisfactory. Because you prefer the company of serious-minded people today, invite some co-workers or close friends to your home. Spend some time reflecting on how to balance your own emotional needs with your duty to others. As a Capricorn you tend to have a well-developed sense of responsibility, but keep in mind that you have a duty to yourself as well. A bad habit could be the cause of a recurrent but minor health problem. You have the willpower to abstain once you make a decision to do so. Any project finished off at home is likely to be a job well done. Put more of yourself into creative work rather than following a pattern precisely.

17. MONDAY. Manageable. Although you have terrific energy and motivation, do not take this to extremes. Otherwise you could find it difficult to get off the merry-go-round and pay attention to important detail. For Capricorns in business, this should be a very profitable time. You are likely to benefit from change or a new beginning in the near future. This is the ideal time to prepare your plans. You may have been generous to a fault recently, but other people may not appreciate what you have done for them or even resent it. Adopt a more businesslike attitude to those who would take advantage of your good nature. Handle any outstanding business involving long-term financial security for you and your loved ones.

18. TUESDAY. Challenging. Developments today coincide with a great deal of activity in your established partnerships, both personal and business. It is slowly becoming clear that changes are unavoidable. It is a question of removing emotional baggage and deadwood from your life so that you are ready to make a fresh start. Your mate, partner, or an older family member is in a strong position to give sound, constructive guidance. You may find it difficult to communicate with certain people who seem to be lost in a fantasy world of their own. Financial success is likely if you make a determined effort to put your talents on display for all to see.

19. WEDNESDAY. Disquieting. This is a good time to be more positive, to force others to be open and direct, and to let colleagues see that you are not about to give in on certain key issues. The planetary arrangement gives you a greater amount of freedom of choice, which can be a little overwhelming at times. However, it is becoming increasingly obvious that you cannot continue to be swayed by the whims and fancies of other people. Squabbles are likely to erupt between you and a close family member. Guard against making a mountain out of a molehill. At home is one place where you can afford to back down without losing face. Events are about to take a surprising turn, with unusual people entering your sphere.

20. THURSDAY. Demanding. A desire to salvage a floundering relationship may be strong. With the right attitude and a show of true affection, there is every chance that you can make amends. However, do so only if you can admit to yourself that you believe the relationship is worth working at and saving. If you are in an adventurous mood, consider hopping on a bus or a train just to see where it takes you. New friends and acquaintances are sure to be stimulating company. A strange coincidence that binds you together in a significant way could stir up strong memories and feelings from the past, but do not look for a replay of a memorable evening.

21. FRIDAY. Changeable. Because you have been overdoing things lately, you are apt to tire easily today. Pace yourself. Try to arrange a quiet day followed by a relaxing evening at home tonight. Do not be afraid to act on impulse or spontaneously; this is the way to get the most fun out of the day. Conditions favor buying or selling and also seeking out new opportunity. Do not let the appearance of a prospective employee fool you. If you overhear a secret, it might give you the edge you are looking for to outfox your competition. A tax rebate could be in the mail. Capricorns who are not currently romantically involved could be attracted to a workmate, but guard against becoming involved in a romantic triangle.

22. SATURDAY. Fortunate. This is an ideal time to make an important decision; you should have no trouble seeing the forest for the trees. Only make your move if you have had plenty of time to mull it over. Guard against undoing weeks of good work because of a course of action you decide to take in haste. Your powers of concentration are excellent. Focus on getting ahead in your work and handling home paperwork, especially bills and contracts. Any thorny problem can be constructively resolved at this time. Do not splurge on an expensive gift simply to impress a love interest. They are undoubtedly more interested in your personality than your wallet. Make some time to be with an older family member.

23. SUNDAY. Pleasant. This is an ideal time to get away from it all with that special person in your life. Capricorn parents may be able to get parents or in-laws to look after youngsters for a while. You could also spend some happy hours browsing through vacation advertisements or brochures. Consider a trip to a place of cultural interest such as a museum or art gallery. Anything of historical significance is likely to appeal to you. If the weather is good, a picnic can be fun with a group of congenial friends. Or seek out an exclusive restaurant for an intimate dinner for two. Later on, relax with a long soak in a bubble bath or hot tub.

24. MONDAY. Good. The start of the workweek is a good time to turn your thoughts to career matters and promotion prospects. Attend to routine important tasks. Influential people are likely to be impressed by how organized you can be. Keep the communication lines open with former as well as current co-workers and employees. An informal tour of the workplace can elicit the honest opinion of staff members. You are likely to get some interesting and constructive feedback from them. Take a guarded approach when it comes to personal finances; there is a possibility that you are looking at this aspect of your life through rose-colored glasses. The advice of an accountant or financial planner could be invaluable.

25. TUESDAY. Excellent. You are going from strength to strength in almost every area of your life. Spectacular configurations are favoring your sign. You are reaching a pinnacle that gives you many opportunities and many new choices. Once you get there, do not rest on your laurels. You need to consolidate your position if you are to remain at the top. Do not hesitate to go after your heart's desire. If you are looking for employment, a promotion, or a career change, do all that you can to take advantage of the main chance. Romance, too, can benefit from a more aggressive attitude on your part.

26. WEDNESDAY. Unsettling. After the giddy heights during the past few days, coming back to reality may feel more like a sharp bump. Try not to become worried or overly cautious. This is not a turn for the worse, only a return to normal. With all the effort you have been putting into obtaining your aspirations, there is a chance you have been neglecting loved ones. They are likely to voice some displeasure, but do not allow them to take the wind out of your sails. This coming weekend might be a good time to devote exclusively to them as a way of making up. An older member of the family is likely to cross swords with you; be ready to do things their way.

27. THURSDAY. Frustrating. As a Capricorn you can doggedly face adversity and frustration and can keep going long after others have given up. Today you need more than your fair share of determination and grit in order to cope with current conditions. The good news is that these adverse influences are going to be short-lived. By the end of the day you should be able to breathe a sigh of relief as you realize that the worst is probably over. How you handle bad news or any unexpected downturn in your fortunes depends on whether you think it is better to quit while you are ahead or dig in until conditions improve. Either way, you are likely to gain from the experience.

28. FRIDAY. Demanding. An acquaintance may be eager for an opportunity to talk over a personal problem with you. Consider volunteering your time rather than your money to a charity organization whose objectives you believe in strongly. An old friend may look you up. Do not hesitate to suddenly change your plans in order to get together. Check that your car has sufficient gas as well as tire pressure before starting any journey. There is a risk of overheating in a traffic jam or of having a flat. Your circle of friends may change as a new interest begins to take up more of your time. You could benefit from a brainstorming session. Computer technology can help you refine your ideas, especially a creative project.

29. SATURDAY. Profitable. For Capricorns who work on weekends, this is another day when those in authority are likely to be aware of all that you are doing. You should be able to make mileage out of this, especially if your work involves public relations or selling. Pooling your resources with a friend or relative could prove mutually beneficial. Word from an older family member may be revealing; something they tell you could bring a skeleton or two out of the closet. Your desire to uncover hidden or forgotten aspects could lead to a growing interest in archeology or genealogy. You may unearth something that has more than mere historical value. News of a legacy or inheritance is possible, probably from a distant relative you hardly knew.

30. SUNDAY. Changeable. Working in the garden can be rewarding, especially clearing weeds and preparing the ground for new plants. However, too much physical work can prove exhausting. You may not have as much stamina as you think. By all means get some exercise, but take it slowly. Regular workouts are much better for you than sporadic bursts of activity. Knowing where you stand with regard to a partnership or teamwork venture can be particularly difficult. Someone may be withholding pertinent information. Do not let a stranger into your life, whether at home or at work, unless you know their background. This is a time when you can be too trusting.

31. MONDAY. Challenging. You cannot afford to sit on the fence any longer. Business partners, in particular, may press you to state your intentions. If you are confused and uncertain, it is probably better to say so. Trying to respond under adverse circumstances is only likely to confuse others. Allow for the possibility that someone is deliberately throwing up a smoke screen in their desire to gain an advantage over you. They could have an ax to grind, even though they seem detached and objective. Take advantage of friendly introductions; they are likely to do far more for your prospects than your established contacts. Offer to do your part in a club or other group, perhaps bringing refreshments or staying to clean up after a meeting.

JUNE

1. TUESDAY. Calm. Conditions favor doing some deep thinking about what you really want out of life. Spend some time reviewing your personal goals and plans for the future. At the same time, you would be wise not to put selfish desire above the needs of those you love. If you are in the mood to change your appearance, consider a new hairstyle or a type of outfit you have never considered wearing before. Ideally, try to arrange to stay at home today. Simply puttering around the house can be a wonderful tonic, and the solitude can be a good stimulus for your imagination. Ideas that bubble up at this time could eventually enhance your reputation and build up your bank account.

2. WEDNESDAY. Manageable. Consider taking some lessons to develop a sport skill or a creative interest. When it comes to speculation or taking a gamble, seek the opinion of an older person you respect and trust; their experience is likely to prove invaluable in steering you in the right direction. Leave any form of experimenting with new solutions to old problems until another day. The tried-and-tested methods are most likely to work best for you at this time. Accept an invitation to lunch or dinner. Be sure to look your best; new people are coming into your sphere. You may find yourself in demand when it comes to parties and barbecues. This is a favorable time to start a daily journal, but do not write anything too personal.

3. THURSDAY. Exacting. Tensions in your working life could cause you to erupt in anger. Be wary of using minor annoyances as a reason to argue in order to avoid more serious matters that you find difficult to face. And do not imagine that the world is out to get you; there is a real danger of taking everything too personally. Try to keep a sense of perspective in all of your dealings, especially with your workmates. This long-term view coupled with your famous sense of irony can help you deflate overblown egos and awkward situations. Resist the temptation to criticize what other people are trying to do. The advice and support of a friend is likely to be right on target, although you may resist it for a while.

4. FRIDAY. Cautious. Risky ventures may deplete your bank balance if you do not cut your losses soon. If you have recently been overindulgent with hobbies or leisure activities, pull in the reins. Use supplies on hand. Tackling a backlog of bills or other outstanding chores with discipline can improve the situation rapidly. You are in the right frame of mind for all forms of mental hard work, viewing problems as challenges rather than obstacles. However, these two positive attitudes might not be enough to keep you from becoming impatient with your daily routine. Discuss a long-standing difficulty with a colleague or a superior, and a resolution to the deadlock should result.

5. SATURDAY. Satisfactory. This is a good day for concentrating on work designed to yield a profit and increase your income, even if you do not normally work on the weekend. Your possessions and your home are assuming greater importance. Shop for items to make your home more comfortable and secure. Being surrounded by familiar objects which remind you of the past can be very comforting and reassuring. This is a starred day for buying a pet for children. Your overall health should be good. A minor ache or pain is nothing to be concerned about. However, seek medical advice if any health problem has been causing you worry.

6. SUNDAY. Mixed. Children can be especially annoying, but guard against reacting to them without thinking. Even if you are not in contact with children today, patience is the watchword. An encounter with an old flame could force you to look at your past actions and reconsider what you really want out of a current romantic situation. Although this self-examination may not be comfortable, it could prove very useful. You are likely to appreciate the company of serious-minded people who are concerned about the deeper aspects of life. There is a risk, however, of becoming too introspective. A leisurely walk, even if only for a short time, can give you better perspective about your options.

7. MONDAY. Exciting. If you recently moved, this is an excellent day for exploring your neighborhood and for introducing yourself to neighbors and local shopkeepers. An unexpected windfall is possible, most likely a cash prize. A minor domestic crisis could arise because you cannot agree with your loved ones about how money should be spent. Planning a family outing at a theme park might put a smile on everyone's face. A burst of mental energy could enable you to expand your creative ideas. You may even surprise yourself with the ingenious methods you devise for dealing with routine matters in order to give yourself more free time.

8. TUESDAY. Useful. Your mate or partner is in a good position to offer practical help with home improvements. Together you can come up with a plan for increasing the value of your property as well as making it more attractive and comfortable. This is a good day for reviewing your home insurance and home security. You may want to contact an agent, but you are under no obligation to sign until you have thoroughly reviewed all the small print. Guard against a tendency to let your mind wander; you may fall prey to obsessive thinking. Share your dreams with that special person in your life. You are apt to discover that your hopes and wishes are not so far apart, although your priorities may be different. Compromise is the key.

9. WEDNESDAY. Variable. Quarrels may break out at home because loved ones think you are devoting too much time and energy to your work or other outside interests. As a consequence, they could be feeling left out. Juggling your time between career and family obligations is not simple. It is all too easy to get the balance wrong on occasion. You may experience excitable feelings and become easily irritated by frustrating delays. This, too, can be a sign of overwork and excessive stress. Take time out to relax with your loved ones. If you are thinking of redecorating your home, a bold and original fabric or dinnerware pattern is likely to appeal. Use it to set the overall color scheme for every room in your house.

10. THURSDAY. Pleasant. The morning is the best time to enjoy private conversations. Be ready to give and receive kindness, friendship, and support from your loved ones and friends. Single Capricorns should guard against becoming too possessive toward a love interest. Jealousy could give rise to trouble between you; you both need space to breathe. If you are in a sentimental mood, by all means enjoy your memories, but do not dwell on the past obsessively. Alcohol, caffeine, or chocolate may strongly appeal to you, and its effect is likely to be more potent than usual. Curb a tendency to overindulge; stay away from what can be all too tempting.

11. FRIDAY. Difficult. Trying to live up to other people's expectations could be the cause of some of your current worries. Consider the possibility that someone is deliberately trying to manipulate you by making you feel guilty. Put off making any crucial decision concerning joint finances. You may not be thinking clearly, your emotions clouding your better judgment. Play your cards close to your chest when it comes to new investments or to spending money on luxury items. You can easily wreck a chance of getting the best deal for yourself if you are too forthright and blunt. Do not be deceptive, but let the other party ask any pertinent questions they may have without you volunteering the information.

12. SATURDAY. Lucky. This is an especially auspicious day for Capricorns involved with artistic work or creative effort of any kind. You have to knuckle down to some extra work, but it is likely to bring you special benefits in the long run. Conditions favor pooling resources; try to arrange a partnership venture with someone whose skills augment your own. This arrangement is apt to have a very uplifting influence on your work. You might rediscover hidden or forgotten talents. If you resent someone close to you, be honest about how you are feeling. At the same time, however, guard against overreacting or making a mountain out of a molehill. Live and let live is a good motto to follow.

13. SUNDAY. Rewarding. Focus on ways and means of furthering your career prospects, even though this is a day of rest and relaxation. Your mental capacities are accelerated and energized. In addition, your heightened ability for long-term planning ensures that you can keep several steps ahead of your rivals. Although it is unlikely that you will see the fruits of your labor for some time, the eventual reward will be well worth the effort and the wait. Perseverance with a difficult job at home can also pay good dividends. Extra attention to detail guarantees admiring compliments as well as self-satisfaction.

14. MONDAY. Useful. Concentrate on domestic and family matters. Home conditions are congenial and your domestic relations should be harmonious. Working in and around the home, finishing up chores and projects, can give you a great sense of achievement. For Capricorns who must work today, personal magnetism should be working very well in all professional dealings. Although financial negotiations could become intense, you have the ability to persuade other people that you understand and sympathize with their needs. Consequently, your mutual interests and your finances are likely to prosper. This is a good time to improve your economic security by investing in what promises a high rate of return over time.

15. TUESDAY. Manageable. You are unlikely to be in the mood for frivolity. Discussions which are stimulating and have some depth are apt to hold your interest more than gossip. As a Capricorn you have a great sense of obligation. Also keep in mind, however, that you have a duty to yourself as well as to others. Consider raising a delicate matter with your loved one. You may be surprised to discover that you both are not happy with the current situation. There is no need to worry about it; you can come up with a mutual agreement you can both live with. Seeking a trusted second opinion can give you an extra boost of confidence to carry through with a special plan.

16. WEDNESDAY. Disconcerting. A clash with someone close to you could erupt in the early part of the day, but do not let this bad start color your overall mood. If you cannot shake it off, you are likely to be irritable and prone to rash action. It may seem to you that other people are being difficult, or even deliberately trying to hold you back. It is possible that your aggressive stance, intended to push forward your ideas, is only putting people's noses out of joint. Later in the day try not to let a minor worry involving shared finances prey on your mind. Check your bank statement before making any accusation; there is a chance your bank has made an error. Keep long-distance phone calls short and to the point.

17. THURSDAY. Changeable. Conditions continue your tendency to be emotionally excitable and impulsive. You may be in for a pleasant surprise when it comes to the value of a family heirloom, but get it checked by an expert before you start computing your profit. A feeling that you are marching to a different drummer than everyone else is likely to be just a fleeting mood. Resist the temptation to become involved with a risky get-rich-quick scheme; there is a danger that you will incur heavy losses. The only gains you are apt to make today are through the fruits of your own dedicated labor. Indulge in a beautiful item for your home if it is a bargain, but guard against overspending.

18. FRIDAY. Productive. You have to take the bull by the horns when it comes to discussing finances. Your mate, partner, or business associate is likely to keep an open mind if you show that you are aiming to improve matters for both of you. Today you have the drive and enthusiasm to delve into any problem in depth. Your determination to succeed makes you more likely to come up with new solutions. Transactions which have been dragging on can be brought to a close now. Negotiations with a business corporation or bank are also likely to proceed well. As a Capricorn you are able to make it clear to others exactly where you stand, and you can do so without offending anyone.

19. SATURDAY. Stressful. Patience is the key to coping with today's stresses and strains, even if it means biting your tongue to keep your cool. If your job is frustrating and is leading nowhere, consider taking a course to broaden your education or technical skills. Gaining a degree may appeal even if you are hesitant about returning to the classroom. An older person may be able to give you sound practical advice. As a Capricorn you understand the value of discipline, but sometimes it is better to wave a carrot rather than use a stick, especially when it comes to dealing with children. Guard against being too exacting with youngsters; an overly stern attitude could upset them now and in the future.

20. SUNDAY. Satisfactory. Contact with people in distant places may take quite a lot of your time. News from friends in the form of e-mails and telephone calls is likely to flood in. This is an especially good day if your work involves business overseas or with people planning a trip abroad. Take advantage of the weekend to finalize the fine points of your plans. If you are involved in community or religious activities, your sensitivity to the whims and wishes of those around you will be much appreciated, and you can expect the same kind of treatment from them in return. You are in a good position to help those less fortunate than yourself by donating some of your time rather than giving money.

21. MONDAY. Changeable. Pay close attention to your dreams. Not only are they refreshing to the spirit but they can also point you toward a direction you have not considered or even thought about. Give your business dealings a touch of flair and originality.

As a result you could achieve your ambitions and objectives in unusual and unorthodox ways that are very productive. However, stick to the rules when it comes to obtaining authorizations and approvals, especially involving budgets and finances. This is also a favored day for Capricorns earning a living by helping people in need, especially in a hospital or other institution. Conditions favor reorganizing furniture, storage facilities, or your filing system.

22. TUESDAY. Tricky. Keep your ear to the ground in all of your dealings; dramatic developments could lead to unexpected improvements in your career and finances. A bold, innovative idea is likely to evolve from what you learn. Your superiors are apt to be suitably impressed by your work, leaving you on cloud nine. Celebrate your good fortune, but do not get too carried away. Arrange your schedule so that you can spend a little more time with loved ones. Catering to them can be a good way of showing how much you care. Stick to doing one job at a time; your concentration is not at a peak, and there is a risk of constant interruptions.

23. WEDNESDAY. Sensitive. Early in the day there is a risk of acting hastily concerning personal or business finances. Put off making any major decisions in such matters until later in the week. Capricorns who are looking for work should not be too aggressive in going after a new job. Be sure you have the right experience; otherwise a tough interview could include some awkward questions. Old grudges are likely to resurface. In matters that are not of crucial importance, the best policy is to compromise. If you take a stubborn line, it could put a damper on your reputation or even cost you a friendship. This is too high a price to pay to get your own way.

24. THURSDAY. Demanding. Let friends know in advance if you cannot keep a social engagement or just do not want to. Think of a plausible excuse if you do not have a genuine one. In that way you are less likely to be accused of keeping friends at arm's length. Taking a risk or gamble with money you actually cannot spare is not smart, even if you have a strong hunch. It could be a long time before you recoup your loss. If you have been experiencing difficulties in a certain personal relationship, it may be because of a deep-seated insecurity. Give your loved one some time and space, and do the same for yourself before making a permanent decision.

25. FRIDAY. Buoyant. You are likely to encounter mental stimulation and intellectual conversation throughout the day, whether it is playful banter or serious debate. Even arguments or controversy are apt to appeal, rather than bland communication. Conditions favor signing a contract or entering into contractual negotiations. Good news about a financial investment is likely to prove that you were in the right place at the right time. If you are hiring for work or home, do not hesitate to ask for credentials and references. Someone may be trying to use you as a front for their rather dubious activities; put a stop to it. If you feel sentimental about your family or an old friend, get in touch by a letter.

26. SATURDAY. Inactive. Spend as much time as possible away from other people. You should be far more effective if left to your own devices. Otherwise the demands made on you may result in you becoming overtired and a little resentful. Difficulties are possible in matters relating to real estate or home maintenance. If you intend to sell your house, agreeing on a listing price is an important first step before doing any redecorating or sprucing up. Do not worry too much about losing the house you want to buy; earnest negotiations should lead to an agreement. Guard against revealing personal secrets to comparative strangers. Turn to someone you trust absolutely if you want advice.

27. SUNDAY. Pleasant. Someone you admire may pay you a sincere compliment. Although this gives you a boost, take it in the way it is intended. A romantic involvement could benefit from a lighter touch. Otherwise you both may take what should be a happy state of affairs far too seriously. The more you relax, the more you are likely to enjoy what the relationship has to offer. Get involved in other people's affairs only at their invitation or they are likely to resent the intrusion. If you are looking for a new home, shop around for the best mortgage deal. Plan on going out for a relaxed dinner with that special person in your life.

28. MONDAY. Variable. You Capricorns who are prepared to be daring and enterprising in business or professional matters are likely to reap the rewards from your actions. Family members are likely to be supportive. If you work now to make your home and personal life more secure this will help you in time of any future troubles. The indications are that you can put plans for home improvements into action. But there is a danger that legal conflicts regarding house extension plans could force you to examine your position more thoroughly. Later in the day guard against being too demanding of a loved one; try to see their point of view.

29. TUESDAY. Demanding. Children may be making heavy demands on your time. For a while it may seem to you that they are being too clinging, but a quirky smile or a funny turn of phrase from them is likely to make you realize how much you enjoy their company. For Capricorn singles, a new love affair may be challenging in some way. Face up to whatever is troubling your loved one; sweeping emotions under the rug can only result in them coming back to haunt you. There is little reason to feel insecure; all the signs are that your relationship can and will weather the storm. Spend some time this evening with friends. You are in a good position to offer more than just tea and sympathy if one of them decides to confide a personal matter. Give advice without revealing too much.

30. WEDNESDAY. Deceptive. Your own personal needs and desires may be at odds with the demands of your business or professional life early in the day. Guard against irritability and rash action, which will only be counterproductive. Later in the day you could discover that someone has lost an item they borrowed from you. However irritating or upsetting this may be, try not to let your disappointment show too much. Confusion over the details of a financial contract could mean you lose more than you gain. Seek out professional advice before making your next move. Be extra vigilant when it comes to agreeing to a new deal. There is a chance that someone is trying to pull the wool over your eyes, or worse may be trying to cheat you.

JULY

1. THURSDAY. Disquieting. Even the most minute details of your financial affairs need to be carefully reviewed with your famed Capricorn pragmatism. Take steps to protect your interests by avoiding even the slightest tendency toward wastefulness. Double-check the fine print before committing to any financial agreement. There is a possibility of a misunderstanding between you and the other interested parties, or worse that someone is trying to pull the wool over your eyes. When it comes to emotions, you may be somewhat confused about your feelings and not able to fully put in words what is troubling you. Vague forebodings can often herald change, which is not necessarily a bad thing. Get to bed earlier than usual tonight.

2. FRIDAY. Mixed. Although the general atmosphere is positive, finances may continue to be troublesome. Sudden surprises or last-minute changes may force you to think fast. An important meeting is apt to be postponed or canceled. Nevertheless, there is ample opportunity to make progress, even if it is not in quite the way you expect. You are likely to have a lot of questions and even more suggestions. Be tactful or you risk offending just the people you want to impress. Have your fun, but do not be tempted to make anyone a butt of your jokes or you could inadvertently cause offense. Give yourself a rest tonight by being a follower, not an organizer.

3. SATURDAY. Fair. The morning hours are the best time to make yourself heard. An aggressive stance is likely to be interpreted as a will to win by those who matter. By afternoon, however, the emphasis changes to routine matters. If you go out traveling, you can expect to have a bumper day. Allow extra time for a journey, traffic delays or disruptions are indicated. Capricorns who are at home this weekend can profit from a shopping spree. So long as you do not go overboard, you can expect to pick up some bargains at rock-bottom prices. Consider buying furniture for your home at a close-out sale or at a garage sale. Plan a quiet evening at home.

4. SUNDAY. Pleasant. Do all that you can to support a local charity or community event. A trip out of town can be enjoyable and potentially rewarding, although shopping for bargains is of secondary importance. You will get much more out of social contacts than you expect. If you are spending this holiday with your family, an afternoon barbecue should be fun. If you cannot organize one at home, find somewhere quiet you can linger together after eating. A member of the family who has recently moved or taken a new job or a job test should have some good news to tell. This is a favorable time to sign up to take or to teach a class. Get to bed early so that you can face the coming week with your batteries fully recharged.

5. MONDAY. Demanding. Unexpected responsibility that is foisted on you today could prove a little daunting at first. However, this chance to prove what you are capable of doing can ensure the promotion you have been seeking. Avoid saying anything out of turn to your boss or another higher-up. Keep new information under wraps; it is too early to make your intentions known. An older relative may express some extreme views. Avoid getting drawn into an argument or debate; you are unlikely to change their opinion. Guard against letting your irritation show; this is likely to result in a serious disagreement. Make the most of any lull in the day to relax and perhaps reconsider a spontaneous decision.

6. TUESDAY. Changeable. High hopes could be dashed. Tense conditions are likely to confirm what you already know. Associates appear unreliable; situations which depend on them may be very difficult to sustain. Do not commit wholeheartedly to any new project. You do not yet have all the necessary facts to make the right choices. Keep your options open. Although it can sometimes be an uphill climb to reach your goals, you have the necessary drive and determination. Certain issues that you glossed over in the past could come to the fore again. There is a chance that an important initiative may not succeed. Adopt a more cooperative stance and be prepared for frank discussion.

7. WEDNESDAY. Stressful. Although cool by nature, you may find it almost impossible to evade certain emotional persons or situations. Avoid the temptation of locking yourself away. Instead, take this chance to set the record straight. In this way you are more likely to restore your peace of mind. Surprising new facts may come to light. Because you are likely to have little room to maneuver, now is the time to force certain issues with colleagues. If you are in a position of authority, demands can sometimes be more productive than requests. Guard against a tactless or thoughtless remark. Take any setback in a romantic liaison in stride; the signs are that you have not reached the end of the affair but may benefit from a temporary separation.

8. THURSDAY. Disconcerting. If a speculative venture is not performing as well as you had hoped, it would be better to cut your losses now rather than sinking more money into a losing proposition. You may have to deal with unruly children. Although as a Capricorn you know the value of firm discipline, you may be reluctant to exercise control. However, this is one of those occasions when you must take charge if you are to retain control. A favorite leisure pursuit may have to be canceled or postponed. Take steps to insure valuable equipment, whether at the office or at home; there is a greater risk of it becoming damaged or stolen. A good book can be good company tonight.

9. FRIDAY. Rewarding. Romance is in the air. You are likely to be strongly attracted to a person who seems dangerous but exciting. Let yourself go a little, but only with someone you trust. This is a good time for exploring certain boundaries with your mate or partner. A golden opportunity at work should be grabbed with both hands, even if it appears too good to be true. If you hesitate you will probably kick yourself later. By all means confirm any rumor that is floating around, but then act quickly to take full advantage of this unusual and unexpected opening.

10. SATURDAY. Tricky. Working Capricorns need to keep a low profile during the first part of the day. If you are at home, take care of household chores before going out. News of a prime or unexpected dividend is likely; take a little time deciding how to spend or use it. If you spread your good news too quickly, other people may pressure you into buying what they want. A high-risk strategy is likely to pay off only if you check your facts and figures carefully before signing on the dotted line. Read the small print, which could hide a small bombshell. Arrange a night out on the town with friends, especially if it has been a long time since you last partied together.

11. SUNDAY. Enjoyable. This is a starred day for socializing and enjoying good company. An afternoon get-together can be memorable, especially if you are a guest rather than the host. If you are organizing a family gathering, all should go extremely smoothly although you might find that it is much harder work than you anticipate. Do not be shy about roping in help so that you, too, can make the most of the occasion. If you are in a steady relationship, you can look forward to a romantic interlude with your loved one this afternoon. For Capricorn singles, this is a good time to ask that all-important question. A liaison can be put on a firmer footing, but only if you are ready to make a commitment.

12. MONDAY. Successful. You can expect a particularly rewarding day. You or someone you have been tutoring is likely to do well in an exam or interview. Do not hesitate to put some extra effort into what may now seem to be a lost cause. Your extra effort might be just enough to turn disaster into roaring success. This is an excellent time to try out some of your new ideas. Talking them over with your mate or partner can shed light on the best way to implement your plans. You may also want to experiment with some of your wackier schemes, but concentrate most of your energy on those that will work. Later, a competitive game such as tennis, chess, or bridge can be particularly instructive.

13. TUESDAY. Sensitive. Today marks the start of a new phase in your intensely personal relationships. For some Capricorns, this could be the time to end a relationship, but only if you are sure that it cannot be salvaged. Capricorns looking to set up a business would do well to find a partner. Look for someone whose skills complement your own; a person born under the sign of Cancer is apt to have special business acumen. Settling the money side of any partnership is unlikely to be trouble-free, however. This aspect should be left until current conditions pass. Keep a friend at arm's length when it comes to tricky personal or joint finances.

14. WEDNESDAY. Confusing. Financial matters may continue to bewilder and confound you. However, you are in a good position to start to discuss them with other people. Try to get a clear understanding of all the angles before you make your next move. A factor as yet unknown could put a cloud on your plans, but a close contact may then be able to shed some light on them. Do not try to impress a love interest by buying expensive gifts. People are likely to be suspicious of your motives or might take offense. A sob story from a friend may churn up a lot of sympathetic feelings. However, consider the possibility that you are being emotionally manipulated.

15. THURSDAY. Slow. Although this should be a fairly uneventful day, you may suffer from minor aches and pains. Avoid spicy food, and shy away from caffeine and any nonprescribed drugs. People may ask small favors of you, but do not overload yourself in an effort to please. If you own a pet, a routine visit to the vet may be overdue. You are likely to be irked by petty officials, but the best policy is to grit your teeth and get through the formalities. Cutting through red tape is apt to be counterproductive in the long run. If you are looking for a home to rent or buy, you may find just what you need through a classified ad. If you are looking for ways to make some extra cash, consider renting out a spare room or garage space.

16. FRIDAY. Fair. If circumstances permit, consider getting away for a long weekend. Conditions are just right for a short holiday or even a mini vacation at short notice. A change of scene and climate can be a great pick-me-up. For Capricorn students, this is just the right time to polish off an assignment or essay. Although you may not win extra points for submitting your work early, accomplishing a milestone is sure to have its own satisfaction. This is the right time to sign a contractual agreement or legal document. A contract that is finalized today is likely to prove trouble-free and lucrative. A friend may be holding back some personal information, hoping you will ask or notice.

17. SATURDAY. Satisfactory. An unexpected phone call from someone at a distance may be a pleasant shock. Your special skills may be needed to help them out of a jam. This might be the start of a change in your life. You can be confident in negotiating the best possible deal for yourself; your particular abilities are apt to be in great demand. A friend who is already in business may offer some helpful advice. Be prepared to travel in order to achieve your objectives, even if it means an overnight stay away from home. This is a good time to review your position with respect to a legal situation. A second opinion could clarify a legal point and reassure you about the choice you are making.

18. SUNDAY. Manageable. An ambition you have long held is likely to finally come true, and in a most unexpected way. However, keep in mind that all that glistens is not necessarily gold. Be pragmatic about all that is going on and you are less likely to get carried away by the hype and the glitz. Although this is usually a family day, your thoughts may turn to career matters. Update your resume even if you are not now actively looking for a job. It can do no harm to find out what you are worth in the open market. If you go out, keep a close eye on youngsters. There is a greater risk of them tripping and getting hurt. Also be especially alert for children if you are driving locally.

19. MONDAY. Productive. Attractive new career prospects may come to your attention. Your superior organizational skills are unlikely to go unnoticed, which could result in being groomed for a leadership or managerial position. However, this is no time to brag about your talents or your possibilities. Jealousy and rivalries are apt to result if you come on too strong. This is a good day for buying a gift for that special person in your life. However, resist the temptation to buy jewelry unless you know your loved one's preferences very well. You are in a good position to give other people some direction. Proceed slowly; in your eagerness to race ahead, guard against leaving them feeling a little bewildered. Patience is vital in giving instructions.

20. TUESDAY. Frustrating. An unavoidable problem at work may force you to let loved ones down. You are likely to be as disappointed as they are. Take what a friend has to say with a grain of salt. Someone may be exaggerating the merits of a new idea because they are so enthusiastic about it. This is not the time to commit yourself, especially if cash is involved. A few searching questions about past performance of an investment or savings plan could show that it is not such a good bet. Keep your eyes and ears open for the latest gossip on the grapevine. What you hear about a co-worker's intentions could work to your advantage. Change can be both frustrating and beneficial.

21. WEDNESDAY. Challenging. When your back is against the wall, you can use your Capricorn perseverance to find a way to climb over it. A certain financial situation may leave you wondering if you only have one option. Farfetched plans can sometimes work, but look into all options before taking any extreme measures. Your vitality and energy may be at a low ebb, but at least you are receptive. This means you can consider and adopt other people's ideas more readily than usual. Let someone else take the reins, even if this might be unusual for you. A setback in your schedule is likely, but do not become discouraged. The trend toward a slowdown or reversal is not long-lived; just persevere and it will pass.

22. THURSDAY. Quiet. Friends and colleagues could let you down. Try to ignore what they say or do and carry on in your own way. There is little point blaming others for a situation for which you alone are responsible. Guard against being possessive, particularly when it comes to close friendships. While other people's behavior may not meet with your total approval, this is no reason to take a high-handed attitude with them. Something you hear from a co-worker could turn out to be of vital importance, even though it may not seem so at the moment. Adopt a wait-and-see attitude to the outcome of current events rather than fighting the odds.

23. FRIDAY. Variable. This is a good time to enlarge your circle of friends and acquaintances. All the signs are that they will hit it off very well. You are in a good position to finish up your work early. Take advantage of the lull this afternoon to clear your desk and your administrative duties for the week ahead. In this way you can start next week ahead of the game. Review all the transactions on your credit card bill; there is a risk that an error has been made. If you are thinking of making vacation reservations, check the small print for hidden extras or restrictions. There may be more to the deal than meets the eye. A secret told to you in confidence can give you the edge over your competition, but play things close to your own chest for the time being.

24. SATURDAY. Useful. Although you may be unusually sensitive to the influence of other people, it is possible to get your own way even if you have to use some rather strange methods in order to do so. Commit yourself to a project only after you have given it careful and deliberate thought. Once you are committed, keep up the pressure to meet the deadline. This is a favored time for taking a calculated risk or gamble. By all means double-check the facts, but you can then rely on your good Capricorn instinct to tell you when to take the plunge. If you have been tired or run-down in the past few days, current conditions should put a spring back in your step. Enjoy an evening with good friends.

25. SUNDAY. Cautious. The little extras you do behind the scenes can give you the most satisfaction, especially because you are apt to be content to remain in your shell today. However, you can expect appreciation and thanks for your efforts from those who are closest to you. Your home may turn into a hub of activity as people constantly drop in or call you up. There is unlikely to be any social situation that you cannot handle, but you are probably most at ease within your own four walls. Call rather than going to the trouble of visiting. Loved ones need lots of encouragement if you want to get the best from them.

26. MONDAY. Tricky. Personal and professional plans should go according to plan. However, this is not to say that you can avoid putting in the necessary time and effort to clear up any difficulties. Communication problems, in particular, should be dealt with as soon as they crop up. Try not to delegate too much responsibility to inexperienced people. By all means give them a challenge, but do not be tempted to use them as a way of avoiding an unpleasant duty. Opt for a change of routine. This is just the time to alter those aspects of your life that you know are misguided or in some other way not quite right. If you are upset about an argument or harboring past resentments, try to adopt a policy of forgive and forget.

27. TUESDAY. Deceptive. This is a good day for altering your appearance in some way. If you are thinking about changing the color of your hair, use a temporary dye rather than a permanent one. Do not let others pull the wool over your eyes, especially if you have had differences in the past. The overtures they make to you now could have an ulterior motive. Do not leave any travel plans to chance. If you are going out of town, give yourself plenty of time. Try not to overload your schedule or you may not get to finish an important task on time. You cannot afford to ignore other people's advice, although you may choose not to follow it.

28. WEDNESDAY. Disquieting. Cooperative ventures could reveal that someone is not behaving as you expect. A clash between you and this person appears inevitable. However, try not to allow things to get out of hand. Concentrate on your own workload so that you achieve some satisfaction from the progress you make. Emotional matters from the past may again begin to prey on your mind. You could be accused of being too sensitive; if you take a little time to look at things calmly, this accusation could have an element of truth. With all its ups and downs, this promises to be a very busy day. It may become necessary to jot down things to do so that you remember everything.

29. THURSDAY. Unsettling. It is important to express your views, but not in a confrontational or antagonistic way. Do not lose sight of other points of view in your eagerness to get your ideas across. You may be tempted to ignore rules and regulations as way of gaining an advantage. However, this strategy is apt to backfire on you. Take a cautious approach to your personal finances. What appears to be a restriction or limitation can actually turn out to be a blessing in disguise. Find a way of making this day your own without treading on anyone's toes in the process. Give priority tonight to your mate or partner's desires.

30. FRIDAY. Sensitive. Social arrangements may have to be postponed or canceled, especially if they involve traveling out of the area. Although as a Capricorn you like to plan ahead, take this opportunity to put a little spontaneity into your life. This is a good time to do all that you can to encourage unusual situations and to stimulate relationships in ways that you have not considered before. Take advantage of this excellent period to explore your artistic and creative talents. Even if it is a simple matter of planning some changes at home, the ideas you come up with today are likely to be inspired. Do not be reluctant to make on-the-spot decisions; they are apt to be the best ones.

31. SATURDAY. Exciting. This is an excellent day for putting some of your new ideas into practice and for lifting your sights a little higher. Get routine chores done as quickly as possible so that you have time to experiment with some of your plans. Conditions are excellent for making new friends and contacts. Seek out people who excite your imagination. You can also depend on the willing help of a friend or neighbor to help with your personal plans; accept all help with gratitude. Some bright, stimulating, and very interesting news is coming your way. Even if everything does not conveniently fall into place for you, your sheer force of will is likely to win the day.

AUGUST

1. SUNDAY. Buoyant. Negotiations, matters involving contractual arrangements, or signing agreements are all likely to work out in your favor. Communications with other people will be easy, whether you are telling a loved one how you feel or are dealing with business contacts by phone or in person. Capricorn salespeople are likely to find business booming, even on this weekend day. New contacts could provide you with valuable leads and information. Later in the day you are apt to be extremely sensitive to the moods of others. Seek out the company of cheerful, positive friends and family members. Enjoy the opportunity to reminisce about shared events from the past and to consider joint plans for the future.

2. MONDAY. Useful. Clearing out items you no longer use or want can be very satisfying. This activity is also likely to help clear the decks for new ideas. Try to get better organized so that you can find what you need when you need it. Do not wait any longer to purchase some kind of electronic gadget for the home or office to keep you in closer touch with all that is going on. You have a clearer vision of what you would like to achieve and can make firm resolutions regarding your personal aims. Relations with a loved one are improving; this could be a time of real understanding and harmony if you are willing to apologize or to accept an apology. However, guard against becoming too possessive.

3. TUESDAY. Confusing. Communications at home, particularly with your spouse or partner, are likely to be troublesome. There is a danger of being so overwhelmed by your feelings that you are deaf to rational arguments or explanations. If you have a problem with someone, try to remain as objective as possible as you air your differences. Holding back could mean you wind up holding a grudge, resulting in more bitter feelings between you. Do not be tempted to change your views every time someone disagrees with them, just for the sake of keeping the peace. If you are undecided about your views, be honest and admit it. Talking to cover up your confusion can turn off those who might be able to enlighten you.

4. WEDNESDAY. Disquieting. Although as a Capricorn you usually have your feet planted firmly on the ground, guard against letting fantasy and illusion take a hold over you. Dreams of reaping riches from some form of gambling, such as a lottery or sports bet, cannot be depended on; the reality is that you have to work hard for your money. A craving for excitement could lead you to take risks you would normally avoid with your finances. There is a greater danger of a dispute arising with those who are closest to you. You may find it difficult to hide your true feelings from loved ones and close friends. Although there is a line that should not be crossed, be true to your own personality.

5. THURSDAY. Enjoyable. There are good opportunities for you to meet and talk with friends, neighbors, and others you normally see daily but do not take the time to talk with at any length. If you feel protective of someone, possibly a young child, this may seem to be quite a responsibility. However, your relationship should be improving as you give them the support and encouragement they need without feeling diminished or drained yourself. As a consequence, you will probably feel quite proud of their achievements in the future. This is a good time to check out what deals are available for fall vacations. You may even get a chance to visit a locale of your dreams at an affordable price thanks to a special promotion.

6. FRIDAY. Variable. Capricorn whose day-to-day work involves creativity can make excellent progress. This is a day when financial rewards are likely for your efforts. You may also have strong sympathy for the problems of others, putting yourself in their situation. There may be a conflict between your need to focus on daily routine and your personal obligations. Your desire to help a friend could cause you to miss a deadline at work. Your desire to support and protect people who are important to you is strong. However, guard against treading on other people's toes and trying to limit their choices. Ultimately you can never know what is best for another person, no matter how well you think you know them or how much experience you have.

7. SATURDAY. Unsettling. The time has come to let a friend know how you feel about their attention-attracting behavior. Do not wait until circumstances become intolerable and you want to break off with them. If you do not take control of the situation soon, change may be forced on you. The events of the day are apt to reveal aspects of your attitude toward money and possessions that surprise you. It is possible that you have been expecting others to share with you while you are less willing to do the same with them. Focus on what you have, not on what you wish you owned. If you make a promise to yourself, be sure to keep it.

8. SUNDAY. Pleasant. Life is likely to feel richer and more rewarding because loved ones and friends are becoming even more important in your everyday affairs. You are more likely to enjoy being with those closest to you, showing concern for them and having fun together. A feeling of mutual trust and support is growing even stronger between you. This is a favorable day to go on a family outing. A trip to a new place away from your immediate neighborhood can be particularly enjoyable. Or you may want to curl up on the sofa with a novel and lose yourself in the story's intrigue. You are apt to be fascinated by customs and lifestyles that are different from your own. A new relationship can give you excitement that has been missing in your life.

9. MONDAY. Frustrating. Current influences favor putting your energies into group activities. After some resistance on the part of other people, you should be able to help unify the group while continuing to take a leading role. Getting the financial backing you need for a planned project might not be as straightforward as you anticipate. Beware of reacting irritably to what you perceive as petty restrictions that are holding you back. The events of the day could reveal a few weaknesses in your approach and point out where you need to build greater confidence in yourself. An older, more experienced friend or family member may be able to give you wise advice if you discuss a concern with them honestly and openly.

10. TUESDAY. Mixed. Early morning is a good time to talk about your feelings with someone close to you. Later in the day you could be very sensitive emotionally and, as a result, may not perceive situations very accurately. If you are out and about, keep a close eye on your wallet; there is a risk of being pickpocketed. Protect your shared finances. Do not allow yourself to be persuaded to gamble with resources which are being saved for a special purchase. Resist the temptation to overspend in order to please a loved one or to let your generosity lead you to lend money unwisely. Even if you are upset by current circumstances, guard against withdrawing into your own private world.

11. WEDNESDAY. Difficult. A dispute over handling group or business funds is apt to be heated and intense. Failure of communication and genuine misunderstandings with others are also likely, especially with those at a distance. Channel your energies into team or group activities. Be willing to take a supportive role in the background. In this way you can stay in touch but not have to coax and cajole other people. This approach is best no matter how much patience and forbearance is needed on your part to carry it out. The demands of today are likely to be directly opposed to what you would rather be doing. You may have to bite your tongue and do what you are told without comment.

12. THURSDAY. Fair. Focus on socializing in order to meet new people and expand your social and business contacts. In this way you can almost guarantee an easier time for yourself. Others are likely to respond warmly to your open Capricorn manner and genuine feelings. You may have a strong urge to take a break from normal routine. Travel could be beneficial, but there are other escape routes as well. Consider going deeply into a subject of study that has appealed to you for a long time, or taking up a creative hobby. Guard against giving in to a sudden impulse to buy an item you cannot really afford. This form of escape is not going to be good for you in the long run. A lost or forgotten document is likely to resurface when you are looking for something else.

13. FRIDAY. Favorable. Conditions are much calmer than they have been in the past few days. Discuss any problems you may still have with an older person you respect. You are likely to get some practical answers to questions that are troubling you. Taking a short break away from your usual scene can provide an opportunity for you to contemplate what moves you want to make next. Working independently without the restrictions of team pressure is the most effective approach for you today. Perform every task with steadiness and responsibility; even though this might take longer, you can be satisfied at having completed the job thoroughly and to your high standards.

14. SATURDAY. Deceptive. Your creative and artistic abilities can help bring you success and public recognition. This is a favorable day for promoting your work by showing it to the public. If you are involved in discussions or negotiations concerning property or finances which are jointly held, guard against being confused or overwhelmed by too much information all at once. Do not count on others understanding your point of view, even if you are sure you have made yourself absolutely clear. Avoid making any permanent commitments or decisions based on what you learn today. In a day or two conditions will change to such an extent that you may come to totally different conclusions.

15. SUNDAY. Good. An urge to make changes in your personal environment could inspire you to do some cleaning, repairing, and reorganizing at home. Although it might take a while for other family members to adjust, the end results should be constructive. Your desire for excitement may lead you to venture into new places and spend time in unusual surroundings. If you are focused on professional and business concerns, conditions favor working as part of a group. Because you are sensitive and responsive to the general mood, you can easily win others over to your point of view. Beware of setting unrealistic objectives for yourself. There is a chance of becoming so obsessed that you lose track of other equally important obligations.

16. MONDAY. Disquieting. This is not a good time to get involved in a lawsuit or any kind of legal or contractual dispute. You are apt to be somewhat careless over details and inclined to turn a blind eye to elements which do not fit into your grand plan. Resist the temptation to take a risk which would jeopardize finances you share with your mate or partner. Guard against being rigid in your communications, especially if discussing problems concerning property or finances. These can best be resolved if you remain flexible in your point of view and do not assume that you have all the answers. Also avoid being too optimistic about money matters and being self-indulgent when buying for yourself or your home.

17. TUESDAY. Unsettling. You could have difficulty assessing the reality of situations involving friends. Misunderstandings concerning money may arise; you may feel put upon by a friend who wants you to help them out of a financial difficulty. Coercion tactics rarely work with Capricorn people. There is a danger your friendship could be compromised as a result. Capricorn singles may feel hemmed in by the demands of a blossoming romance. Your feelings are likely to overwhelm your reason, making it all the more difficult to get your views across. Count to ten or take a walk around the block before you dive into a confrontation.

18. WEDNESDAY. Stressful. Guard against discussing provocative subjects with friends or acquaintances. You are apt to become easily irritated and could find it difficult to stay calm. In matters involving an organized group, avoid making demands or threats. There can be little good stemming from an attitude where you are thinking only of getting your own way at the expense of the needs of the group. In any case, people are less likely to support your unorthodox ideas. As a result, you may feel out on a limb. Do not let your disappointment show by becoming irritated and insensitive. Instead, look for a way to compromise so that everyone gets something.

19. THURSDAY. Cautious. Tensions concerning joint finances may be brought to the surface early in the day. Worries over money have been demanding much of your attention recently, and you are likely to be feeling stressed out as a result. If you have been taking a partner for granted, this is the day to start correcting the situation. Later in the day you may be tempted to spend time alone. However, because you are very sensitive to other people's moods, you will feel better in the company of positive people. There is a chance of meeting someone whose ideas have a profound effect on your thinking. Be willing to explore new beliefs and ideas far different from your own.

20. FRIDAY. Disconcerting. Strong feelings could distort your sense of perspective regarding a romantic entanglement. Relations with a loved one are unusually intense. Beware of being ruled by possessiveness or jealousy. However, you should be able to express yourself and your emotions. The insight you have into your own feelings enables you to offer effective help to others. There is a possibility of meeting someone who becomes a catalyst for dramatic changes in the way you earn your living. If you are applying for a bank loan or mortgage, negotiations should go well.

Conditions favor reviewing joint finances and revamping your budget to make it more realistic.

21. SATURDAY. Happy. This is a beneficial day for working alone at home. Try to complete neglected tasks so that you can free up time for making your surroundings more attractive. You are in harmony with everyone around you. This inner peace and serenity can draw others to you; joint activities should be very pleasurable. Married Capricorns should find this a time of greater understanding. You may feel more protective toward a loved one; it could be a good time to take out an insurance policy or make investments for future security. Enjoy a quiet evening at home doing what you like best with that special person at your side.

22. SUNDAY. Buoyant. A pleasant sense of well-being is likely to keep you in high spirits all day. There should be no problem being warm and friendly toward everyone you meet. As a result, new friends will warm to you and give you affection and support in return. Helping others is sure to help you as well. Being with children could prove rewarding. Capricorns working in a creative or artistic field may have the chance to make more money than usual as a result of increased public attention. You now have greater freedom for self-expression and will not find it necessary to promote yourself aggressively. Sit back and enjoy being in the limelight.

23. MONDAY. Manageable. You are likely to have a more disciplined approach to creative work, whether or not you are directly involved in artistic work. Take advantage of this attitude to put recent good ideas into practice. Applying your energies to group activities could bring personal benefits and rewards as well. As a Capricorn you tend to be ambitious and may be hankering after a leadership role. The signs are that you will have the chance to do just that. However, beware of being too blunt or saying things to shock. This tactic can sometimes be effective, but current conditions do not favor this approach. Even if there is a difference of opinion, others are likely to listen to your point of view if you back it up with hard facts and figures.

24. TUESDAY. Exacting. There is a possibility of delays concerning finances. If you recently applied for a bank loan or mortgage, or for a new credit card, matters may not proceed in a straightforward manner. You could be too demanding of loved ones; tensions may ride high, with quarrels arising as a result. Avoid insisting that you are right and others are wrong. A spirit of compromise is necessary. Focusing on the imperfections and flaws of plans, projects, or the people around you is likely to make you depressed. By dwelling on the negative side you are only seeing part of the truth. Guard against being with people who reinforce your pessimism. Instead, get together with those who have a can-do attitude.

25. WEDNESDAY. Demanding. Delays or restrictions in money matters may make you want to rebel. Do all that you can to get to the root of the problem. Strive to clarify certain issues concerning joint finances. This is not a good time to enter into a contract or make any investments which involve shared money. Children may act up, making you impatient with them. People in authority are likely to challenge your basic assumptions. Guard against becoming overly defensive. Putting exaggerated emphasis on material possessions can blind you to the value of the people in your life; they are the true treasures. Give romance top billing tonight.

26. THURSDAY. Stressful. Intense involvement in a close relationship is important to you. You could be feeling extravagant and run up high expense buying items for yourself and your loved one. However, you may regret this later. You can make a good impression without spending a lot of money. Guard against letting minor irritations get under your skin. If you are unhappy about a friend's behavior, air your feelings as honestly but tactfully as you can. That way, the communication lines can be kept clear and the problem resolved. You have to work hard to maintain the right balance between your home and professional life. If you must work late, be sure to let family members know in advance.

27. FRIDAY. Fair. This is a good day to become involved with a group activity in your community. Working together with neighbors should prove beneficial for all concerned. Spending time with a friend's child is likely to be enjoyable; there is sure to be good rapport between you. If your business involves antiques or the arts, focusing on in-depth research concerning these matters can result in a good investment or business deal. There is the possibility of finding a bargain at an auction. Use your spare time to pursue an interest in art or music, whether on the creative side or as a connoisseur.

28. SATURDAY. Fortunate. Tasks which require precise thinking and concentration are especially starred. Do not hesitate tackling difficult problems; view obstacles as a challenge that you can overcome. If you are involved in work on a community project, have the courage of your convictions. There is no need to worry about how others feel about where you stand on a particular issue. You are sure to excel at any form of public communication, especially speaking in front of an audience. The belief you have in your ideas is likely to make you daring and bold in your actions. Conditions also favor trying out a new leisure activity or taking a trip to a locale you have not visited before.

29. SUNDAY. Challenging. Do not hide your sympathy and compassion for others. Consider working as a volunteer to help less fortunate individuals, either personally or through a charitable group. You are apt to have some original ideas regarding how to carry out this work. You may even feel like shaking up other people who seem too passive in responding to the problems of the needy. Family affairs and home comforts require sensitive handling. There is a danger that family members are worried and upset; an emotionally exhausting encounter could occur as a result. Bring some of your famous Capricorn steadiness and pragmatism to bear on the problem. Opt for a low-key course of action, at least initially.

30. MONDAY. Stressful. Although this is the start of a busy working week, you may want to spend a little extra time at home with loved ones. You are apt to be feeling rather lazy and not in the mood to get much done. One area where you may feel inspired, however, is how to make your home more comfortable and attractive. Consider investing in some antiques or in well-designed furniture. Be careful if you go out; there is a danger of an accident, especially when walking or driving. Clashes with a friend could arise because you misinterpret an off-the-cuff remark as a provocative challenge. Give everyone the benefit of the doubt until and unless they prove you wrong.

31. TUESDAY. Cautious. Communications with loved ones early in the day about shared finances are likely to proceed well. Conditions favor getting away from your usual environment. If you do not do so, events may force you to make radical changes in an area of your life which you know is not working very well. People in authority may wield strong power over you. Avoid a serious confrontation with these types, but try to get the support of an independent but equally powerful person. Communication problems with people at a distance may need attention, especially if a fax machine or computer network is involved. Later on in the day enjoy going out with friends to a concert or show.

SEPTEMBER

1. WEDNESDAY. Disconcerting. Be careful not to jump to hasty conclusions or react negatively to news, especially where money matters are concerned. A younger family member is likely to badger you for extra money; help them finds ways of earning it if you cannot give it to them outright. You are apt to do the exact opposite of what is suggested. Although this response can be a liberating experience, you may find yourself acting in ways you would usually never consider. You have to work hard in order to enjoy yourself today. A strenuous workout or the company of serious-minded people can restore your sense of balance. Chances are you will have to look after an older or infirm person.

2. THURSDAY. Disquieting. Friends are likely to be a source of irritation because you are in an emotionally excitable mood. You may be rather impatient as well, far less tolerant of other people's quirks and foibles. Guard against arguments just for the sake of being obstinate. Later, you may find it difficult to keep from daydreaming. Routine work must be attended to, but with a little extra effort you can turn even this into a creative or artistic activity. Beware of letting your heart rule your head. There is a tendency to overreact to ordinary problems and situations. You can avoid open controversy by agreeing in public, even if you have some questions or reservations you want to discuss in private.

3. FRIDAY. Exciting. This is a good day for making sweeping changes in your personal life. Although other people may be shocked by your sudden moves, they will eventually come around to accepting your changes. If you deal regularly with the public or with groups of people, this is a good time to advocate change and new policies. A date with an exciting new partner is likely for Capricorn singles. Because you are likely to make them feel good, you can easily build quick rapport. Avoid the temptation to let others do all the running for you. Meet challenges head-on rather than looking for an easy way out. Try to absorb as much new information as you can; it is likely to serve a useful purpose soon.

4. SATURDAY. Variable. Spend the day with your nearest and dearest. You are more likely to be at ease with them than with new acquaintances or strangers. Include your mate or partner in a new scheme you are hatching, or offer your services to them if they are working on a special project of their own. There are unlikely to be any major upsets or emotional dramas. Just chatting about the ordinary things in life can make you feel closer than ever. If you have a problem you cannot handle, ask someone you respect who lives at a distance for advice. This is a good time to write a letter to people you miss since they moved away. Guard against becoming obsessed with a single train of thought. It is important to keep an open mind.

5. SUNDAY. Challenging. An older, wiser person could have some pearls of wisdom to share with you. Take advantage of their vantage point. This is a favored time to tackle odd jobs around the house. You are apt to be even more thorough than usual. Once a job is done, it is unlikely that you will have to worry about it again for some time. At some point in the day consider performing a good deed with no thought of reward. You may want to volunteer for a charity or club event. Find time to get away by yourself in order to practice meditation. You may develop an interest, even fascination, with sports or other exercise that can raise your spirits while toning your body.

6. MONDAY. Mixed. You may be laboring under a misapprehension about a certain matter that involves a joint bank account or shared resources. Guard against taking what you see and hear at face value; there could be more to it than meets the eye. This is a good time to accept a leadership role. You are able to speak directly and openly without being in the least bit offensive. You are also radiating inner excitement, as though ready for immediate action. Do not put off starting short-term projects, although this is not a favored time to begin complicated work. It should be easier to keep your main objective and strategy clearly in mind. Beware of getting bogged down in petty or inconsequential details.

7. TUESDAY. Cautious. Powerful feelings are likely to be stirred up by someone you like at work or in your neighborhood. Pursue this potential relationship if you are single. If you are already attached, however, this can be a hurtful experience unless you handle it appropriately. Getting to know a newcomer could turn out to be an enriching, rewarding experience. A strong urge to blow your budget on an impulse purchase could be nearly impossible to resist. Resist a tendency to act disruptively, especially in your family relationships. Give loved ones the same respect and consideration you give virtual strangers. This evening you are apt to be in a lively mood, ready for a social gathering or party.

8. WEDNESDAY. Sensitive. There is danger of a needless dispute due to hasty action or words that you blurt out in anger. This tendency is most likely in your dealings with people who are at a distance from you. Capricorns in business would be wise not to rule out any possibilities quite yet. Petty annoyances with other people could be masking a deeper and more serious resentment. Getting away from it all for a day or even an evening can put you in a much better frame of mind. This is an excellent time to launch a new publication or an advertising campaign, but do not overdo your exuberance and enthusiasm. If you get too excited there is a chance that everything will fizzle out when you face the first major hurdle.

9. THURSDAY. Useful. This is a much easier day when it comes to dealing with other people. They are likely to warm to your ideas rather than trying to oppose or resist them. You are in a good position to offer both practical and emotional support to whoever needs it. Cultivate connections at a distance; new opportunities are opening up for you. You are likely to be inspired by a lecture, seminar, or book and may even decide a career matter on the strength of it. If it seems that life has been out of control recently, today's conditions should put you firmly back in the driver's seat. Stand up for what you believe is right even if your views are not popular.

10. FRIDAY. Manageable. Conditions are beginning to be much more settled, which should be very reassuring news for you. Use the morning hours to finalize a deal or transaction connected with faraway lands. Make the most of today's stellar influences by polishing off an essay or report, or writing an important letter. If you have just begun a new venture, this is an excellent time to consolidate your position by laying down a solid foundation. In this way you can ensure lasting success. Your concentration is good, allowing you to tackle any thorny problem or task that requires sustained effort. Keep your feet firmly planted on the ground and take a practical approach to all that you do.

11. SATURDAY. Excellent. If you are entertaining you are likely to be at your most efficient and are bound to make a big impression. Paperwork can be signed with confidence that you are making the right move. However, guard against rushing headlong into a commitment that you know in your heart you may not be able to meet. Fixed opinions are subject to outside influence. You may well find yourself changing your mind about a friend or neighbor. Consider the possibility that work interests are beginning to make you neglect your loved ones. Obtain their okay before accepting an invitation from a work colleague to attend a social event. Your hunches about a new person on the scene are probably correct and should not be ignored.

12. SUNDAY. Satisfactory. Attend to routine paperwork such as paying bills or balancing your accounts. Catch up on business correspondence if you have access to a typewriter or word processor. For dedicated Capricorn professionals, this is a good time for furthering negotiations or participating in informal discussions. Even if the money side of such negotiations seems satisfactory, there could be some problems to iron out when it comes to staff and equipment. Think twice before making a promise to your loved one, no matter how eager you are to show them how much you love them. Capricorn singles should play it cool; do not wear your heart on your sleeve.

13. MONDAY. Confusing. Try not to worry too much about plans, schedules, and upcoming events. They will tend to go more smoothly if you simply let them take their own natural course. This is not the best day for traveling. Trying to cram too much into your waking hours is likely to leave you exhausted and less efficient. Affairs relating to friends and co-workers should be put off until later in the week or even next week. Stick to routine tasks that you can do without having to read a manual of instructions. New projects you attempt now are likely to result in confusion and disappointment. If there is a job that you would like to apply for, do not let anyone or anything stop you. Asking for advice from too many people is only going to confuse you.

14. TUESDAY. Difficult. A confrontation that erupts during the morning or early afternoon could leave you wondering about a certain friend. At the same time, guard against being oversensitive or beginning to imagine things. The person in question probably has no intention of hurting or offending you. Do not overdramatize the situation by making it into what it is not. Someone may want to entrust you with their valuables or money on a temporary basis; be realistic about the responsibilities you are taking on. There are so many distractions and interruptions today that you may not make much headway. Putting in a little overtime which stretches late into the evening can be a good idea if you must meet a deadline.

15. WEDNESDAY. Rewarding. Do a good turn without anyone knowing about it. You can save the pride of a friend in trouble in this way. Hectic though your social life may be, find time for intellectual pursuits as well. You may even be able to combine the two by attending a seminar or meeting in a resort setting. A trip with a friend could be memorable. Conditions are promising for Capricorn people who work from home; a lucrative new contract is indicated. Capricorn students can make good progress by studying with someone else. Tackling a new topic at this time is likely to result in confusion at first, but persevere.

16. THURSDAY. Changeable. Get an early start in order to put your carefully laid plans into action. With your increased energy and vitality, change is indicated: You may find yourself involved in a new business activity or taking a leading role in your community. Your can-do attitude is sure to make others follow you, and you can expect increasing popularity as a result. If you are in a romantic relationship, concentrating on partnership issues may lead to happy results. A love affair that is not working out may be given new life by getting away together for a long weekend. A change of scene could give you a change of heart as well.

17. FRIDAY. Successful. Your intuition is combining well with your sound pragmatism. You can trust a hunch; you have an unerring instinct for the right deal and the right timing. You may argue with a certain friend; a problem you thought you had dealt with earlier this year is likely to resurface and leave you feeling disconcerted. Seeing less of each other for a while could eventually heal the rift. Listen to the advice of a friend, even if it is not what you want to hear. Conditions are right for tackling any problems with an older relative. Disputes over property have a good chance of being resolved. This is a favored time for making a long-term investment providing you have done your homework.

18. SATURDAY. Mixed. The early hours are best for home entertaining. Later on you may want to spend time alone with your loved ones. The day favors do-it-yourself jobs around the house. Going ahead with home decorating plans is unlikely to be a decision you come to regret. It is also a good day for puttering around the garden if the weather permits. If choosing new bulbs or plants for next spring, consider robust varieties rather than more delicate alternatives. Preparing a vegetable and herb garden can be worthwhile. Family members may feel they are getting stuck with the least desirable domestic chores. Talk it over with them and be willing to switch responsibilities on a rotating basis.

19. SUNDAY. Unpredictable. Look carefully into the motivation of those who are urging you to make a move in a particular direction. They may have their own interests at heart. Your professional and career potential is likely to get a boost from expanding your expertise and acquiring new skills. Signing up to take a class could start you on a profitable path. Your ability to respond positively to a difficult situation could be the cornerstone to your future success. Capricorn leadership potential is emphasized. To tower head and shoulders over everyone else, exercise your talent just when other people are beginning to lose heart and give up. Timing is all-important as you struggle with unexpected events.

20. MONDAY. Uncertain. The day starts off on an uncertain and unstable note. Loved ones may be feeling more insecure than they are willing to admit, which is likely to create a generally tense atmosphere. As a result you could start to doubt yourself and your own abilities without any real reason. Be on the lookout for strangers who try to impose themselves on you or win you over to their way of thinking. They could be playing mind games with you and are probably not to be trusted. Delays in receiving a letter, package, or message from someone at a distance could cause some concern. If you are worried, check up on their health and general well-being by phoning a mutual friend. Stall before accepting or declining an invitation.

21. TUESDAY. Good. There is a greater chance of receiving recognition for a certain project or artistic endeavor you have been involved in for some time. A sales contract may be forthcoming. If a youngster is doing particularly well at school or on a sports team, you have every right to feel proud of them and should let them know how you feel. You can be lucky in finding a backer for a speculative or risky venture. If you spread the element of risk there is much less to worry about. Although a past failure or error can be dogging your footsteps, it is important to forgive yourself and put it out of your mind. Even though you often set very high standards for yourself, sometimes you can still get it wrong.

22. WEDNESDAY. Disquieting. This is a good time for putting together a team and for consolidating team efforts. However, do not mix business and pleasure. Avoid an extended lunch that keeps you or others away from work. Any romantic feeling you may have for a work colleague is unlikely to be reciprocated; there is a risk of your pride being hurt if you do not read the signs they are sending you. Guard against prying into other people's private lives; they are sure to resent the intrusion. This is a good day for fund-raising activities, especially those connected with elderly people or those who are confined at home due to illness. Do not overlook returning a library book.

23. THURSDAY. Lucky. This day promises fulfillment of a secret hope or dream you have been cultivating. It is favorable also for all matters relating to people at a distance. Traveling can open up new horizons for you, bringing you what has been missing from your life closer to home. Settling permanently in a faraway city is worth considering seriously. A package that has been delayed or temporarily lost in the mail may arrive at last, much to your relief. During the afternoon and evening, friendship and romance are unlikely to mix well. Think twice before lending money to anyone, unless you are able and willing to consider it a gift.

24. FRIDAY. Exciting. A meeting with business associates could lead to planning a new project. Do not hesitate to try out new ideas or innovations. Follow your good Capricorn instincts, but think through the practical angles before parting with too much money. Avoid going off in many directions at once. Instead, concentrate on what is most important to you, and keep plugging away at that until you are satisfied with your results. What you have been producing for your own satisfaction could become marketable; all you need to do is streamline your methods a little. This is a good time to write a serious letter of intent or explanation in order to improve your chance of getting a new job or a promotion.

25. SATURDAY. Pleasant. Do not try too hard to have a good time. Forcing pleasure and enjoyment is unlikely to be successful. Instead, try to be laid back and take pleasure in the little things of life. Conditions favor creative and artistic endeavors. Avoid becoming too obsessive about getting everything exactly right. The desire for perfection can be Capricorn's undoing. Getting out and about is likely to give you a sense of positive purpose. Stop to chat with neighbors; you may pick up some fascinating bits of information via the grapevine. Loved ones are looking forward to special moments of family togetherness with you. If you choose to go out for dinner, make it a leisurely meal.

26. SUNDAY. Fair. Keep a recent discovery to yourself. Think twice before divulging what you know to officials or any authorities. Although formal social occasions may not be to your liking, you are apt to enjoy a relaxed gathering with friends and loved ones. You should feel sufficiently at ease to talk freely about political, philosophical, or religious matters. Consider planning a trip with your loved one to a romantic location. A blunder you committed recently in dealing with an influential person can easily be rectified if you talk with them in a relaxed, informal setting. Others are just as prepared as you are to forgive, forget, and start the relationship with a clean slate.

27. MONDAY. Mixed. Do not wait for opportunities to present themselves to you. This is a good time to seek out established contacts and call in a few favors. Some good items are likely to come your way at a rock-bottom price. Your optimism and positive approach need to be based in reality. Even when you are thinking big, you instinctively know what can and cannot be achieved. Commercial associates are likely to be inspired and enthusiastic about your grand schemes. Others will probably be attracted to the warmth and sympathy you are radiating and, as a consequence, are more likely to confide in you. They are sure to appreciate your advice as much as they respect your sincerity and concern.

28. TUESDAY. Frustrating. During the first half of the day you could well find yourself chasing a lot of false leads. Try not to personally rush around unless it is really necessary; use the telephone or e-mail instead. People you need to contact might not be easy to get hold of, and you may just have to wait until they are available. There is little to be gained from trying to force negotiations or a contract. If you pressure someone into signing now, you are likely to regret it later. The rest of the day should be smoother. Working with colleagues can be a pleasure. Arrange to meet up with your loved one or a friend after work, even if it is only for a walk around town and some window-shopping.

29. WEDNESDAY. Manageable. A little extra exercise should help keep you feeling fit and on top of all that is going on. This is especially true if you spend much of the day sitting at a desk. Experiment with a routine for getting physical exercise each day; it can make a world of difference to how you feel mentally. Make an appointment to have a dental checkup even if nothing hurts; it will be a relief to confirm that nothing is wrong. Working to a deadline is the best way of completing a job that is beginning to bore you. Doing an adequate job is all that is required; do not aim for perfection. Children are likely to play a role in your evening activities; give them extra time and attention.

30. THURSDAY. Changeable. Whatever you decide to do, it is likely to cost more than you anticipate. You may have to exceed your budget just to keep up with the crowd. Do not allow yourself to be persuaded by a forceful sales pitch that is difficult to counter. Guard against letting anyone in on your secret until you are ready for everyone to know. Carefully choose the moment when you want to make your announcement. You can gain a definite advantage by timing what you have to say to make the maximum impact on the largest number of people. If you follow the same routine day in and day out, you lose the momentum that comes with the element of surprise. It may necessary to prevent friends and a romantic interest from meeting at this time.

OCTOBER

1. FRIDAY. Fortunate. Early in the day is a good time to buy or sell anything of high value and to undertake business matters which require signatures on a document. Conditions also favor dealing with correspondence and writing of all kinds; work you do now should produce benefits in the future. Later in the day is the best time to propose your plans and ideas to other people. Seize any financial opportunities which come your way. A new business partner may be able to help you make financial progress. Gains are foreseen through investment in a new product or starting a new business enterprise. Your goals can be achieved fairly easily once you pinpoint them. Look for new romantic opportunity after dark.

2. SATURDAY. Unsettling. Although normally a day off the job, indications are that there will be some kind of career upset or dispute this morning. Take special care in business matters, especially if you are starting in business for yourself or have to deal with employers or important business connections. The basis of all your recent efforts may be tested by the impact of today's events. Some changes to a partnership arrangement are possible. You may be less responsive to the ideas or appeals of other people, preferring to be alone with your own thoughts. Do not be tempted to take any new financial risks. What you achieve today will be the result of hard work.

3. SUNDAY. Variable. Be extra careful if signing any important document early in the day. There is a danger of fraud and uncertainty in money matters. You could easily be deceived, so be extra cautious in all dealings with others. There could be trouble concerning property as well as upsets in family matters. Guard against extravagance and blind optimism; it is vital to avoid unwise financial speculation and any type of gambling. Your judgment may not be at its best; delay important decisions. Late in the evening conditions are likely to improve. You can enjoy stimulating conversation with friends providing you are willing to listen as much as you talk.

4. MONDAY. Changeable. The first order of business is to complete any neglected or unfinished tasks in order to clear the way for new operations. Do all that you can to get to the root of a financial problem. Spend time working alone behind the scenes to further group efforts. There are likely to be delays in seeing the results of your efforts, which could lead to a temporary cash-flow crisis. Take care not to work so hard that you reach the breaking point. Try to take any unsatisfactory or surprising developments in stride. Despite changes or unusual conditions regarding finances, you should find new opportunities for making money in unexpected ways. Be sure to schedule time for relaxation at the end of the working day so that you can unwind.

5. TUESDAY. Rewarding. A sudden and unanticipated change could enable you to take vigorous and decisive action regarding joint finances. Your energy level is likely to be high. This, coupled with wise channeling of your Capricorn drive and initiative, should help you achieve at least one of your ambitions. Do all that you can to pass on your enthusiasm for a new project to others; talk them around to your point of view as well as inspiring teamwork. A close emotional relationship may be developing with someone you recently met. This is a day when you find it easy to express your feelings directly and in person. Home life is smooth. You could make financial gains through work done by your mate or partner or through a family legacy.

6. WEDNESDAY. Mixed. Unusual for the Capricorn temperament, you are apt to be feeling restless and might even get itchy feet. Consider the possibility that you can gain more from broadening your mental horizons rather than changing your base of operations. Spending time on new interests and ideas could provide some of the excitement you are looking for. A more studious friend may stimulate you to use your own mental abilities to achieve your plans and goals. Personal finances may be in a chaotic state. A loss is foreseen, either though an error of judgment on your part or because of deception by others. If you are thinking of buying or selling a car through a newspaper advertisement, take extra care with any contract or agreement. Nothing is quite as it seems.

7. THUSRDAY. Cautious. If you are making a tentative outline for a new business proposal guard against trying to plan too precisely. Your immediate goals may be thwarted now, but careful long-term planning should bring the results you want in the future. Resist the temptation to get involved in a get-rich-quick scheme or similar uncertain ventures. Any success you attain will be the result of concentration and hard work. Interacting with other people may seem difficult, but avoid losing your temper or provoking a needless dispute. Even if you have a genuine grievance, keep a level head. Any buildup of inner tension is likely to negatively affect your concentration. If you drive while your mind is preoccupied, there is the risk of a minor accident. Also take extra care if using sharp instruments such as knives or scissors.

8. FRIDAY. Useful. Bring imagination and creativity to bear on business changes. Artistic work should progress especially well and can bring you the prestige and recognition you deserve. Strange as it sounds personal gains are foreseen if you work for those who are less fortunate than you. It should be easier to empathize with their problems and offer practical solutions at the same time. Consider contributing either time or money to a worthy cause. This is a good day to get down to repairing and reorganizing, whether you do the work yourself or hire someone to do it. Look for bargain buys, especially in equipment to make domestic tasks easier. As far as romance is concerned, Capricorn singles may be ready to consider a long-term proposition.

9. SATURDAY. Satisfactory. Your plans may be affected by sudden and unexpected changes that seem to come from out of the blue. Although this might not be quite what you were hoping for, you have a good chance of making events work in your favor. Conditions indicate that this is a good time to start a business for yourself. Opportunities for making money in unusual ways are present. If you are taking part in a meeting or conference, you could be instrumental in helping the group reach a decision that is agreeable to everyone. As a consequence of advocating change and new policies, you may be asked to assume a leadership role. You are unlikely to balk at the prospect of being in charge even though you realize the hard work it will entail.

10. SUNDAY. Easygoing. With less pressure coming at you from all sides, you should feel considerable relief. People will tend to leave you alone, respecting your need for privacy and your ability to get on with your own affairs. You are in an ideal position to do whatever seems most important. Put aside any concerns you have for an older family member; there seems to be little need to be worrying about their needs or what you think they want. Adopt a pragmatic approach to your own needs, your desire to get ahead, and your drive for creativity and self-fulfillment. By being a little more tactful than usual, there need be no clash or conflict with those around you as you follow independent but intertwining paths.

11. MONDAY. Misleading. A new friend who is serious about studying may stimulate you to make better use of your own intellectual abilities. This is a good day for starting new studies, although you need to develop concentration in order to make the most of your new interests. There may be tension over money matters. As a result of recent extravagance or unwise speculation, your finances could be in a state of flux. This is not a day for reinterpreting the ground rules to suit your present situation. You are not in a strong enough position to dictate terms and conditions. Instead, you have to follow rules and regulations to the letter. Allow time for relaxation during the day to help prevent stress and inner tension. Getting some outdoor exercise can be good preventive medicine.

12. TUESDAY. Quiet. This promises to be a more tranquil day for you. Friends or a former colleague may come calling, or you may decide to visit them. Financial progress is likely to be at a standstill. If your goals have not yet been fulfilled, it could be useful to review them. Make sure they are not the result of emotions and drives from the past which are not relevant to your present situation. Better budgeting can help, too. Friends are apt to be somehow involved in your business activities. It might become important to ensure that the money side of a close association is clearly understood by both sides. Spend part of the day in contact with a group or club whose goals and aims you support.

13. WEDNESDAY. Challenging. Creative ideas and inspiration should come easily to you no matter what field you are working in. You are likely to be drawn to unusual people whose lives are very different from yours. Take care, however, in relating to them. Keep your home and all domestic matters distinctly separate from your social affairs. Consider sorting through drawers and closets and getting rid of items stored in dark corners. Although much of it is unlikely to have material value, you may want to keep some mementos for sentimental reasons. Although you may be eager to put fresh ideas into action, constant interruptions are likely. Rather than getting upset and frustrated, give in to these circumstances gracefully. Conditions will soon change to favor your plans and projects.

14. THURSDAY. Buoyant. This promises to be an interesting, memorable day. A friend from the past could come back into your life unexpectedly, providing a welcome opportunity to get away from your usual environment for a while. There are valuable new possibilities for making money. Capitalizing on an interest in a technical subject such as electronics might open the way for you to make a good income. Ideas and thoughts are likely to flash through your mind at great speed. However, allow for the possibility that you might not be able to fine-tune them right away. Brainstorm ideas, jotting them down as you go so that you can work out the details at a later time. Guard against pushing yourself too hard mentally or nervous tension could result.

15. FRIDAY. Frustrating. For every step you take forward, you are likely to take two steps back. It is particularly important that you do not lose your nerve, especially if you are venturing into new territory. Allow yourself some time to become familiar with any new situation; other people are likely to give you room to experiment and learn. Guard against revealing a secret to a relative stranger, particularly if you are in close quarters with them while traveling or attending a performance. On the other hand, there seems to be no need to play your cards close to your chest with those you know and trust. Capricorns with young children or working with youngsters can expect a full schedule. You may want to consider giving a home to a needy child or supporting a child-related charity.

16. SATURDAY. Slow. Being cautious can be an advantage if it causes you to stop, think, and review carefully. This is particularly important if you are signing any document or finalizing any agreement. This can help clear your mind and prevent needless worry. Conditions favor making plans intended to bring benefits in the future, but do not expect immediate results. If you are renewing an interest in the arts, visit an art gallery for inspiration. Romance is likely to flourish, with an easy flow of feelings between you and your loved one. You are likely to make a good impression entertaining visitors who have traveled some distance in order to be with you if you act naturally and do not put on any airs.

17. SUNDAY. Sensitive. Financial matters demand tact and care. Any underlying tension between you and family members are likely to surface today, especially if a loan is involved. Caution is indicated in making changes which affect your career or ambitions. If you give close attention to problems as they arise, there should not be any serious long-term effects. You are apt to be low in energy and not up to par healthwise. As a result you may have difficulty dealing with an older relative whose eccentricities you find hard to tolerate. A fairly quiet schedule is the best way to get through the day. Taking occasional breaks while you are working or thinking can keep levels of concentration sustained and your interest right on target.

18. MONDAY. Unsettling. There may be continuing problems regarding finances and home affairs. There is a chance you have overcommitted yourself in making a purchase agreement. Your bank may be able to restructure the terms of a loan so that repayment becomes easier. Or you may decide to consolidate debts into one lower-interest loan. There is apt to be some intrigue and resulting anxiety concerning home affairs. Guard against being deceived by a close member of the family over finances. Consider new ways of earning a living. There are valuable new business opportunities just waiting to be seized upon. You are likely to be drawn to the kind of work where you are operating alone, away from the public eye and the scrutiny of an everyday boss.

19. TUESDAY. Disquieting. Although change may seem exciting to you at this time, look before you leap. All is not quite what it seems to be at first. Go over your plans carefully. Avoid committing yourself to any important agreement until you have analyzed every angle. There could be some kind of upset with a friend. If you have loaned money to a friend, repayment could be delayed. Do not get carried away by new developments in matters of the heart; any romantic liaison formed now is likely to be intense but brief. Children are apt to be unruly, especially if you need them to help you make a good impression.

20. WEDNESDAY. Useful. Important contacts are likely to look favorably on any request you make of them. Significant changes are possible. This is a good day to get involved with a new enterprise, especially one that involves a new partnership. Gains can be made through wise investments. You should be feeling more energetic than at the start of the week. If you are able to harness your additional energy in a constructive way, much progress can be made. Later in the day you may decide to travel to meet friends for an evening's entertainment together. A suspicion that begins to dawn on you is likely to be based on a realistic assessment of the situation, but follow your hunch discreetly. Avoid making any accusations.

21. THURSDAY. Variable. Whether at home or at work, you are apt to be on the move. Friends want to include you in their plans. Consider helping out a loved one who is making repairs or working on or in their house. This is also a good time to do some thorough cleaning. Clothes that no longer fit or are not in fashion should be given away. An inventory of your kitchen gadgets may reveal that you do not need many of them and they are only in the way. If you are eyeing a major purchase for later in the year, consider saving for it in a special account that earns interest. The generous side of your Capricorn nature needs to be controlled; give your time, not money.

22. FRIDAY. Satisfactory. Opportunities for increasing your social activities are likely, although you need to examine your attitude toward the groups with which you are currently involved. Conditions favor taking up a new interest. This is a good time to become active in a charitable group working to help others. Consider dropping in on a neighbor to catch up with the latest gossip. Reading a news magazine can help fill you in on world events you have been too busy to follow on a daily basis. Guard against becoming irritated with a person who is still in the learning stages, even though their questions seem irrelevant and perhaps a little naive. Later in the day you can enjoy relaxing at home, away from the hustle and bustle.

23. SATURDAY. Inactive. Although today lacks a certain vital spark, consider this lull in a positive light. If you bide your time, you will soon find that opportunity is not far away. Someone is working on your behalf behind the scenes. The fruits of their labor are likely to come to your attention as they begin to have an impact. Guard against making a unilateral decision, especially if a close family member will be affected by it. Check through your bills; there is a possibility you have overlooked one and could incur a penalty because of late payment. If a gentle reminder does not shame someone into paying a debt owed to you, be more direct rather than letting the matter drop.

24. SUNDAY. Exciting. Propose your ideas or plans to those who may be able to help you put them in motion. Financial affairs should progress well. Although you may feel physically fit, your energy might not be well coordinated. The different areas of your life could be working against each other, with the demands of your work competing with your home and social life. Taking a vacation is likely to appeal to you. There can be a surprise from visiting a city you have not been to before. This is a good time to discuss a problem in a close relationship. You are able to be objective and should not get carried away by impractical ideals. Watch your diet; you could be strongly tempted to overindulge in rich foods.

25. MONDAY. Deceptive. You would be wise not to believe everything you hear. Also be guarded in what you say; a casual remark might be misinterpreted and used by someone for their own purposes. Work hard or play hard, but do not attempt to do both. Although you have plenty of energy in reserve, you could find yourself slowing down well before the day is done. Quiet periods spent clearing up a backlog of work can balance the more energetic periods of the day. Even if you are having a change of heart about a certain financial investment, stick with it for a little while longer. Conditions are too unstable now to make drastic changes in any area of your life until you see what develops.

26. TUESDAY. Mixed. Early in the day an old prejudice may take precedence over your more reasonable judgment. Consider the possibility that this is at the root of difficulties you encounter today. Problems could arise with written work, especially an important report. Later in the day, conditions switch to emphasize domestic affairs. Getting involved in some kind of craft, such as making new furnishings or bed coverings for your home, could be the most positive way to direct your energy. Friends are unlikely to turn you down if you enlist their help with a pet project of yours. If you are planning a new health regime, consider joining a health club for daily supervised exercise. Dismissing an older person's opinions as old-fashioned or outmoded could be counterproductive; at least consider them seriously.

27. WEDNESDAY. Changeable. Accepting additional work now may mean you are not able to honor your existing commitments. Accept a new offer only if you can reschedule your other tasks or delegate them to someone else. Cutting corners as a way out is likely to backfire on you. Guard against getting into a heated argument. If you must get involved, try to remain neutral without seeming to be indifferent. Your attitude or recent behavior may have unwittingly put you on the wrong side of a relative. This could explain their short temper and sullen mood. It is up to you to bring the matter out into the open. A little flattery can help break the ice and clear the air. Privately rehearse an all-important meeting you have scheduled; first impressions count for a lot.

28. THURSDAY. Manageable. Concentrate on domestic and family matters. Redecorating your home can increase its value, giving you real satisfaction. You may overspend a little on items for the home, but it is not likely to hurt your budget. Try to clear up any domestic difficulties. Turn to your family for support if you have any personal problems. Conditions favor making your family and personal life your main priority, so that it is a source of support and comfort. As a Capricorn you are not particularly demonstrative even with your loved ones. However, you should now be feeling affectionate toward those who are closest to you, even if there are no blood ties. Keep track of all your social engagements; there is every chance that it is filling up rapidly.

29. FRIDAY. Fair. Overall, this should be a successful day. There are good opportunities for meeting new people and your social life should be flourishing. Even so, your attention is likely to focus on your most personal relationships, which are apt to seem much more important. Any conflict with loved ones may be more emotional than usual. There is no need to resume a war of words or to take sides in a battle that does not involve you directly. Rehashing an incident from the past will only serve to make someone uncomfortable; it is wiser to let sleeping dogs lie. An angry or disconsolate family member could disrupt your set plans. Patience is required in all joint activities, even if it means biting your tongue more often than usual.

30. SATURDAY. Variable. A loved one can help to broaden your experience by introducing you to new interests. You may be attracted to people who are very different from you. New contacts could be with people from another country or culture, or someone who has traveled more than you or who seems to be better educated than you. Eagnerness for a change from home conditions may lead you to neglect domestic chores which need to be done. The frustrations and compromises you have to make may tempt you to stay out late tonight. Other people are likely to see your need for independence as a sign of aloofness. Try to keep communication channels open even through this rather turbulent day. Making demands or threats is unlikely to be a useful ploy.

31. SUNDAY. Disquieting. The usual peace and quiet you have come to expect on this day of rest could be marred by a conflict surrounding property or possessions. Guard against getting involved in a boundary dispute with a neighbor. If necessary, check the title deed of the property to verify the dividing line. Low vitality and disappointment could add to your problems. If you have been taking someone for granted, a small crisis may make it necessary to give them more attention. Resist the temptation to allow one idea to dominate your mind; it could put you under stress without you realizing it. If you are fretting about a work worry, a leisurely walk outdoors might be the only way to get things back in perspective before you reenter the fray tomorrow.

NOVEMBER

1. MONDAY. Calm. Concentrate on ways to increase savings so that you do not have to constantly scramble for necessary funds. Look for one area to cut and not miss it much, such as bringing lunch to work occasionally instead of eating out. Ignore what the people next door seem to be accumulating in a material sense. Trying to keep up with them is likely to be a futile and frustrating exercise. Instead, focus on your real needs, not what you think you need in order to impress others or gain their approval. Consider a long-term investment which offers returns over a number of years. If you are looking for work, a large corporate environment is favored over a small firm because there will be better opportunities to advance.

2. TUESDAY. Variable. This is a good day for taking out or updating a life insurance policy or retirement policy. Any new project started at this time should proceed well. Your judgment is sharp, putting you in good position to finalize a contract. Capricorns thinking of going to live or work abroad could find deep personal fulfillment by following through on such plans. However, steer clear of any dubious deals or people. A misplaced sense of generosity could lead to you losing a lot of your hard-earned money. Even if you are feeling thwarted in career matters, do not try to force the issue; patience is the best policy. Talk through your problems with someone you trust absolutely.

3. WEDNESDAY. Useful. Learn more about a subject that holds special appeal to you. Browsing in a library, museum, or art gallery can stimulate your creative senses. You are ready for a new challenge that uses all of your Capricorn talents. A letter delivered before the close of business can open new doors for you; call to obtain particulars. It can pay to be the first or the last; those in the middle are apt to get lost in the shuffle. If you are trying to make a lasting impression, put more of yourself into all that you are doing. Surprised attention is better than none at all. A new partnership is favored along with community involvement. Donate your time rather than money to a worthwhile cause.

4. THURSDAY. Excellent. Contacts with connections at or from a distance should run smoothly. Dealings with foreigners in general are likely to prove worthwhile. You may find yourself daydreaming about faraway places or about living abroad. Talk to someone close to you about these fantasies; they may be more possible than you imagine. Also, sharing your dreams for the future with others could open up new horizons for all of you. If you identify closely with someone whose religion is very different from your own, learn more about it. Your imagination can be a rich source of inspiration; allow it to roam freely as you expose yourself to new ideas. Studying a subject you did not enjoy while you were in school could turn out to be fascinating.

5. FRIDAY. Challenging. The day starts on an auspicious note. Someone occupying a position of power may contact you informally to pass on some good news. Be sure to keep a confidential matter secret. Betraying a trust that has been placed in you could backfire in the future. Trying to get youngsters to settle down can be difficult. Mildly bribing them to do their homework or chores could work better than trying to lay down the law. As a Capricorn you tend to work all-out even when you reach a state of exhaustion, which can cause your health to suffer as a consequence. Use some of that determination and willpower to kick a habit that you know is not good for you. Schedule rest and relaxation as part of your day.

6. SATURDAY. Difficult. Life continues to be demanding and busy. No matter how willing you are to finish up a particular project, you have to face your limitations and accept that you cannot do it all by yourself. While the gains from working hard may be plentiful, especially in terms of how much you are valued, you may need to get away from it all for a while. Family members may try to persuade you to socialize, but you are more inclined to spend your free time on your own. Something from your past could stir up uncomfortable feelings, interfering with your ability to concentrate on what you are supposed to be doing. The sense that you are not on the same wavelength as everyone else can be quite disturbing, but this mood should soon pass and your natural optimism return in full force.

7. SUNDAY. Uncertain. Children are likely to be quite a handful, whether they are your own or are youngsters in your care or even in the neighborhood. When it comes to risk taking, do not push your luck too far even if you seem to currently be on a winning streak. Partnership and teamwork endeavors are favored. Unexpected new prospects are about to open up for you which would not be possible if you had insisted on going it alone. A change of scenery can do you and your loved one a world of good. With some quick thinking later in the day you can finish a repair or redecorating job well ahead of time. Be on the lookout for a labor-saving device or gadgets that could speed home chores and thus give you more free time.

8. MONDAY. Sensitive. Be alert to what is going on out of your earshot. Pick up on clues from what people say and, more important, what they do not say. This is not a good time to be involved in anything clandestine or underhanded. If you back out now while you still have the chance, your reputation is more likely to remain intact. Try to restrain an impulse to spend extravagantly, especially for a person you love. Your time and attention are the best gifts you can offer right now. A child may need special encouragement in the face of a disappointment; help them find an alternative that is likely to work for them. A friend may want to talk about a problem but not yet be ready to listen to your advice or alternate views.

9. TUESDAY. Manageable. Do all that you can to finish off neglected work so that you can clear the way for new opportunities that are on the horizon. You can probably achieve more if you work alone. It might be difficult to resist making cutting remarks, especially if you become drawn into office or neighborhood gossip. Strangely, however, you may have difficulty expressing how you feel to those who matter most to you. In discussions with superiors, use extra tact and diplomacy. It can even help to play up to them. A friend or relative who is sick or recovering from an operation is bound to appreciate your sympathetic attitude. Some gentle exercise at the end of the day is a good way of dispelling tension.

10. WEDNESDAY. Buoyant. You should be feeling really good about all that is going on. Health and appearance are increasingly important to you. You could well decide to plan a weekend at a health farm or retreat. Even if it is expensive, you deserve the pampering it promises. This is a particularly favorable day for personal and business money matters. If you have been thinking of asking for a pay raise, you now have the confidence and charm to get what you want. Your employer is likely to be in a generous mood toward you, recognizing how valuable you are. A shopping spree could be rewarding. You may find a special item that is just what you have been looking for, and at a bargain price.

11. THURSDAY. Satisfactory. Make things as easy as possible for yourself. Do not write if a phone call will do. Take a cab or bus rather than walking. Delegate as much as you can to people you can depend upon to do a thorough job. As a Capricorn you can be very effective in a managerial role. And you can be even better if you pull the strings quietly from behind the scenes rather than taking an obvious leadership role. Pay more attention to etiquette and good manners. Be as polite to those you know well as you would be to a total stranger. Taking someone for granted can swing a happy relationship into an antagonistic one. Be wary of allowing a minor disagreement to create a chill breeze that could lead to a separation.

12. FRIDAY. Variable. Be wary of trampling on the rights and sensitivities of other people. What you want could be in conflict with plans that are already underway. Give in a little and others are more likely to meet you halfway. Lack of money could put a damper on your efforts. You may have to settle for less expensive seats to see a show, or watch a sports event on television rather than paying for a stadium seat. An activity you normally enjoy could seem somewhat burdensome. Make an excuse to get out of it if possible. It may be time to think about revising chore assignments at home. Such changes can renew your vitality and participation in your own household. If you own a pet, a trip to the vet may be necessary.

13. SATURDAY. Mixed. Do not hesitate to speak up about any important issue in order to gain public support. You can enhance your public reputation by being reliable and thorough. The key to success in pursuing your goals is to work hard in a disciplined, practical manner. In that way you guarantee good results. The incisive logic combined with a flash of intuition which Capricorn people are famous for can help you make the right decision concerning your long-term ambitions. Guard against impulsiveness or impatience, however, which could undo any progress you make. Family and career interests can best be handled by making slow, steady progress toward long-term goals. Try not to be swept off your feet in a romantic situation.

14. SUNDAY. Unsettling. What seemed to be a sure thing at the beginning of the month now is something of a problem. Conditions can go either way depending on how much you are willing to push, plead, and compromise. A positive approach is an almost certain guarantee of success. Once you know exactly what you want, you stand a better chance of getting it. Write down your goals for the remainder of the year. Be clear about where you are willing to give in and where you will not budge. Take advantage of a break at lunch or after work to get together with a person whose company you enjoy and who does not want anything from you. A movie or good novel can take your mind off whatever is troubling you.

15. MONDAY. Fair. Do not count on friends or associates doing any special favors for you. They are likely to feel compromised or even threatened by any such request and may feel that you are trying to exploit your relationship with them. Go easy on personal spending. Impulse buying can prove disastrous to your budget. Something that seemed perfect in the store may turn out not to suit you at all once you get it home. In dealing with younger family members who are about to go out on their own, it may be difficult learning to confide in them, especially when it is a matter of revealing your own uncertainties and fears. However, their sympathy and understanding are not only likely to make you feel better but can also help you solve problems by taking advantage of their less emotional perspective.

16. TUESDAY. Manageable. Get your priorities lined up in order of importance. Begin the day with what is most urgent, then move on down the list. A professional may be able to complete a job much more quickly and thoroughly than if you try to do it yourself. Your budget should be able to stand the extra expense this would entail, and the cost would be worth the hours you save.

Pace yourself throughout the day. Take occasional breaks to stretch your muscles and clear your mind. Accept without hesitation if asked to join a group that has interested you for a long time. If you turn down an invitation for any reason, you could miss out on future opportunity. Do not stand on formalities when it comes to friendship; pitch in where you are needed without waiting to be asked. The more you give, the more you will get.

17. WEDNESDAY. Slow. The more quiet and privacy you can arrange for yourself, the better you are likely to feel. Although this is an unusual interlude for you as a hard-working Capricorn, it is necessary from time to time. As a result of your introverted mood, other people may misinterpret your views as vague and noncommittal. They may be only too willing to point out the fact that you are not as decisive as normal. For the moment, at least, there is very little you can do to change things. Any option to get out of your usual environment should be considered. Even a short outing can lift your spirits, but do not eat or drink too much attempting to comfort yourself.

18. THURSDAY. Lucky. A surprising offer can ease the workload and give you a welcome respite. Do not allow yourself to become too relaxed, however. Even work that you have delegated should be checked. Tactfully offer suggestions for improvement after the work is done rather than standing over their shoulder while they are working. A person who you believe held you back in the past may now want to join forces with you. Give them the opportunity, but also be aware that they may back out if they change their mind. If you are the one who has a change of heart, ask a friend to act as an intermediary for you. Put off until another day all but the most vital purchases.

19. FRIDAY. Good. If you feel the need to clear out old clothes and personal possessions, this could reflect an underlying need to clear someone or something out of your life. This is a very favorable time for making a new start or moving into new ventures. If you are looking for a job, undertake some quiet background research designed to improve your prospects. Bring your resume up to date. Although you could feel a pull to faraway places, the demands of problems closer to home can limit your options. If you are working under a lot of unceasing pressure, participating in active sports can help relieve tension and aid relaxation. Win or lose, you will gain from competing.

20. SATURDAY. Sensitive. Gossip may be weaving its web in the neighborhood this morning. Do not pay too much attention to what you hear. Those who are close to you may be doing more than their fair share of telling tales and repeating rumors. If a reputation is in the process of being tarnished, do not add fuel to the fire or you could find yourself being taken over the coals. Continual interruptions make it almost impossible to get ahead with your day's schedule. Taking the phone off the hook or turning on the answering machine could be the simplest solution, especially if you have pressing work that you must get done. Do not expect an easy time in reaching an agreement for evening plans. You may give up and decide to stay home.

21. SUNDAY. Pleasant. Enjoy a day with family members and close neighbors. You may want to host an informal get-together to watch sports on TV. Keep it simple and make the game the main entertainment. A friend's casual remark can stir you into action before evening. Something you have suspected for a while but not been able to verify could now become crystal clear to you. Your good intuition can give you a head start on what needs to be done. Problems are unlikely to intensify if you do not think about them or try to resolve them for a day or two. Enjoy what is left of the weekend by spending a relaxing evening with a best-selling novel or working on a creative project.

22. MONDAY. Disconcerting. The question of popularity may well rear its ugly head. You may be forced to decide just how far you are willing to go in pleasing friends and living up to their expectations. The key is a personal integrity that has to do with conscience, and which only you can know or understand. This is definitely not a day for taking gambles of any kind, especially in business and professional matters. It is important to subordinate your personal creativity and self-expression in favor of the needs of others who are part of your team. In group or club activities, one dissenting or rebellious voice can unfortunately cause a fair amount of discord, but guard against taking sides.

23. TUESDAY. Changeable. This promises to be a good start to the day where romance is concerned. Love will eventually win through, whatever the problem or however intense the misunderstanding. Letting a minor matter blow over is the best policy instead of getting too emotionally involved. A journey with someone you love, admire, and trust can be an eye-opener. There is a greater risk of business plans being blocked by government officials or other bureaucrats. Unfortunately, there is little that you can do except wait. Consider presenting your case again at a later time in a slightly different format. Do not take any rejection too personally; keep your sense of perspective.

24. WEDNESDAY. Fortunate. Build on the inroads you made yesterday. Act immediately on what was decided in a meeting. Look for ways to publicize a cause that you believe in strongly. Keep in mind the old adage that what is worth doing is worth doing well. Do not opt for the easy way out unless you are convinced it is the most effective solution. When verifying facts for accuracy, it may not be enough to check just one source of information. A trip promises to be pleasurable as well as a successful conclusion to a project. Combining business and pleasure is a wise tactic. You may be able to make a purchase that adds to the excitement and value of a collection you have been acquiring for some time.

25. THURSDAY. Satisfactory. Someone who has apparently been avoiding you now seems ready to sit down and talk face-to-face. Make time for them on this Thanksgiving holiday. Be prepared to bury the hatchet now that you have reached this turning point. Abandon an exciting idea only after you have worked through all the implications. Do not allow others to pour cold water on your dreams or convince you to do what goes against the grain. A family member may be ultraconservative in their outlook, causing dissension with a younger person on account of their straitlaced views. By all means follow your instinct, but do not throw all caution to the wind. Although luck is on your side, it is basically your good Capricorn common sense that is propelling you forward.

26. FRIDAY. Mixed. People close to you may urge you to put work aside and enjoy socializing for most of the day. However, indications are that you would much rather focus on finishing up one or two pressing matters. This is an ideal time to consider taking out a home improvement loan. Keep both beauty and practicality in mind when making redecorating decisions. Your mate or partner's point of view could turn out to be the key to solving a long-standing problem. You are in a good position to deal with associates in a firm but fair manner. Making an offer to help with a personal problem is likely to be gratefully received. Avoid driving after dark, especially if you have a few drinks; alcohol is apt to have an especially strong effect on you.

27. SATURDAY. Variable. Do not get caught up in a pack mentality if you do not approve of what is being proposed. Although it can be very isolating to be the lone voice, what you have to say can help everyone keep a balanced perspective. Start to cultivate a wider circle of friends. Capricorn singles might consider a reputable dating agency or advertisements by other singles in a high-class magazine. Look into your insurance documents; there is a chance you may be able to reduce your payments and save yourself a tidy sum. A secondhand store can be an interesting place to buy clothes and accessories with a distinctive style. Try to keep in contact with someone who recently transferred. It pays to have a way to get inside knowledge of employment opportunities at a distance.

28. SUNDAY. Disquieting. Sensible concern about joint finances is useful, but worrying about them unnecessarily can wear you down. It is possible that you are fretting over investment matters more than is really necessary. Once you have made what seems like a wise decision, stick to it rather than continually questioning whether you have done the right thing. Do not let fear of the future or the unknown prey on your mind. Even if someone close to you has recently had a bad experience in their financial affairs, take this as a lesson to make the very best out of life both for yourself and others. Life is a challenge without guarantees. All you can do is your best. In all matters today, make a point of giving credit where credit is due.

29. MONDAY. Confusing. Do not become deluded by pipe dreams. When it comes to fantasizing, you can be your own worst enemy. With your vivid Capricorn imagination, it is easy for you to substitute empty dreams for reality. If you let down your partner or a colleague, you may live to regret it. People are looking to you for advice and wisdom, even if it seems to you they are unwilling to offer you the same. Double standards can be particularly difficult for you to understand, but there is little to be gained from violating your own standards or pointing out their possible hypocrisy. Be sure not to accuse others of the very faults you share because you are as humanly vulnerable as they are.

30. TUESDAY. Fair. Make an extra effort to work with people whose views are different from yours. Together you might come up with the best possible plan for all concerned. If the weather is good enough, take a lunchtime stroll in the park or to window-shop. This can give you a welcome change of scene from your usual environment. A trip should be enjoyable, especially if it is solely for sociable purposes. If you are traveling out of town or to unfamiliar territory, be sure to take a map along. Do not let anyone or anything tarnish the good name you have managed to build up for yourself. Now is the time to aggressively promote your career and your personal interests.

DECEMBER

1. WEDNESDAY. Productive. Spending part of the day day-dreaming about future success can open your eyes to new possibilities. Although it can be useful to have a goal to work toward, attaining it requires practical day-to-day effort. Capricorns involved in artistic or creative work may find unexpected opportunities for career advancement. There is a good possibility that your work will reach a wider public and be in greater demand. New ideas are likely, making this a very productive day. Domestic life should be harmonious. If you feel sympathetic toward the problems of an older relative, be willing to make an extra effort to personally help them out in any way you can.

2. THURSDAY. Difficult. This is the right time to put into action the get-rich-quick scheme or plan to increase your income that you have only been thinking about until now. Your enthusiasm and drive is infectious and can help to overcome any obstacles you encounter in the outside world. Although conditions favor new beginnings in your career, you first may have to put some troubled times behind you. The hard work you do now is sure to bring benefits to you later. Do not let overwork cause you to forget those all-important domestic affairs. Attempts to repair a broken appliance are apt to be fruitless; a complete replacement might be the best answer.

3. FRIDAY. Changeable. Business matters demand your time and attention. Extra duties could be delegated to you, perhaps being asked to help with plans for holiday decorations at your place of work or an office party. Your working relations should be smoother than they have been of late. Your popularity with co-workers is on the increase, and those in authority are favorably inclined toward you. There is a possibility of a special relationship developing between you and an older colleague. Long-lasting ties with co-workers that are deepened now can help you in the future. Handle relations with family members with kid gloves, however; do not take a loved one's generosity for granted.

4. SATURDAY. Stressful. There is a danger of getting involved in an argument with a friend. It may seem to you that a certain friend has let you down over a joint business venture or purchase and that money has been squandered. Clarify such misunderstandings as soon as possible; they could prove almost impossible to sort out if you leave them until later. Dreams and ideas you have for helping people less fortunate than you may not become the reality you were hoping for; scaling them down could be useful. The failure of your enterprise is likely to give rise to worrying circumstances regarding finances. Do not let feelings of envy over an acquaintance's success cloud your judgment about the next step that you should take. Try to relax this evening by keeping your expectations within reason.

5. SUNDAY. Unsettling. Having tried all obvious means of getting what you want or need, the time has come to consider more creative ploys. It may become necessary to issue an ultimatum or even a veiled threat to get a friend or family member to realize that you mean business. This is especially true when it comes to demanding payment for an overdue debt. If you are longing for more space or a change of scene, this is a good time to analyze your options. A move to another area could be the answer for you, but consider renting for a while if you are not completely certain of what you want. Unclear desires are likely to get you in hot water and could cost you money to undo at a later date.

6. MONDAY. Satisfactory. Early in the day is a good time to talk seriously with a friend. Conditions favor developing a better rapport with those in charge. Capricorns involved in political activities should make a good impression speaking on topical issues to a group of supporters. Later in the day, give yourself the opportunity to work on a creative project or simply to reflect and dream a little. Talking about your plans with someone you trust can be enlightening. This is a good time to make changes at home. Radically altering whatever you are currently dissatisfied with at home can prove very rewarding. Rearranging furniture can be as useful as buying new.

7. TUESDAY. Profitable. Conditions favor working alone to improve your income. If working with others, you need the freedom to do things your own way. Taking a leadership role can give you the authority to make the changes you want. Contacting important people who can help you advance your cause is starred. This eventful day heralds the start of a new phase. However, at first the changes are likely to be so subtle that you may not recognize them for what they are until later in the month. A secret ambition is attainable, although you will have to wait patiently before you reap the benefits of your current effort.

8. WEDNESDAY. Confusing. What seemed to be a sure thing at the beginning of the month now is beginning to be in doubt. The outcome could go either way; it largely depends on how much you are willing to plead, cajole, and compromise. Consider making your New Year's resolutions early so that you know exactly how much you are willing to compromise. Having a good idea of what you want increases your chances of getting it. Write down your intentions so that you can review them as you go along. At lunchtime or this evening, seek out the company of a friend who makes no demands on you. A movie or blockbuster novel can also help take your mind off your current concerns.

9. THURSDAY. Easygoing. Home life promises to be harmonious and relaxing. Entertaining visitors at home is favored, or planning an upcoming get-together. Certain troublesome influences have receded, so you should be feeling happier and more at peace with the world. Your more cheerful mood is bound to be infectious. A shopping expedition for clothes should be successful. If your business involves buying or selling, trade is likely to be brisk. Belonging to a group and relating to friends is especially rewarding at this time. However, beware of expecting problems to evaporate into thin air or expecting other people to go out of their way for you. Try not to neglect your own responsibilities.

10. FRIDAY. Mixed. Concentrate on long-term planning for your family's future. Effort to secure a steadier, more stable income should be made now. It may be necessary to make some changes to your intended course; the new plans could enable you to reach your goals sooner than you expect. Working steadily and cautiously, performing tasks thoroughly and carefully, should bring the success you seek. You may have to work very hard now, but the result is likely to be long lasting. Guard against doubting your abilities. Nor should you become discouraged by negative remarks from people in positions of authority.

11. SATURDAY. Cautious. Although as a Capricorn you tend toward being quite conservative financially, you could be lured into taking a gamble. Enjoy flirting with fate, but avoid acting impetuously just to prove a point to yourself or to others. This is a good day for all matters relating to home and family. Do not put off clearing the air regarding a subject you have been reluctant to discuss. However, tact is indicated; there is little point in voicing the kind of honesty that hurts people's pride or feelings. Before you go on a holiday spending spree, check your credit card limit or bank account balance. You may be disappointed to find that you have less money available than you think.

12. SUNDAY. Variable. Take a break from normal routine and do something out of the ordinary. This is a good time for delving into an obscure subject or doing some investigative work behind the scenes. As a fact-finder, you can be remarkably successful. You have a gift for sniffing out the information that really counts, no matter how dusty it has become or how hard someone has tried to cover their tracks. This is also a favored time for a secret errand. Expect a surprise visit from a long-absent friend. Guard against leaving your mate or partner out in the cold. Small children are apt to be especially demanding. You need every ounce of your patience and inventiveness when it comes to keeping youngsters occupied.

13. MONDAY. Good. You are apt to be happiest and most confident in the company of those who know you well and with whom you have strong emotional ties. Concentrating your efforts on making your surroundings more comfortable and secure may make you feel more settled. If you are thinking of buying a new home, conditions favor making an offer for a house or for another real estate investment. A leisurely lunch can lead to scintillating conversation, but guard against getting into a debate about politics or religion. Your very strong feelings about a subject are likely to come across as arrogance. Try to keep an open mind; you have a lot to learn.

14. TUESDAY. Unsettling. Communication problems with family members are foreseen. Strong feelings and emotions may overwhelm your ability to think rationally. There is a possibility of a dispute over ownership or use of property, which can lead to stony silence or even a lawsuit. Because you are likely to be feeling rebellious, relations with authority figures could be difficult unless they allow you plenty of freedom. Be extra vigilant when it comes to handling sharp tools or dangerous machinery. Guard against wasteful spending. Although you may have a strong desire to accumulate possessions, you are unlikely to be satisfied with impulsive purchases which you do not really need.

15. WEDNESDAY. Disquieting. There may be conflict between your sense of responsibility where family members are concerned and wanting to accept an invitation to go out and have a good time on your own. If duties and obligations keep you from joining in pleasant activities with friends, accept the situation rather than fighting it. Otherwise your Capricorn conscience is likely to bother you. At the same time, guard against building a wall between you and your friends by not explaining your situation. You may be surprised how understanding they are and how willing to help out. Computers and communication equipment are prone to breaking down now. If you own a computer, check for viruses.

16. THURSDAY. Mixed. There could be some confusion or misunderstanding concerning a recent purchase or a contract to buy.

It may be that you change your mind about the price you already agreed on. However, do not let the seller pile on the pressure if you are now sure about what you want. Disagreements with superiors at work could leave you feeling that you are not getting your point across. Keep calm or you could damage your chances of promotion at work. Your vitality and energy are at a low level; a quiet schedule with plenty of breaks is important. If you are working at home, turn on the answering machine or turn a deaf ear to the telephone so that you can work uninterrupted.

17. FRIDAY. Challenging. Do not wait any longer to discard some outmoded habits that are preventing you from moving forward with confidence. This is a good time to sign up to take a course in assertiveness training or to study a book about it. Also consider a course to polish your public speaking skills. Expressing yourself openly and sincerely to others can help you be successfully assertive in any confrontation. At the same time, guard against provoking a fight because you have a somewhat restless desire for excitement. A permit or other permission that is still being reviewed by the authorities may have gotten lost in the shuffle. Make one or two phone calls to nudge officials into action sooner rather than later.

18. SATURDAY. Useful. Early in the day should be an easygoing time for home affairs. Propose your ideas and plans to family members and try to enlist their help with projects at home. Consider inviting close friends or relatives to lunch to discuss a do-it-yourself plan. Your finances may be in good shape, but guard against being lulled into a false sense of security. You could be tempted to overspend or take unnecessary risks with money. If you are concerned about the health problems of a relative, researching which method of treatment might help them most can be the best way of assisting them. Be careful not to give one certain idea more attention than it warrants.

19. SUNDAY. Difficult. It can be all too easy today to look on the downside of every situation, especially in regard to emotional relationships and friendships. Little annoyances are not worth getting upset about; genuine grievances should be talked over calmly. Letting off steam can leave a trail of destruction in your wake. Try to free yourself from some responsibilities for a while. Taking part in group exercise or martial arts is a good way to release tension. Avoid getting caught up in a domestic argument that does not involve you directly. Even though loved ones may try to drag you into it, keep a safe distance. Younger members of the family need to learn the fine art of give-and-take.

20. MONDAY. Challenging. Do not hesitate to rethink your working life and your means of earning a living. Scientific and occult subjects are likely to draw your interest. On your own you may find a new solution to an old problem. Go out of your way to meet new people and discover new sections of your community. Consider spending time improving your photographic skills or honing your skills in a practical craft from which you derive personal satisfaction. Your best work and thinking are likely to be done alone, but take time to share your ideas and opinions with other people. Keeping secrets can undermine the confidence that has been placed in you.

21. TUESDAY. Disquieting. You may feel like breaking away from the normal round of responsibilities and duties. Wanting to find a more exciting way of earning a living could cause you to make changes which startle other people but which are likely to be constructive. Try to put emotional considerations aside in order to attend to immediate practical necessities. Be careful of being too critical of those around you. If a heated conflict arises, there is a danger of your feelings overwhelming your reasoning. Take the time to stand back from a stressful situation and view matters more objectively. Say what must be said.

22. WEDNESDAY. Variable. Get an early start. Focus on harnessing your energy and mental powers so that you can make progressive, constructive progress. Conditions favor working closely with other people. The enthusiasm you radiate, together with your ability to persuade others by showing you understand their needs, enables you to be an effective leader of a group. You have the necessary drive to start new projects and also to use your own resources in order to complete them. Goals can be achieved with reasonable ease and within your time limit. Home affairs should progress well. Enjoy getting together with your family or old friends this evening.

23. THURSDAY. Productive. Whatever you achieve in partnership matters will probably be the result of your own hard work and concentrated effort. As a Capricorn you are very conscientious in all you undertake to do. Avoid any risky investments or speculative deals; these could result in serious losses. Arrange to spend some time mulling over your own thoughts and feelings. You are apt to prefer the company of serious people. This is a good day for finalizing some serious long-range planning. The practical experience of older, wiser family members or colleagues whom you respect can help you make a difficult choice. A loved one or partner could ask you for support; do all that you can.

24. FRIDAY. Deceptive. If you are going out with friends or colleagues you should have an agreeable time. However, resist the temptation to overindulge in food, drink, or gossip. Single Capricorns may be strongly attracted to a member of the opposite sex. All the signs are that this is going to be a wild, short-lived affair if it is based purely on physical attraction. With little else in common, you are likely to soon drift apart. Later in the day, take extra care with finances. You might not feel like dealing with the details of life, but some confusion over property matters or joint finances may demand your attention. There is a danger of being deceived by a stranger and becoming a victim of fraud.

25. SATURDAY. Merry Christmas! Whether you are spending Christmas with loved ones or apart from those to whom you feel closest, this can be a time which brings up memories from the past. Be careful not to fall into negative thinking about yourself and your achievements. If you are going to be with people you do not know well, you might find yourself upset by them in some way. However, they are filling a need for you now and can only act naturally. Your feelings and emotions are likely to be intense, making any intimate encounter very powerful. Put your Capricorn passion and energy into the day and it should be richly rewarding. Be sure to express special thanks for a handmade present.

26. SUNDAY. Calm. Nostalgia about the past is likely to be reawakened by information you receive from a family member or an heirloom you are given. You could feel sentimental and want to be surrounded by people or things reminding you of earlier times. Go out of your way to be warm and supportive to friends and relatives. However, try hard to focus on the present; otherwise there is a chance you will miss out on the continuing festivities. Home life may not be totally peaceful, but try to remain calm no matter how difficult it might be. It is important not to be too possessive of others or to restrict their freedom.

27. MONDAY. Buoyant. You are likely to be feeling more energetic than usual and able to be single-minded in working hard on a project designed to further your own personal interests. Although you may not be keen to expend your energy working for someone else's benefit, your inner calm and strength is drawing others to you. Relations with the opposite sex should be especially easygoing. If you are in a steady relationship, there should be special harmony with your partner. An older friend might be able to offer support or suggest practical answers to any worries you have. Taking up a new interest can add spice to your life.

28. TUESDAY. Happy. The joy of the season may be extended as you continue to see old friends and enjoy mutual entertainment. Arrange to get together with people to whom you feel closest. If you are involved in any type of legal proceedings, you are likely to find these matters working out in your favor. If you are promoting a business or commercial venture, there is a good chance you can negotiate a personally advantageous deal. This is also a good day for study; new ideas can intrigue you. Try to increase your understanding of subjects needing deep thought. Self-discipline allows you to be mentally creative and to make good progress.

29. WEDNESDAY. Fair. Career matters are again coming to the fore in your affairs. Showing sensitivity and empathy toward the people you work with can win them over to your way of thinking. Your ability to be responsive to the general mood should help you establish a good position for yourself. You may find certain people in your life more irritating than usual, but guard against a public outburst of emotion as a result of your pent-up frustrations. If you have been dragging your feet about getting ready for the new year, this is the day to do some serious straightening up and throwing away. Also find time to carry out any repairs that are needed.

30. THURSDAY. Good. Take time to review the year that is coming to a close. Consider making some much needed changes to enhance and improve your economic situation. The demands on your energy are likely to be high because the nature of your work could be changing. Or you may have to figure out how to satisfy a new boss. The signs are that you will be assuming a leadership role and advocating new policies. A surprising event may lead you to spend part of the day with people you normally do not come into contact with at work. These events can be turned to your advantage. Visiting a new place this evening should satisfy your craving for an enlarged circle of friends and acquaintances.

31. FRIDAY. Sensitive. You may feel torn between wanting to take the day off from work to spend more time with your family and wanting to push ahead with new developments on the job. The best policy is to concentrate on work early in the day when you can progress well and be very productive. At that time you are likely to have the energy and drive that creates success. Later there may be busy social activities involving friends and neighbors. Be careful not to get too caught up in the revelries. The indications are that you will be at the center of the action when it comes to ushering in this very special new year. Any resolutions you make should be long term and not too specific.

CAPRICORN
NOVEMBER–DECEMBER 1998

November 1998

1. SUNDAY. Mixed. This is a starred day for social networking. A certain person is likely to be a source of inspiration. Talking openly about your ideas and future plans can help motivate you to take action. Home life should be peaceful. Find some personal space to focus on private matters. Confide in a family member if you are struggling to find a solution to a perplexing problem. Whether this trouble is emotional or practical, discuss the difficulty. In this way you are likely to be able to solve it. Set a deadline for yourself if you go out tonight; you need a good night's sleep.

2. MONDAY. Quiet. You should be able to make marked progress in completing a project. More peace and quiet than usual at work provides the right surroundings for pressing ahead. If you have been out of work, come up with a plan for looking for a new job. Family and domestic matters are apt to take priority in your thoughts overall. This is a favorable time for planning a redecorating project. Consider the practical aspects involved before getting too upscale. The simpler you keep things, the better the results will be. Good news about an educational endeavor or school project is likely to reach you.

3. TUESDAY. Uncertain. Negotiations in relation to property matters are likely to leave you feeling confused or taken advantage of. Whether you are interested in buying or selling, do not rush the decision. It is likely that you do not have certain facts. Try to be patient. A gift you are planning to purchase for a loved one could turn out to be more costly than you expect. Come up with an alternative if you cannot afford your first choice. Expenses in relation to one of your family member's interests and activities are likely to be unusually high. It may be time to rework the family budget.

4. WEDNESDAY. Good. Concentrate on broadening your leisure interests. If you enjoy a game such as bridge or chess, venture out to a local club. Dancing and swimming are both good stress relievers. If you have not exercised regularly for some time, this is a favorable day for joining a health club or pairing up with a neighbor who regularly walks or jogs. Getting a fitness video could motivate you. Travel for pleasure is likely to be very fulfilling; in another environment you may be filled with inspiration. Trips are likely to be especially stimulating if you have an agreeable travel companion.

5. THURSDAY. Disquieting. Although you want to get a great deal done today, be careful not to cram your schedule too full. You are apt to feel far too stressed if you do not pace yourself carefully. If you must manage a set workload, especially if you have deadlines to meet, take reasonable breaks throughout the day. What you hear via the grapevine at work is apt to worry you. While there is often no smoke without fire, it is not wise to believe even half of what you hear. Deal with facts, especially if you are about to make a major decision.

6. FRIDAY. Stressful. Work and travel do not blend well today. If you are traveling for any period of time, you are likely to worry about what you are not getting done in the workplace. On the other hand, if you have many detailed tasks you may be stuck behind your desk all day without sufficient time to make an important trip. Cancellations or postponements may be the best answer. If you have to be out of town, leave clear instructions to those who are covering for you. Also be sure to leave an emergency number where you can be reached.

7. SATURDAY. Difficult. The partnerships in your life should be smooth at the moment. Spending more time with your loved one is likely to be pleasurable for both of you. Make some plans for the future when you are together. For single Capricorns, this evening favors going out socially in hopes of meeting new people. If you have recently been introduced to someone who could be a potential romantic partner, try without delay to strengthen your connection. Do not be too inward looking; you tend to worry about matters more than is really required.

8. SUNDAY. Excellent. This is another starred day where partnerships are concerned. The friendship part of a love relationship can be deepened by unhesitatingly supporting each other with your individual plans. If you go away on a trip you are bound to have a memorable time. A recurring problem can be smoothed over if you make more of an effort to communicate. Single Capricorns can advance a new romantic link. If you have not met anyone special yet, today brings increased opportunities to do so. Your self-confidence is likely to shine through when you find your match.

9. MONDAY. Uncertain. You and your partner may disagree on matters involving your home life. This is not the best time to discuss redecorating or ideas for improving joint property in other ways. You are unlikely to see eye-to-eye. It might be hard to admit that your partner perhaps knows better or has better taste. Confine discussions to more intimate matters. You may come up with a worthwhile scheme where joint finances are concerned. It is wise, however, before making a commitment to do a bit more research just to be sure.

10. TUESDAY. Demanding. This is not an especially favorable time for involving more than one other person in your financial or business ventures and negotiations. If a group is involved, you are likely to find it hard to agree on anything. A committee decision could turn out to be a disaster. If you are thinking of moving, consider your choices very carefully. It might be appealing to move in where the rent is cheaper because more people are sharing. However, consider if this really suits you in a practical sense, especially if you are used to your own space. If buying property, check tax rates and special assessments.

11. WEDNESDAY. Productive. Where joint financial or business negotiations are concerned, you should be able to conclude an important deal. Signing a contract is likely. Property negotiations can also be finalized. This is an all-around helpful day for finishing up ongoing tasks before moving on to something new. If you have investments, check to see how they are faring. Blue-chip stocks are favored over new issues. In any event, be sure your interests are being adequately monitored by you or by someone you pay to take care of such matters.

12. THURSDAY. Stressful. If you are driving a long distance be sure to take some breaks along the way. Otherwise it is probable you will get far too tired to concentrate properly. At work you need to strike a balance between current demands and long-term expectations. You may have future plans which you wish to develop, but there are neglected tasks which demand your prompt attention. By doing a little of both you should make good headway. Prioritize in order to handle the most important matters first. If you are looking for new work, wait to hear about an interview earlier this month before sending out any more resumes.

13. FRIDAY. Fair. Business negotiations are apt to become quite heated. Nevertheless, creative results are likely to flow from the discussions. Long-distance travel is highlighted. Try to take any journey at an easy pace. Too much rushing around can work against you in one way or another. Allow plenty of preparation time before departing. If you are visiting friends, your time together is likely to be very pleasurable. This is an ideal time for a reunion with people you have not seen in a long time. This is also a fruitful time for striking up new friendships far from your normal base of operations.

14. SATURDAY. Easygoing. Focus on your career ambitions. Today's peace and quiet allows you to concentrate on matters which require a great deal of careful calculation. A new job opportunity is likely to include an unusual financial or material incentive. Weigh the pros and cons of the offer. Older people are especially good company and may have some useful advice to impart to you. If you need a favor, this is the right time to ask. If any of your relatives or associates share a secret with you, be sure to keep it strictly to yourself.

15. SUNDAY. Good. Discuss an embarrassing emotional issue with an older member of the family. You may assume that your elders are old-fashioned but could be in for a pleasant surprise. Those with more experience in life tend to assume a compassionate attitude along with their worthwhile advice. A trip which involves good friends is likely to be very pleasurable. If you do not have any special social plans, call up a few people and arrange a spontaneous party. You could get others to bring some food so that you do not have to spend a lot of time shopping and cooking.

16. MONDAY. Deceptive. It may be difficult to make important decisions, partly because you are doubting yourself more than usual. A harsh comment from someone who knows you well could hurt more than you want to admit. As a Capricorn you are not usually overly sensitive. However, at the moment you are likely to take too much to heart. Where your career is concerned, it is vital to believe in your capabilities in order to make progress toward achieving your ambitions. Do not allow opposition from an employer or other higher-up to throw you off course. It may be that you are simply not seeing eye-to-eye.

17. TUESDAY. Variable. If you belong to a social or sports club, dues renewal could turn out to be more than you expect. This may cause you to reconsider whether you are getting value for the money. Avoid getting friends involved in your financial and business activities; complications are likely, and it is possible that someone will end up offended. In social activities with friends, you should have an enjoyable time. A problem that has been troubling you can be resolved if you talk it over in a group and listen to varying views.

18. WEDNESDAY. Enjoyable. It is likely that you can strike up a series of new friendships. This should be especially good news if you have had just about enough of a particular friend or set of friends who seem to be taking you too much for granted. This is a favorable day for networking. Make more effort to stay in touch with relatives and neighbors you do not see all that frequently. A long-distance trip should be worthwhile. The change of environment can serve as a pick-me-up for your spirits. Time spent in a warm climate should be especially enlivening.

19. THURSDAY. Fair. Thinking intensely about a situation that has been troubling you may bring an answer to mind. If you occasionally meditate, use those skills now. Aim to maintain a low profile. You can accomplish more without other people loading new tasks on you; catch up first with the current backlog. An unexpected financial bonus is likely just when you are beginning to worry about upcoming bills. Compliments from people who admire you will boost your self-confidence. If you feel physically under par, a medical checkup should put your mind at ease, showing that there is nothing wrong.

20. FRIDAY. Sensitive. Time spent alone should be particularly profitable. Communing with yourself is likely to help solve a vexing problem. You may not have as much time to yourself as you would like, however. Expect a flurry of telephone calls and even drop-in visits from people you see only occasionally. If you cannot bear being constantly interrupted, turn on the answering machine and ignore any knocks on your door. Try to make an effort to catch up with neglected tasks rather than starting a new project. Less running around is advised; take life a little easier and be good to yourself.

21. SATURDAY. Variable. Try not to be too isolated today. As a Capricorn you sometimes keep problems to yourself, which can lead you to become quite negative and depressed. It is better to try to get worries and tensions out of your system. Pouring them out to a close friend could help. Overall, physical rather than mental exercise is likely to be your best tonic. Getting out to do something exciting should help move you out of the rut you are stuck in. If someone you care about is hospitalized, make an effort to a visit. An elderly person, in particular, needs to know that someone cares.

22. SUNDAY. Buoyant. Focus on ways of fulfilling an important personal goal. A dream which you let go of a while ago can be reinstated now that you realize there is actually a way of turning it into reality. Friends and acquaintances are likely to be a great support to you both emotionally and practically. Encouragement for your plans can help you accomplish them with greater confidence. If you have been planning a change of image, this is a favorable day to work at it. If you decide to change your hair color, allow yourself time to get used to it before facing other people.

23. MONDAY. Rewarding. This is a favorable day for networking. If you have been thinking of joining a club, this is the ideal time to do so. You should end up making more new friends and contacts than you expect. You could also develop new personal interests. Long-distance travel is favored, especially to visit relatives. You might also want to make a personal pilgrimage; this is likely to be highly fulfilling. Do not be surprised if some family members oppose your plans; do not let them stop you. Extending your education can guide you in a fruitful new direction.

24. TUESDAY. Fair. If you are trying to get a personal project off the ground, get friends in on the act. It is likely that they can not only relieve some of the burden but will also have some useful advice to pass on. Financial developments are apt to be positive. There is a good chance of an unexpected windfall thanks to a prize or inheritance. If you owe money to anyone, pay it off quickly before spending money on yourself. Behind-the-scenes negotiations are likely to be useful in renegotiating a loan or obtaining new financial backing.

25. WEDNESDAY. Good. Get an earlier than usual start to the day. Negotiations behind closed doors should work to your advantage. If you are coping with a problem do not discuss it with more than one or two people. Take it to the few you feel sure will be able to help you. Be sure this is someone you can trust to keep a secret. You may need to make investment arrangements that no one will know about, not even your partner or family members. As a Capricorn you are an excellent planner. There is no reason to feel guilty about protecting your private and personal interests.

26. THURSDAY. Mixed. Money is making your world go around at the moment. This is a propitious day for bringing financial negotiations to a satisfactory end. If you are looking for a second investment opportunity, you may stumble upon it while reading the newspaper. Socially, it is best to maintain a low profile. Someone nosing into your private affairs and asking personal questions can put you in a very embarrassing position. It is best to avoid too much individual contact with relatives or neighbors; they may not understand your situation. If someone has confided a secret in you, guard against revealing it just because others pump you for information.

27. FRIDAY. Profitable. This is a favorable day for shopping. As a highly organized Capricorn you may already have your Christmas shopping list. Now is the best time to check the sales. You are likely to be able to make helpful new contacts both in the business world and in your social life. Be careful however, not to entrust anyone new with a confidence. Trustworthy as individuals may seem on first meeting, you do not yet know enough about their motives. There may be nothing to worry about, but it is better to be safe.

28. SATURDAY. Fair. If you are intending to buy or sell property, this is a favorable day for concluding a deal at the right price. Think twice about purchasing an old property, however. Although its character is likely to be appealing, you could have to do a lot of work to get it in good shape, and this could be costly. Private time alone is vital for weighing the pros and cons of any key decision. Spend some time in peaceful surroundings if your home is crowded and noisy; the library could be your refuge. Romantic intrigue can spoil a date tonight, making you tense and suspicious. Speak up, and your partner will reassure you.

29. SUNDAY. Exciting. Today favors property viewing and deals. If you are hoping to sell, a buyer could appear out of the blue when you least expect anyone. In fact, a speculator could track you down if you have an unusual property or valuable land. Behind-the-scenes negotiations are likely to work in your favor. For homebound Capricorn people, good progress can be made with a do-it-yourself project. Quality upgrades and attractive additions are sure to add value to your property.

30. MONDAY. Interesting. This should be a productive day if there are ongoing tasks you need to finish up immediately. You should be able to conclude negotiations on a key business deal. Romantic opportunities abound. However, watch your spending in relation to romantic and social plans. If you are out to impress someone new, it is better to be honest about a temporary shortage of funds rather than set a precedent you may not be able to live up to in the future. Avoid going to a restaurant that is too expensive and upscale to be comfortable. Travel is likely, either today or later in the week.

December 1998

1. TUESDAY. Misleading. Beware of hidden expenses in your social life. An early Christmas party could turn out to be a lot more expensive than you expect. There is no reason to stay away from most of the festivities, but be discriminating in the invitations you decide to accept. Increased contact with friends and neighbors should be heartwarming. Single Capricorn people could hear from someone special through the mail, or there may be a telephone call to look forward to. Catching up with neglected tasks at work should pay off in greater prestige for you.

2. WEDNESDAY. Mixed. Although you should start the day in fine fettle, this could all change if you try to cram too much into your schedule. A flurry of telephone calls this afternoon could call a halt to your continued progress. If you go to a meeting, do not be surprised if you come back to a stack of messages on your desk. Put off what you cannot do rather than exhaust yourself mentally or physically. There is much to be gained from pushing ahead with work, but you probably cannot fulfill every single commitment. Superiors are likely to be supportive in assigning additional staff if you are pushed for time with a deadline looming.

3. THURSDAY. Variable. This bright and breezy morning is a good time for catching up on any work backlog. Get routine matters in order; it pays to be organized. For Capricorns who have been out of work, an unusual and lucrative opportunity is likely to arise; snap it up. As with yesterday, avoid overdoing physically or mentally. You cannot be in two places at the same time, so guard against double booking. Being stuck in a meeting is likely to put you behind on routine tasks. It is a good idea to delegate some of them to another person if you can trust them to do a good job.

4. FRIDAY. Slow. This is a favorable day for finishing up tasks that have been neglected while you handled other matters. An important deal may go through today. Attention to detail is vital. Do not expect to get much good work done in a hurry. You can benefit from a slower, even plodding pace to ensure that tasks are carried out properly. Trying to cut corners will probably backfire on you in the long run. Legal documents, in particular, require meticulous attention. You could have a lot to be angry with yourself about later if you overlook a vital clause or detail.

5. SATURDAY. Good. If you are going shopping bring along a good friend or your loved one. Together you can handle the crowds better and can also turn the expedition into an enjoyable event instead of a chore. This is a good day for catching up on neglected work at home. If you have a problem on your mind, a private discussion with an older person is likely to be helpful. For single Capricorn people, this is a key time for strengthening social links. You can get to know an intriguing newcomer better through shared, routine activities.

6. SUNDAY. Disquieting. Avoid spending too much time at home. You are likely to bicker with loved ones. If you are in the middle of a decorating project, aim to stay out of each other's way. Criticism from the person who is not doing all the work is bound to be aggravating. Get out for a breath of fresh air and some stress-relieving physical exercise. Money matters need careful handling. Double-check the details of a proposed investment scheme before writing a check. Prove that you are capable of handling whatever comes your way.

7. MONDAY. Fair. Control your spending. This is one of those days when impulse buys are more appealing than usual. If you are shopping for gifts, your total bill could be more than you have budgeted. The more you plan ahead, the better. The cost of items for which you have not done any comparison shopping can come as a bit of a shock. Quiet time alone is useful if you are trying to sort out a personal problem. Where business matters are concerned, hold an important meeting behind closed doors so that clients or business associates feel free to speak openly and frankly.

8. TUESDAY. Rewarding. This is another day when it is advisable to hold key meetings behind closed doors. If you need to discipline a staff member or someone in your immediate family, be firm without casting blame. It is better to simply lay out the facts rather than pass judgment. An investment opportunity which has caught your attention is likely to be sound, but do some background research to be absolutely sure. Time spent with your family this evening is likely to be rewarding, giving you a chance to iron out an emotional problem that has been causing tension at home.

9. WEDNESDAY. Successful. A change of scene is likely to be refreshing. However, if you are doing the driving on a long-distance journey, it could be quite tiring. If you cannot share the chore, at least be sure to take plenty of breaks along the way. Avoid drinking and driving, even though it may be tempting with the Christmas spirit around. However, if you are tired, or have a long journey ahead, the combination can lead to an accident. This is a favorable day for catching up on neglected tasks. Secret negotiations can be finished up, freeing you to start a new project.

10. THURSDAY. Stressful. This is another day when long-distance travel could be quite tiring. Using public transportation, if possible, is a better alternative to driving. Routine tasks are likely to keep you quite busy. A number of people may call with inquiries and gossip. It is important to be discriminating with these people and only talk at length to those with key information to impart or urgent questions to be answered. Because you do not have time to do everything you set out to do, prioritize. Get important matters out of the way early in the day.

11. FRIDAY. Frustrating. A break from your usual surroundings should be helpful. However, if there is a problem weighing on your mind, you are unlikely to be able to escape from it no matter where you go. It could help to talk to a loyal and trusted friend who might be able to help you see things from a different perspective. This is a starred day for career planning. If you are considering changing jobs, or are looking for new work because of a layoff, a golden opportunity is likely to come your way. Avoid cramming meetings into your day one after another or you may become muddled.

12. SATURDAY. Profitable. Discussions with authority figures can be helpful where money matters are concerned. You may unexpectedly meet a highly influential person at a social gathering who offers to do you a favor. Aim to get key responsibilities handled, especially anything that you had to put off during the past week. A discussion with an older person is likely to be helpful if you have an emotional problem to solve or a moral dilemma to work out. The right choice is likely to be clearer to you by the end of the day if you are open to advice and suggestions. Some Capricorns may be honored now for a past achievement.

13. SUNDAY. Mixed. Confidential discussions should be productive if you need a favor from an important person. Expect some opposition from someone in authority, or a delay where authorization of some kind is needed. Try alternative channels in order to get what you want. Your home life is apt to be disjointed. It may irritate you if other household members are not pulling their weight. Now is the right time to reassign tasks to keep your home running smoothly, but try not to be heavy-handed about it. Although you may want to put your feet up when there are still important tasks to do, get your priorities in order.

14. MONDAY. Changeable. Friends and acquaintances are supportive and encouraging in relation to your personal plans. If you are going to host a big celebration soon, get other people in on the planning. It can be helpful to seek the advice of someone who is used to organizing parties or catering to large groups of people. It is not a good idea, however, to involve friends in business matters at the moment. If your business involves selling, there could be difficulties when one of your clients cannot pay on time. Do not part with merchandise before you have received payment.

15. TUESDAY. Exciting. This promises to be a lively, fast-paced day. You can move your plans forward with the help of friends and acquaintances. Social functions are likely to go with a swing. Accept invitations that come your way, so long as you can fit them in. There is a chance to make new friends and contacts. For Capricorn singles, a new romance is foreseen. If you are struggling with financial difficulties, seek the advice of a counselor. A professional financial adviser or accountant could offer helpful tips to reduce your taxes.

16. WEDNESDAY. Satisfactory. Close, intimate meetings are highlighted. If you are meeting a special friend at lunchtime or this evening, choose a quiet restaurant where you can chat rather than a noisy spot. At work, concentrate on catching up with neglected tasks. Also contact people you have been meaning to call. A financial bonus could come your way as the result of sticking to your principles despite a lot of opposition. If you are hoping to change direction in your career, insider information is sure to be useful. Keep all meetings and discussions as low-key and discreet as possible.

17. THURSDAY. Fair. You are apt to feel sensitive and vulnerable. A private matter could be too embarrassing to share with anyone else. It is best to maintain a low profile, especially at work. If you need to be out in public today, you have to work hard to appear in top form. It may not be something negative that is troubling you, only a past indiscretion that is over and done. If you have fallen in love recently, your feelings may be uncertain and your fears heightened. Whatever the case, do not let your feelings show in public and on the job. More important, do not confide romantic secrets to anyone who might broadcast them.

18. FRIDAY. Manageable. You are entering a new phase when it is imperative to handle problems which you have avoided in the past. Although this may seem to be a tall order, it is likely to be easier than you expect. In getting a major difficulty resolved once and for all, you can relieve yourself of an immense burden. Any problem in relation to a future course of action should be discussed with the family member you consider most experienced in similar matters. Build on what has been successful in the past.

19. SATURDAY. Calm. This is an excellent day for pressing ahead with personal plans and ambitions. You should feel calm and confident. There is less need to compromise in relationships and bow to other people's preferences. As a Capricorn you have a knack of often being the life and soul of any party. If you go out socially this evening, you are likely to be the center of attention. If you have a number of events to attend in the next few weeks, invest in at least one new outfit. Do not hesitate to wear clothes that help you attract favorable attention, even turning a few heads.

20. SUNDAY. Variable. Unlike yesterday, there is apt to be some opposition to your plans or some obstacle in your way. However, it should be nothing that you cannot handle. With careful negotiation you should be able to obtain the approval or authorization which you need. If you are meeting someone influential, make a point of talking more about them than yourself, and of listening more than you talk. It is likely that this person needs to have their sense of importance reinforced. If you are looking for a favor, be ready to strike a bargain. In your current mood you may do just about anything in order to achieve a particular aim.

21. MONDAY. Confusing. Do not expect to make rapid progress with your personal plans and aims. You may have to temporarily divert your attention to other areas of life, such as your home and family. A loved one may need your help with Christmas shopping. Be watchful when making purchases. What appears to be a bargain or special offer could turn out to be a sales gimmick. If you receive a check, be sure that the sum is correct; it is possible that a mistake has been made. Although it probably can be easily rectified, you may have to wait a while to get the cash.

22. TUESDAY. Disconcerting. This is a favorable day for financial planning. You probably have spent a lot of money lately. Now spend some time adding up your bills and settling your accounts. Your credit card bill may have to be paid before the end of the month. It is to your benefit to pay in full in order to avoid high interest charges. Be careful with your wallet if you go out to any public place. Pickpockets are likely to be taking advantage of crowded streets and stores during the busy shopping period. Quiet time alone this evening can help you catch up on personal tasks.

23. WEDNESDAY. Good. There is a good chance that you can conclude a business or property deal. Money due you could come through now. If you have been studying an investment opportunity, this is the key day to make your move. Spending more time alone can help you find the solution to a long-term problem. A complete change of scene could be especially useful. Get out at lunchtime to somewhere peaceful. A local park is just the place to mull over plans, dreams, and schemes for the year ahead. Now that your Capricorn birthday period has begun, make firm resolutions for developing a creative talent.

24. THURSDAY. Fair. This is a good day for renewing contact with acquaintances. Spread the merry Christmas spirit; call up a few people and offer season's greetings. As a Capricorn you come into your own at small, intimate gatherings. At a social celebration you are likely to be the center of attention. Guard against drinking too much and then attempting to drive home. Instead, call a taxi or rely on public transportation. If you receive a gift from someone but do not have anything for them, do not become embarrassed. Just say a sincere thank you.

25. FRIDAY. Merry Christmas! This promises to be a spirited, lively Christmas day. You are likely to take center stage wherever you go. This could be quite a relief to a busy host or hostess in whose home you are a guest. Capricorn people who are spending today apart from loved ones can overcome a feeling of loneliness by making good use of the telephone. And you could be receiving a few welcome calls yourself. A get-together at a local restaurant later in the day is likely to bring single Capricorn men and women into contact with other singles who have romantic notions.

26. SATURDAY. Mixed. Home and family life should be wonderfully rewarding. With the pressures of the actual holiday out of the way, everyone can relax and enjoy a quiet day. Although you have been at the center of most social gatherings recently, you probably need a rest from this now. Try to spend some quiet time alone. If you must be around family members at home all day, reading a good novel could be an enjoyable way of mentally escaping. Avoid getting into serious conversation with a relative who loves to argue.

27. SUNDAY. Sensitive. For most Capricorns, this is a favorable day for relaxing at home. Nevertheless, Capricorn professionals who are virtually indispensable at work could have to spend some time in the office or on the phone with colleagues, offering practical help as well as advice. Try to keep such an interruption in your personal life as brief as possible. It is important to have time to wind down after the busy seasonal festivities. In addition, there could be a disagreement with a loved one if you stay away too long. Total harmony at home may not be possible, but you can help it by being available and upbeat.

28. MONDAY. Demanding. There are more burdens to carry to-day than you have experienced for a while. You could have to go on a shopping trip for groceries or other necessary supplies. Family responsibilities might include driving relatives back home or to the airport. Do not expect to have an easy, relaxed day. Your social life should be lively, however. The only problem is that you may not have much money to spare after your Christmas spending. Decline an invitation if you know it is likely to cost more than you can comfortably afford. Get to bed early tonight.

29. TUESDAY. Pleasant. This promises to be a good day overall for social activities and leisure pursuits. Accept an invitation from neighbors or relatives. It should lift your spirits to get out and about, especially if you have been spending a lot of time at home. If you are still off from work, take advantage of opportunities to get to know a new neighbor and catch up on the news in your local community. If you have not seen people you hoped to visit over the holiday, give them a call. This is especially important if you had to decline a social invitation from them.

30. WEDNESDAY. Rewarding. This is a task-filled, busy day. You are likely to be quite rewarded for your efforts. If you are back at work, try to ease into new projects. It is not a good idea to plunge into work and other responsibilities after the recent break. There is a tendency to take on too much and end up feeling exhausted. Focus on catching up and on tying up a few loose ends, but try not to get heavily involved in anything new. If you are at home, slowly get back into your usual routine. Finish clearing up around the house. Be sure to write thank you notes.

31. THURSDAY. Satisfactory. You should be able to make very good progress with work matters and other routine tasks. There could be an unexpected financial bonus in recognition of your efforts. If you need help or approval from an authority figure, it is likely to be forthcoming. Avoid spending too much time alone this evening. Join in a New Year celebration rather than staying alone and pondering the future. Make some resolutions, but avoid being too inward looking. It is counterproductive to give yourself a hard time about what you have not achieved in the year just gone by. Be positive in looking to 1999.

Having A Good Psychic Is like Having A Guardian Angel!

Love, Romance, Money & Success
May Be In Your Stars....

Get a **FREE** Sample
Psychic Reading Today!!!

1-800-799-6582

FREE
Love
Advice

Does he really love me?

Will I ever get married?

Is he being faithful?

Call To Find Out How To Get Your

FREE Sample
Psychic Reading!

1-800-869-2879

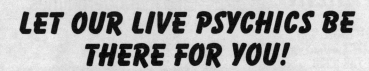